How to Build a Successful
Application Using Agile Without
Sacrificing Data Management

Building the
Agile
Database

first edition
Larry Burns

Technics Publications
New Jersey

Published by:

Technics Publications, LLC

966 Woodmere Drive
Westfield, NJ 07090 U.S.A.
www.technicspub.com

Edited by Carol Lehn
Cover design by Mark Brye

ISBN, print ed.   978-1-9355041-5-3

First Printing 2011
Library of Congress Control Number: 2011931258

ATTENTION SCHOOLS AND BUSINESSES: Technics Publications books are available at quantity discounts with bulk purchase for educational, business, or sales promotional use. For information, please email Steve Hoberman, President of Technics Publications, at me@stevehoberman.com.

Contents at a Glance

Contents

To my loving Aunt, Sarah McPherson, who inspired in me a life-long love of books, learning and teaching, and to the memory of my parents, Keith G. (Bob) and Mary (Peg) Burns.

And, always, to Becky for her continual love and support.

Acknowledgements

I would first of all like to acknowledge and thank my mentors in the data management profession, in particular John Dart, Dave Wells, Tim Feetham, Bill Stewart, Roger Paulsen, and Jim Bigej. They gave me my start in this business, and guided me with their wisdom and experience along the way.

I would like to thank my colleagues at DAMA International, in particular Deborah Henderson of the DAMA Foundation and Mark Moseley of the Chicago chapter of DAMA, who gave me the opportunity to contribute to the Data Management Body of Knowledge (DAMA-DMBOK). Also, of course, my friends and colleagues in the Puget Sound chapter of DAMA, who have let me bend their ears and try their patience at numerous monthly meetings, gave me the first opportunity to explore some of the ideas in this book, and provided me with excellent feedback.

I would like to thank all of my colleagues, especially those in the Software Development Center and in the Data Services group. I have learned a lot from working with all of these wonderful people, and many of their thoughts, ideas, suggestions, and comments have found their way into this book.

In particular, I would like to thank Bill Sheboy of the SDC, and Bill Stewart of the Data Services group, for reviewing the manuscript of this book and providing many excellent suggestions. To the extent that I took their advice, this is now a much better book.

I would like to thank Steve Hoberman of Technics Publications for shepherding the manuscript through its various revisions, and helping it see the light of day. His advice was invaluable, and this project would not have seen completion without his guidance.

Last but not least, I would like to thank my long-suffering wife Becky who, at many points in the creation of this book, probably wished she had married a long-haul truck driver. Thanks, sweetheart!

Foreword

I have often wondered how two of the hottest trends in information systems – Agile development and data governance – can coexist and reconcile their differences. In my consulting work, I typically see three scenarios: Agile development supersedes data resource management, data management limits agility, or two groups work at cross-purposes with a high degree of conflict.

Building the Agile Database is an unprecedented and much needed book that describes a very pragmatic approach to resolving tension that is common between application development and enterprise data management. From the developer perspective, it seems that data management creates barriers to fast and adaptive development. From the data management point-of-view, Agile development appears to ignore or discard many of the best practices of data asset management. The conflict is driven by different motivations – developers driven by a short-term need for functionality, and data managers motivated by a long-term need for high-quality business data.

This isn't a new problem; it has been with us for decades. The very same dilemma existed back when I was an application developer in the 1980's and 90's. Agile methods didn't exist, and we practiced something called Rapid Application Development (RAD). The premise with RAD was that we could quickly prototype functions when working with a stable data model. In other words, we could be fast once the hard work of database design was finished.

Today the approach is agile development, with development cycles much faster than those of RAD. Business cycles are faster and urgency greater, making agile development an imperative. At the same time, the stakes are raised for data management. Regulatory compliance and business analytics are among the factors that make data quality, continuity, and cohesion critical; and the variety of data and database models is much more extensive – relational, dimensional, columnar, unstructured, and so on. We have the same developer-database dilemma in a faster-moving and more complex environment.

Fortunately, Larry Burns answers some of the hard questions that must be tackled to resolve the conflict. Larry begins by making data administrators and database administrators "Agile aware" with understanding of the *what* and *why* of agile development. Next, he describes the principles of data management that are in apparent conflict with agile: Performance, Reusability, Integrity, Security, and Maintainability (PRISM). Now, with the stage set, Larry describes several concepts and techniques for design of agile databases. Many of the techniques may be familiar – abstraction, virtualization, and normalization, for example. New insight is in the application of the techniques and their implications for agility.

When I first met Larry Burns, he was an application developer at the University of Washington. Today he is a data management professional with more than a decade of experience. Larry is the right person to author a book of this kind. He has walked both sides of the street; he sees the conflict from both perspectives; and he offers pragmatic solutions born of experience as a practitioner in the field.

Building the Agile Database doesn't have all of the answers, but it makes big steps in the right direction. Every database administrator, every application developer, and every information systems manager will learn from this book.

Thanks, Larry, for stepping up to this long-standing problem.

Dave Wells
Information Management Consultant and Mentor

This book is meant for a broad audience that includes all of the application development stakeholders whose roles are explained in Chapter 1: application developers, database developers, database administrators (DBAs), data managers, data analysts, Quality Assurance (QA) managers, QA testers, project managers, business managers, enterprise architects, operations managers, and application support managers.

The early chapters of the book will focus on general, business-oriented principles that will help all stakeholders understand the roles and needs of the other groups, and explain how they can work together effectively, in the context of Agile development. The middle chapters explore the book's central theme of separating the work of data design (the logical, or business requirements view of data) from the work of database design (the physical, or implementation-specific view of data), and introduce the important concept of data virtualization. The final chapters show how these principles can be practically applied to Agile database development, and will be of interest primarily to application developers, database developers, and DBAs. The book concludes with a section explaining how to develop an "Agile Attitude" that helps people on Agile development teams work together more effectively. Everyone involved in the process of application software development will find something of value in this book!

The following outline briefly describes each chapter's content:

- **Chapter 1: Taking the Business View**. This chapter explains the importance of taking a business-focused, stakeholder-oriented view of application development, summarizes the economics of application development, and explains the importance of data – and of good data management practices – to the enterprise. This chapter should be read by all readers, as it provides much of the justification for the approach this book recommends.

- **Chapter 2: Agile Explained**. Explains how Agile has transformed software development, examines the implications of an Agile approach, and explores some of the critical issues in Agile Development. Data management professionals will want to be sure to read this chapter, as it describes the justification for an Agile approach. Even Agile practitioners will want to read this chapter, since it explains the difficulty that people in some roles will have in adapting their processes to an Agile model.

- **Chapter 3: Agile Data Management**. In this chapter, an Agile approach to data management is described, based on the five PRISM principles. Different ways of looking at what a database is are examined, and a defense of the "intelligent" database is proposed. The information in this chapter is central to the book, and should be read by everybody.

- **Chapter 4: Data Management Roles and Responsibilities**. Describes the roles and responsibilities of data management professionals in application development, enterprise data management, and operational support; explains how these roles are evolving, and describes how their work is affected by an Agile approach. The information in this chapter is essential to understanding data management work, and should be read by everybody.

- **Chapter 5: Managing the Logical-Physical Divide**. Examines the root cause of what Agile practitioners call the "object-relational impedance mismatch", the disconnect between the logical (requirements) and physical (implementation) views of data. The consequences of confusing these two views of data are explored, and the central concept of the Virtual Data Layer is introduced and explained. At this point, the focus of the book shifts to material that will be mostly of interest to application developers, data analysts, and DBAs, although I would recommend that project managers, application architects, and data managers read and understand this chapter as well.

- **Chapter 6: Agile Data Design**. Explores the logical side of the data divide to determine how best to do requirements modeling in the context of an Agile project. Since Agile emphasizes a minimum of design work, how and when can data modeling be done? The role of normalization in logical data modeling is explained. The material in this chapter will be of great value to data analysts, and to anyone involved in understanding and modeling data requirements for an application or business process.

- **Chapter 7: Agile Database Design**. Explores the physical side of the data divide to determine how best to do database design and implementation in the highly-iterative context of an Agile project. The role of normalization in physical database design is explained. This material will be of value to DBAs, application database developers, and anyone involved in designing and creating data structures for applications.

- **Chapter 8: Agile Modeling and Documentation**. Examines the concept of an "Agile Model" to determine how much – and what kind – of documentation can and should be produced from the logical and physical data activities. Agile developers, data analysts, DBAs, Scrum Masters and project managers will find this chapter useful.

- **Chapter 9: Building the Agile Database**. Examines different approaches to data virtualization, both relational and object-oriented and describes how to implement data requirements in the database. This chapter will be of value primarily to DBAs and application developers.

- **Chapter 10: Refactoring Made Easier**. Explains the Agile concept of refactoring, and how refactoring is applied to the logical model, physical database design, database schema, virtual data layer, and data. The emphasis is on minimizing costly refactorings at the database schema level. This chapter will be of value primarily to DBAs and application developers, but will also be of interest to QA (Quality Assurance) and Application Support people.

- **Chapter 11: Developing an Agile Attitude**. The biggest determinant for the success of an Agile project is the attitude of the people involved. Each person must make an effort to understand the roles of everyone involved, what they contribute to the effort, and what they need to be successful. Then, everyone must commit themselves to the success of the undertaking. The three Agile attitudes of commitment, cooperation, and communication are explained. This chapter should be read and understood by anyone involved in an Agile project – or in any other sort of application development effort.

- **Chapter 12: Case Study – A Sales Option Management Application**. This case study describes how Agile principles were applied in the development of an application that maintains sales option data for a manufacturing company. The case study is not intended to describe how Agile ought to be practiced, but to illustrate how data management can be done in the context of an Agile project, and how Agile projects can be done in the context of well-defined project management processes and stakeholder groups. This chapter is essential to the book, and should be read by everybody.

Case Study: The Blue Moon Guitar Company

To illustrate the application of the concepts in this book, I've created a fictional company called "Blue Moon Guitar Company". The company designs and builds custom guitars and other wooden stringed instruments to order; that is, it does not mass-manufacture instruments. When ordering an instrument, the customer can specify a number of customization options, such as size, finish, type of tuning pegs and bridge, pick guard design, size and location of the sound hole, type(s) of wood used, type and placement of electronics (if any), and so on. Each model of instrument is associated with a set of these customization options, and each option specified contributes to the total list price of the instrument.

The Sales Option Management (SOM) application will enable the company to input and manage these options, and their relationship to the models of instruments offered by the company. The application will also enable Blue Moon's sales representatives to help customers design their dream instrument, and give them an accurate price quote when all of the options have been chosen.

Introduction

In the decade or so that I've spent working in the field of data management (after many years as an application developer), I've experienced first-hand the challenges of implementing effective data management processes in the context of a fast-moving IT organization at a large global Fortune 500 company.

Most of the existing literature on application development, including much of what you'll read in the online developer forums, highlights the difficulty of getting application developers and data managers to work together effectively, especially in the context of Agile development. In many large organizations, there is often a considerable amount of contention between application developers, who need to get their applications written and deployed as quickly as possible, and data managers, enterprise architects, and other "big picture" folks, who are trying to focus on the long-term needs of the business. Although Agile development methodologies have been around for a decade, we seem to be no closer to resolving this contention. In fact, the rift between the two groups has become so wide at some companies, developers are advocating doing away with databases altogether!

In this book, I intend to demonstrate, in a practical way, how application developers and database developers can work together to satisfy both application (functional) requirements and larger-scale business data requirements. My complaint about much of the current Agile literature is that it is written solely from the point of view of Agile developers committed to the cause of Agile Development. There is no explanation, for non-Agile people, of why Agile is an important, even crucial, methodology (and not just the application methodology *du jour*). Nor is there any explanation, or exploration, of the roles and needs of other stakeholders in the application development effort.

Instead of exploring alternative approaches that would enable *all* stakeholders to do what they feel they need to do, most of the literature on Agile Development simply says, "The Agile approach is the correct one, and everyone else will have to accept it and change." In this book, I hope to educate both application developers and data professionals about how to approach Agile projects in a way that meets the needs of the *entire* organization.

Everybody involved in an application development effort, including business users, project managers, QA testers, DBAs, and developers, is a stakeholder in the outcome, with legitimate interests and needs. To create an effective application development strategy, it is essential to understand what each of these groups brings to the table, and what each of them needs in order to do their jobs effectively. Each group has to learn as much as possible about what the other group is trying to do, and why, and then commit themselves to working together in a positive and professional manner, putting aside preconceived ideas and personal antagonisms in pursuit of the common enterprise goal.

In addition to taking a more inclusive approach to this topic, I also want to define an approach that is more business-focused. Both application developers and data managers need to understand that it's not their money that is being spent and that, personal interests aside, the important goal is to satisfy both the short-term and long-term needs of the business. This requires a complete understanding of the economics of application development, the trade-offs involved in various development approaches, and a commitment to achieving the maximum ROI (Return On Investment) from each project.

I also believe that in any effective approach, the less prescription, the better. Instead of telling people, "This is what you must do, and this is how to do it!", it is better to simply establish some fundamental goals and principles, and let people chart their own course. This is why, for example, I won't be writing anything about the "rules" of normalization (normally *de rigueur* for a book of this type). Instead, I'll talk about what normalization is, how it works (in both the logical and physical realms), and what the trade-offs are in the context of various types of data structures. The rest is up to you.

I'm also going to try to forsake ideology for the sake of practicality. Both developers and data managers tend to have very strong opinions about what is the "right" thing to do, which is why conflicts between the two groups tend to take on the tone of religious disputes. Developers tend to be focused on ease and speed of coding, while data managers search for the Holy Grail of "a single source of the truth". Reality is usually much more complicated than this. As we'll see, getting an application out the door quickly may be the *least* cost-effective thing to do, and an organization's data needs may encompass several views of multiple truths, occurring in different business contexts.

However, my major source of dissatisfaction with most of the books I've read on the subject of application database development is that they don't properly address the critical distinction between the *logical* and *physical* views of data. The common assumption is that a (relational) database will be modeled in third-normal form, and implemented in third-normal form; in other words, there is no distinction made between the logical design (the data model) and the physical schema of the database. In this book, I will show why logical modeling and database design must be treated as two separate activities, each with its own purpose and goals, and its own set of rules, and how failure to do this leads to many common database problems, including what has been referred to as the "object-relational impedance mismatch".

This disconnect becomes most apparent when examining the most common approach to Agile database development – continuous "refactoring" (reworking) of the database schema. Not only is this a difficult, sometimes dangerous, and often unnecessary thing to do from a database perspective, it's also, ironically, one of the *least* Agile approaches from an application development perspective! In Agile Development projects that I personally have worked on, the schema-refactoring approach has resulted in significant rework, project delays, and frayed tempers in both the application and database groups. To make matters worse, many Agile practitioners also recommend performing "normalization after the fact", i.e., starting with denormalized data structures and normalizing incrementally as needed. Unfortunately, this approach often fails when it is discovered that the data needed to populate the new normalized key attributes is missing or corrupted, due to a lack of data integrity constraints.

An alternative approach, which I intend to advocate in this book, is to do as much of the refactoring and denormalization as possible in one or more *virtual* data layers residing above the database schema. This approach accomplishes a number of very important things: from a data management perspective, it helps preserve the critical distinction between the logical (application-independent) and physical (application-specific) views of data, enabling a single database to support multiple applications and multiple uses of business data. From an application development perspective, it helps reduce the coupling that rigidly ties applications to an unyielding and over-normalized view of the data, and enables iterative changes to be made quickly, easily, and painlessly. This approach, which our organization has used in a number of Agile Development projects, has resulted in much faster development and implementation times, less "scrap and rework", more data and code reuse, lower maintenance costs, and greater cooperation between the data and development groups.

Too often, in the past, developers have said to data managers, "You MUST DO this!"; while data managers have said to developers, "You CAN'T DO that!". Nothing is really going to change until both developers and data managers understand that everybody NEEDS TO DO certain things for certain reasons. Any methodology that denigrates the valid business needs of people or groups who must support it is doomed from the start.

As a database developer in good standing (I helped write the chapters on Database Development and Database Operations Management for DAMA International's Data Management Body of Knowledge [DMBOK] and frequently speak at DAMA meetings and conferences), I am committed to an approach to data management that helps companies maximize the business value of their data. As a long-time application developer, I am also committed to helping software developers create high-quality, reusable code that maximizes the return on our company's IT investments. I do not believe that these goals are mutually exclusive; indeed, I don't believe that either can be achieved without the other. My hope is that this book will inspire a broader vision of what both developers and data people can accomplish if they work together.

Larry Burns
Kent, WA

CHAPTER 1
Taking the Business View

Most books on application and database development focus on IT (Information Technology) activities: choosing the application architecture, designing and coding the application, testing, etc. What often gets overlooked is that all IT activities exist (or, at least, *should* exist) to add value to a company's business activities, in pursuit of that company's business goals. At each step in the application development process, we need to ask ourselves: are we doing the right thing, in the right way, to help our company achieve its goals? Are our activities adding value to processes that are streamlined and effective? Are the activities of critical stakeholders in these processes being helped or hindered? An approach that helps one set of stakeholders is ultimately valueless if it impedes the constructive work of others, and ultimately costs the company time, money, and opportunity.

The Importance of Stakeholders

One of the distinguishing characteristics of my approach to data management is my insistence on a stakeholder view. Most books on software development (especially Agile development) are written totally from the developer's point of view – nothing is more important than getting software out the door on schedule. Most books on data management are written totally from the data management point of view – nothing is more important than "a single view of the truth". But in the real world, it's not as simple as that. All organizations and organizational processes involve a large number of concerned stakeholders, whose interests must be considered in any endeavor.

For companies to be successful over the long term, they must consider the interests and well-being of their customers, employees, and suppliers, as well as their stockholders and directors. David R. Vincent, whose seminal work, *The Information-Based Corporation,* is an excellent introduction to the concept of stakeholder economics, goes so far as to include communities, competitors, and regulators in his list of stakeholders.[1] Failure to consider the environmental impact of corporate activities on surrounding communities, for example, has cost many companies millions of dollars in lawsuits and settlements. Similarly, many companies have lost millions of dollars fighting – and losing – anti-trust and patent infringement suits.[2] Other companies have created value for their shareholders by entering into cooperative ventures with their competitors; a consortium of insurance companies in Florida, for example, have pooled customer data in order to expedite the processing of third-party and multi-party insurance claims, resulting in benefits for both the companies and their customers.

In the arena of software development, there are many stakeholders at various levels who have a legitimate interest in the outcome of the development effort. These include:

- *Software developers*, whose livelihoods depend on being able to create useful software applications quickly and cost-effectively.

- *Project managers*, whose jobs depend on being able to complete projects on time and under budget.

- *Business users*, who want to be able to do their jobs as effectively as possible.

- *Product owners*, who are responsible for making sure the application meets the needs of the business.

---

[1] Vincent, David R. *The Information-Based Corporation: Stakeholder Economics and the Technology Investment* (Dow Jones-Irwin, 1990).

[2] Microsoft, for example, paid no stockholder dividends in 2002, and its stock lost 16% of its value, because much of their available cash was tied up in lawsuits and settlements (Source: The *Seattle Times*, November 6, 2002, p. E1).

- *Business analysts*, who understand the needs of the business and can communicate business requirements to the development team in technical terms.

- *Business managers*, who want to obtain the most value for their IT investment.

- *Enterprise architects*, who want to ensure the maximum reuse of enterprise assets at the lowest possible cost.

- *Data managers*, a subset of enterprise architects, who want to ensure the maximum reuse of enterprise data assets at the lowest possible cost.

- *Data analysts*, who are responsible for determining and documenting (modeling) business data requirements.

- *Database developers*, who must design and build databases (and other data structures) that satisfy both business and application requirements.

- *Database administrators*, who must maintain the databases (and the database software they run on), ensure that data can be accessed quickly and easily, and safeguard data against loss, theft, and harm.

- *Infrastructure administrators*, including server and network administrators, who oversee the day-to-day maintenance, testing, installation, and operation of the enterprise's IT infrastructure.

- *Quality Assurance (QA) managers*, who want to make sure that business users get the maximum benefit from new software with the least amount of pain and disruption to the business.

- *QA Testers*, whose job it is to make sure the software satisfies the user requirements and provides a positive user experience.

- *Operations managers*, who want to make sure that the day-to-day operations of the business run smoothly, with no (or minimal) disruptions. They also want to make sure that business operations can be quickly and effectively restored if a disruption occurs.

- *Application Support managers*, who are responsible for both the day-to-day support of IT applications, and for the maintenance and enhancement that enables these applications to maintain their value for the organization over time.

- *Portfolio managers*, who oversee and administer a set of applications supporting a specific area of the business.

- *Resource managers*, who are responsible for allocating the resources (people) needed for the project to succeed. Most of these resources will be divided between several different projects.

Each of these roles contributes some measure of value to the application development effort, and helps ensure, to some extent, the ultimate success of the project and its value to the business. It's important to understand that, while ignoring the needs of one set of stakeholders may provide some short-term advantage to another, the greatest long-term advantage to the enterprise is served by creating processes that enable all stakeholders to accomplish what they need to accomplish for the good of the organization. Taking a stakeholder view gives all affected groups a stake in the successful outcome of a given endeavor. Failure to do this encourages one or more groups to back-pedal, to slow down or obstruct the effort of others. I would argue that most of the internal conflicts that cause IT projects to come in late and over budget can be traced back to a failure to sufficiently consider the interests – and enlist the support – of all the groups whose active participation and cooperation is essential for success.

The Economics of Application Development

I also believe that application development and data management issues should be looked at from a broader economic perspective. This means taking a hard look at the economics of both application development and data management to determine what processes and practices will deliver the maximum business value (ROI) for our IT investment. While it may be true, as Scott Ambler says, that "working software is the primary measure of progress"[3] in an application development effort, it is not the sole measure of value. It may also be true, from an application development standpoint, that "the highest priority is to satisfy the customer through early and continuous delivery of valuable software";[4] but developers, and even end users, are not the only or even the principal stakeholders in the development effort. After all, it's not their money that's being spent! The ultimate goal of any application development effort is not just to put functionality into the hands of end users, but to increase the value and profitability of the company's activities. So, we need to look at the whole "value equation" of application development, which includes:

- The initial cost of development.

- The incremental cost of subsequent changes and enhancements.

- The cost of maintenance over the life of the application.

- The cost of missed opportunities if the application is not deployed in a timely fashion, OR if it is deployed but fails to work as required, OR if the functionality of the application doesn't meet current or future business needs, OR if the time and money spent developing the application could have been better spent on something else.

- The value returned to the company by the application.

- The value returned to the company from subsequent reuses of the application, application components, data structures, and/or application data.

---

[3] Ambler, Scott W. *Agile Database Techniques* (Wiley Publishing, Inc., 2003), p. 9.

[4] Ambler, op. cit.

- The value returned to the company from subsequent reuses of any design artifacts, such as an architecture model, logical data model, or OOA class model.

- The value returned to the company from tools, skills, processes, methodologies, or knowledge created or acquired in the course of the development effort.

This is not a comprehensive list, but you get the idea. The basic objective of Agile Development, to get working applications into the hands of business users quickly enough to take advantage of business opportunities, is a laudable and correct one, but care must be taken to ensure that this is done in a way that doesn't sacrifice the company's long-term best interests on the altar of short-term goals. For example, we will see later on that there is a difference between "time to market" (the standard measure of software project success) and "time to money": the amount of time it takes for new – and often bug-ridden – software to start having a positive impact on a company's balance sheet.

What I'm advocating, of course, is that companies take a somewhat broader view of the application development equation than is usually found in Agile methodologies. I'm going to try not to be too prescriptive here, but would suggest that a more economically viable approach to application development might include the following:

- Establishing a consistent architectural framework of approved platforms, vendors, tools, processes, products, and languages that can support current and future development efforts across the enterprise. It is unnecessary (and economically counter-productive) to adopt a different set of architectural standards for every application or business unit.

- Creating a project management process to ensure steady progress toward the project's goals, anticipate problems, keep the project aligned with business objectives, ensure an adequate return on investment (ROI), and make sure that lessons learned from one project are used to improve the process for future projects.

- Creating a quality assurance process and QA team to make sure that product quality requirements are met, that all functional requirements have been satisfied, that user expectations have been met, and that total cost of ownership (TCO) is minimized.

- Formalizing an implementation/turnover process to ensure that both end users and IT support and maintenance staff have adequate training and documentation, and will be able to use and support the application with a minimum of cost and effort.

This might, at first glance, appear to be smothering the development methodology with a lot of process, and it's true that taking this broader approach to application development involves more project stakeholders and more communication (including, probably, more formal documentation). But it needs to be recognized that these activities involve legitimate company stakeholders, whose interests and activities directly affect the company's profitability. There is no point to a software development methodology that leaves critical stakeholders dissatisfied, and ultimately costs the company money.

The Role of Business Data Management

Much has been written about the so-called "Information Economy", but most people do not understand the economic changes that are driving the new economy. At the heart of these changes are two driving forces: *commoditization* and *globalization*. Commoditization means that everything is basically a commodity; something to be produced as cheaply as possible, used, and then thrown away. Traditionally, manufacturers of goods make profits by lowering costs, creating more efficient manufacturing processes, improving quality, or producing newer or better products. They've spent most of the last three decades reengineering their businesses to create more efficient processes (laying off millions of employees along the way) and moving their manufacturing plants overseas to take advantage of cheaper labor and production costs. Today, most manufactured products are virtually indistinguishable from one another; any given product, regardless of brand, is made in the same way, probably in the same overseas factory, in the cheapest and most cost-effective way possible. Thus, it has become very difficult, if not impossible, for businesses to increase their profits in the traditional manner.

How then, can companies increase value for their customers (and profits for their shareholders)? David R. Vincent makes the point that in the new global economy, business value is created by establishing and nurturing *relationships* with customers, suppliers, and dealers. He makes the further point that the essence of effective relationships lies in *empowerment*; in giving people the ability to do more things for themselves.[5] For example, from the comfort and convenience of my office, I can do all my banking, manage my investments, schedule my travel arrangements, and buy virtually anything anywhere in the world. Thanks to the power of the Internet and the various software applications it supports, we are moving from a service economy to what might be called a *self-service* economy.

To quote columnist Ian Shoales, we live in a data-driven world.[6] Businesses use CRM (Customer Relationship Management) software to identify problem areas and potential new business opportunities in their relationships with their customers; they use ERP (Enterprise Resource Planning) software to supply up-to-date financial information to workers at all levels of the business; they use data mining technology to identify patterns, trends, and possible opportunities for growth; they use intranets to improve their relationships with their employees; and they use extranets to improve their relationships with their suppliers and vendors. All of

---

[5] Vincent, op. cit.

[6] Ian Shoales' column "Data-Driven World" appeared monthly in *Intelligent Enterprise*, a trade magazine for database programmers, from 1997 to 2005. Ian Shoales is the alter ego of writer/performer Merle Kessler.

these different technologies have one thing in common: *they use the power of information to empower people to create value at the lowest possible level.*

Bill Gates, in his book *Business @ the Speed of Thought,*[7] echoes this idea of improving business processes by using information to empower individuals, and cites several examples from his struggling but moderately successful software company. Both Michael Dertouzos[8] of MIT and Thomas Davenport[9] of Harvard use the phrase "information marketplace" to describe a scenario in which economic value is generated through the exchange of information among individuals, much as the traditional marketplace generates value through the exchange of goods and services. They cite examples such as American Airline's SABRE reservations system, which enables travel agents to locate and book flights on any airline. This enabled American to develop a preferred (and highly profitable) relationship with travel agents. Now, of course, online providers such as Expedia and Travelocity have given individual travelers the ability to make their own travel, hotel, and rental car reservations, bypassing the use of travel agents entirely. Vincent gives the example of American Hospital Supply (AHS), which made its order entry system available to its customers, allowing hospitals serviced by AHS to order all their supplies through the AHS system. This not only improved AHS's relationship with its customers, but also gave it an advantageous bargaining position with its suppliers!

---

[7] William H. Gates III. *Business @ the Speed of Thought: Using a Digital Nervous System* (New York, NY: Warner Books, 1999).

[8] Michael Dertouzos. *What Will Be: How the New World of Information Will Change Our Lives* (San Francisco: HarperCollins, HarperEdge, 1997).

[9] Thomas Davenport and Laurence Prusak. *Working Knowledge: How Organizations Manage What They Know* (Boston: Harvard Business School Press, 1998).

To put this another way, we are moving from an economy based on physical value chains (e.g., from supplier to wholesaler to dealer to customer) to one based on what Jeffrey Rayport and John J. Sviokla have called the *virtual value chain.*[10] In the virtual *marketspace* (as distinguished from a physical marketplace), competitive advantage goes to those who can find innovative ways to use information to deliver goods and services. Sporting goods retailer Cabela's, for example, automatically emails discount offers to its customers on goods that are being closed out of inventory. I'm constantly getting emails from Amazon.com: "Dear Mr. Burns: People who have ordered *Fundamentals of Data Analytics* have also purchased Vladimir Nabokov's *Lolita.*" (Not true). (As far as I know).

In contrast to physical value chains, which are discrete and linear, with defined points of input and output, virtual value chains are non-linear and virtually limitless – "a matrix of potential inputs and outputs that can be accessed and distributed through a wide variety of channels".[11] As Rayport and Sviokla point out, a customer not interested in a new compact disk by the Rolling Stones may still choose to download it from iTunes, listen to it on Pandora, or sit in on a chat session with them in the Internet's Voodoo Lounge.[12]

What fuels the information processes that make up the virtual value chain is *data*. Data assets, as Vincent points out, are a special type of circulating (as opposed to fixed) asset. But they are very different from other types of circulating assets such as cash and inventory. They do not disappear when consumed. They can be reused almost indefinitely (unless they become out-of-date), and in an almost infinite variety of ways. And, most importantly, because

----

[10] Rayport, Jeffrey F. and John J. Sviokla. *Exploiting the Virtual Value Chain.* Harvard Business Review, November-December 1995, pp. 75-85.

[11] Ibid, p. 83.

[12] Ibid, p. 77.

value can be created using data assets at minimal cost, the traditional barriers to entry and expansion for new or small businesses are eliminated, allowing almost anyone to become an entrepreneur.

Even for traditional businesses like the global Fortune 500 manufacturer I work for, the power of data assets can be harnessed to reduce costs, improve quality, expand markets, and fuel innovation. For these companies, information can contribute to business value in the following ways.[13]

- Eliminating repetitive or redundant tasks (automation)

- Enabling people to do more work, or to work more effectively (e.g., collaboration and workflow software that lets people work in distributed ad-hoc teams without frequent meetings)

- Designing improved business processes (e.g., Ford was able to shorten its design-to-market time by over a year, enabling it to take significant market share from its chief rival, General Motors. Also, by automating their design-to-manufacture process, Ford's management was able to accept bigger design risks, enabling Ford to break from its conservative tradition and produce car designs that had more customer appeal)

- Enabling business to be conducted globally

---

[13] The examples cited in this section, along with many others, can be found in the article *How Information Gives You Competitive Advantage*, by Michael E. Porter and Victor E. Millar (Harvard Business Review, July-August 1985, pp. 149-160), the article *Exploiting the Virtual Value Chain* by Jeffrey Rayport and John Sviokla (Harvard Business Review, November-December 1995, pp. 75-85), and David R. Vincent's book *The Information-Based Corporation: Stakeholder Economics and the Technology Investment* (Dow Jones-Irwin, 1990).

- Reducing intermediaries (i.e., flattening hierarchies and giving more responsibility to empowered individuals and entrepreneurial teams)

- Adding intelligence to their products (e.g., PACCAR Inc can produce trucks that can communicate their location, fuel consumption, and status to the driver and the driver's dispatcher; if necessary, the driver will be directed to the nearest service dealership, where an appointment for service will have been automatically made)

- Lowering costs (Canon, for example, has built a low-cost manufacturing process around an automated parts selection and materials handling system, delivering parts "just in time" to workers on the assembly line)

- Enhancing differentiation (American Express has developed differentiated travel services for its corporate customers, using information systems to search for the lowest airline fares, hotels, and rental cars, and tracking travel expenses for each cardholder).

The point I'm trying to make here is that, in the Information Economy, competitive advantage is dictated by the quality and reusability of a company's data assets. To maximize its usefulness, data must be managed in a way that ensures its accuracy, timeliness, and business relevance. The data must be easily accessible, consumable, and transformable in a variety of ways. Imagine if, for example, the data in Cabela's inventory system was inaccessible to distributed applications, or if it couldn't easily be consumed and transformed by an email application, or if its customers were being offered discounts on products that didn't exist or weren't available (or that shouldn't be discounted).

It is in this context, the importance of managing high-quality, reusable, and easily consumable data assets to fuel innovative business information processes, that the rest of the material in this book should be considered.

Key Points

- The end purpose of all IT activities (including application development and data management) is to add value to a company's business activities, in pursuit of that company's business goals.

- All business activities should be conducted with the broadest possible view of the stakeholders involved. Enlisting the support of all affected stakeholders is essential to the success of any endeavor.

- All business activities have an economic "value equation" that determines whether the activity will be profitable for the company. In any undertaking, the entire value equation must be considered.

- In the new global economy, companies create value by using the power of information to nurture relationships, empower stakeholders, improve products and processes, and create new markets.

- Companies rely on high-quality, reusable, and easily consumable data assets to quickly create or modify the information processes (the "virtual value chain") that enable them to be competitive in the global marketspace.

- Proper management of business data assets is key to a company's success in the Information Economy.

CHAPTER 2
Agile Explained

There is, I think, a great deal of misunderstanding about what Agile is, and is not. Some people seem to think that an Agile approach implies a complete absence of process or rigor. Others dismiss Agile as nothing more than the latest development fad. We need to acknowledge that Agile is the *de facto* development methodology in many industries, and that some measure of iteration has always played a part in application development. At the same time, it's important to note that an Agile approach is a better fit for some stakeholder roles than for others.

The Importance of Agility

It's no secret that software development is a difficult, expensive, and problematic undertaking. It seems that nearly every week, we read of some organization's multi-million-dollar IT project failure, or the latest survey indicating that 60+% of software projects "fail" (although the definition of "failure" can be somewhat elastic, and can reflect unrealistic customer expectations). The causes of software project failures are numerous and complex, but most failed projects have at least some of the following elements in common:

- Poorly-understood or poorly-communicated requirements
- Insufficient alignment with critical business needs
- Too broad a project scope (trying to do too much in one project)
- Insufficient customer involvement during development
- Lack of attention to product quality
- Unavailability of critical resources when they're needed
- Poor planning, estimation, and risk management
- Rigid and inflexible processes and methodologies

- Lack of collaboration and communication between the various groups involved in the project

- Long delays in delivering the final product, by which time it no longer meets the user needs or business requirements.

In an attempt to address these problems, a group of software developers met in February 2001 and formed the Agile Software Development Alliance (usually referred to simply as the Agile Alliance)[14]. They developed a set of principles (the "Agile Manifesto") that articulated a new vision about how software development should be done. Agile Development guru Scott Ambler has neatly summarized the Manifesto into four general principles of Agile Development.[15]

- *Individuals and interactions over processes and tools.* Success is more often the product of talented, dedicated individuals working in close collaboration than of rigid, formally defined processes and toolsets. Peter Coad and Edward Yourdon introduce their book on Object-Oriented Analysis[16] with the story of a failed air traffic control project in which two teams of analysts, using different modeling processes and methodologies, were unable, after two and a half years, to come to any sort of common understanding or agreement on the project's requirements!

- *Working software over comprehensive documentation.* In the words of the Agile Alliance, "our highest priority is to satisfy the customer through early and continuous delivery of valuable software." Working applications add value to the business and deliver competitive advantage – reams of

---

[14] Further information about the Agile Alliance, and the "Agile Manifesto", can be found at www.agilealliance.org.

[15] Ambler, Scott W. *Agile Database Techniques* (Wiley Publishing, Inc., 2003), pp. 8-9.

[16] Coad, Peter and Edward Yourdon. *Object-Oriented Analysis* (Yourdon Press, 1990), pp. 1-2.

product and process specifications, however accurate and well-done, do not.

- *Customer collaboration over contract negotiation.* In the classic "waterfall" approach to software development, the project requirements are written into an iron-clad "contract", which the user signs off on at the beginning of the project. The project requirements don't change (ideally) until the product is delivered, months or even years later, at which point it is discovered that: a) what the developer thought the requirements were was not what the user thought he was requesting, and b) it's no longer what the business needs, anyway. Successful projects must find a way to keep the product continuously aligned with user and business requirements, even when those requirements change over the course of the project.

- *Responding to change over following a plan.* There are two ways to do anything – do nothing until you completely understand the problem, or do something with the understanding you have, and let your understanding of the problem develop as you solve it. There's nothing wrong with planning, but we must recognize that change is inevitable, that unforeseen contingencies will arise, and that our understanding of the problem will mature over time.

It's important to understand that Agile Development is not just the latest development methodology *du jour.* It is a serious and reasoned attempt to address the root causes of software project failure. For that reason alone, I believe it is important for those of us in the data community to support the objectives of Agile, even if we don't always agree with the specifics of the many and varied approaches to Agile Development.

And, let's be brutally honest here – software developers are trying to save their jobs. When large, complex and expensive IT projects consistently fail, the word "outsource" starts cropping up in management meetings. We in the data community need to understand this; after all, our jobs are just as much at risk as theirs!

Agile Development Explained

Agile Development can be defined, briefly, as the ability to respond quickly and effectively to changes in business requirements and new technology with software that meets critical business needs and delivers significant business value. In today's fast-paced, globalized, and highly-competitive world, it is imperative that companies be able to respond to competitive challenges in real or near-real time. The days of multi-year software development projects, so common in past decades, are over.

The Agile approach is characterized by an emphasis on personal interaction and collaboration, determining the business' needs, and working together to quickly meet those needs. Business stakeholders provide continuous input into the development process. When problems or issues are encountered, the team works together to resolve them, without finger-pointing or blame-gaming. When changes are required, there is a process in place to manage them. Requirements are not "set in stone".

The goal of Agile Development is to quickly produce solutions that are "good enough" (roughly defined as "meeting 80% of the requirements"). This goes back to the old "80/20" rule – since 80% of the requirements can be met with 20% of the cost and effort, that's the part you do. One significant cause of a lot of software project failures is attempting to write software that does everything for everybody, instead of defining those business needs that can be met quickly, effectively, and (relatively) inexpensively with a software solution, and empowering people to take care of the rest. One of the key tenets of Agile is empowering people to handle problems.

Software development occurs continuously and iteratively, with new releases taking place every few weeks. After each release, the product is evaluated by the customer, the requirements (including any changes requested by the customer) are re-prioritized, and a manageable subset of the highest priorities is selected for the next iteration. In this way, the customer gets at least some of the requested functionality early in the development process, with more features arriving at regular intervals. The product is continually tuned to fit customer and business needs throughout the development process; there are no unpleasant surprises when the user discovers he's waited several months for software that doesn't meet his needs.

Continuous testing is built into the development process, so that errors and problems are found and fixed early. Agile teams don't wait until one week before production implementation to start finding and fixing bugs! This helps eliminate a lot of expensive rework.

There is also an emphasis on evaluation and improvement. Each team member seeks to improve his/her skills and capabilities, learning as much as possible about what the other members of the team do, and what their needs and perspectives are. Agile Developers try to become generalists, skilled in many different areas, rather than single-minded specialists. Also, at each iteration in the process, the team tries to assess what went well and what went poorly, and works to continually improve its processes.

Implications of an Agile Approach

Now that we have a basic understanding of what Agile Development is about, let's consider some of the implications of an Agile approach in the context of our current organizations and development processes. What does it really *mean* to be "Agile"?

First of all, as I see it, the ability to reuse application components and data is essential to Agile development. In a truly Agile environment, there isn't the time or the resources to keep reinventing the wheel. The more able an organization is to reuse existing applications, services, and data for new purposes, the more Agile that organization will be.

Similarly, I think the ability to design and build loosely-coupled systems is also imperative. Systems that are tightly-coupled (i.e., applications whose components can't easily be changed or swapped without breaking something; or that are dependent on a particular hardware or software environment) are going to be more difficult to adapt to new or changing business requirements. The principle of coupling applies to databases, as well. As I will be explaining in more detail later, you want to avoid situations in which an application is tightly-coupled to a database schema (such that the database can't easily be changed without breaking the application). You also want to avoid having a database that is tightly-coupled to a single application, so that the database and its data cannot be used to support other applications, or other business uses. Both our applications and our data should be *extensible*; easy to change, and able to accommodate new requirements with a minimum of fuss and bother.

Along with loose coupling, another requirement is the ability to create policy-based (or rule-based) components. This means that the behavior of the component can be altered by changing its properties, or by passing different parameters to it. In a sense, this helps keep components from being tightly-coupled to business rules. For example, we've experienced great anguish in our IT organizations from the government's decision to change the starting and ending dates of Daylight Savings Time. Shouldn't we be able to simply make a change in a registry entry or a configuration file to inform our operating systems and applications of the change of rule?

Agile Development has implications for processes, as well as systems. For one thing, I regard the ability to automate routine tasks as being essential to an Agile process. When deadlines are tight and resources are constrained, the focus must be kept on value-producing activities, not routine housekeeping.

Since the Agile approach does not attempt to anticipate and forestall all possible problems before commencing work, the ability to recognize that problems and exceptions will occur, and to empower people to handle them is important. Traditional projects do a "risk assessment" at the beginning of the project; in Agile projects, risk management is an on-going proposition. This also implies that Agile teams must have the ability to enhance processes based on experience. With each iteration of the project, the team should be able to recognize potential problems earlier, and respond to them faster.

The Agile approach also carries some personal and cultural implications. I've already mentioned the importance of learning to generalize (i.e., understand areas outside your particular domain), as well as specialize (within your domain). Individuals and organizations must be willing to "suspend disbelief" and risk trying new things. Both old processes and new ones should be continually evaluated in light of what is most applicable to a given project, and what has been shown to work best in any particular situation.

Lastly, a customer service mindset and positive ("can do") attitude are required for anyone working in an Agile environment. Agile Development is predicated on the idea that any group of talented, dedicated individuals, committed to the success of a goal, can find a way to overcome any obstacle, and find a solution to any problem. This means abandoning negativity, as well as rigid preconceptions about how things should and should not be done.

Critical Issues in Agile Development

So, all we need to do is abandon our traditional processes and methodologies, adopt an Agile approach, and everything will be perfect, right? No, of course not. No methodology is without its flaws, and none works perfectly in all situations (or, perhaps, in *any* situation). It's also true that any project represents a collaboration of stakeholders, each of whom has different needs and different priorities. In my own experience, I've noticed several aspects of the Agile approach that must be taken into consideration (from the point of view of all of the project's stakeholders) when embarking on an Agile project. None of these issues are show-stoppers, and none should be taken as an irrefutable argument against any sort of iterative approach; however, each project needs to consider whether, and to what extent, each of these issues will have an impact.

These issues also go to the heart of a lot of the resistance to the Agile approach, particularly among data administrators, data analysts, enterprise architects, and other people in similar positions. As a database administrator, what I often hear from the Agile community is "Why can't those data people just *change* (and adopt an Agile approach)? Well, to a large extent, I think they can; that's what this book is about. However, it must be kept in mind that for those of us in these enterprise-focused positions, our jobs carry certain responsibilities that cannot be ignored. Agile Developers ignore these realities at the risk of their projects.

Having said that, let's take a look at some of these critical issues, especially from the point of view of data management concerns:

- **Reusability**. As mentioned earlier, reusability is a key aspect of agility. The ability to reuse code components, application services, processes, and data goes a long way toward enabling organizations to be truly Agile. But here's the rub (as Hamlet's masseuse might say) – designing and coding for reuse takes longer, and under the pressure of project deadlines and resource constraints, most developers don't do this. However, data managers (including DBAs and data analysts) are *required* to design and build for reuse – it's part of our charter, and a large part of the value we provide to the business. Like it or not, companies expect and assume that the data acquired in the course of their business can be used for anything that will benefit the business, at any time in the future.

  This can involve anything, from finding new markets and expanding existing ones to identifying cross-selling and up-selling opportunities; managing inventory turns and improving product quality; identifying poorly-performing dealers and suppliers and rewarding good ones. Companies expect their data to be immediately available and adaptable to any purpose. In other words, Agile!

- **Quality**. Generally speaking, applications can retain a significant amount of functionality and value even if they are "buggy". This is how most software vendors stay in business. It's also why many companies will download and deploy even pre-release "beta" versions of new software. Application errors are easier to detect and fix (or work around) than data errors; in fact, as I've pointed out in one of my online articles,[17] most companies aren't even aware of their data problems until they try reusing the data for some other purpose – and by then it's too late! Fixing data problems after the fact can be problematic. I once worked at a company whose response to any data problem was to run a program to massage the "bad" data. This usually caused other data problems to surface later, which were then similarly "fixed", causing more problems, and so on.

It also needs to be pointed out that, for both applications and data, quality directly affects reusability. A code component written for a single application might get away with having a few bugs in it, but a component intended for general use needs to be perfect, or as close to it as possible. Components that don't work as advertised probably won't get reused. Similarly, data that can't be trusted won't be used. By anyone. Ever.

- **Waste**. Agile methods can and do help eliminate significant amounts of waste in software development. For one thing, as noted earlier, users don't spend months or years waiting for an application, only to find out it isn't what they wanted, or what they need now. Also, the Agile emphasis on continual testing helps ensure that errors and problems are detected and fixed as early in the development cycle as possible. However, the iterative nature of Agile Development, coupled with ever-changing requirements and an emphasis on coding over design, means that Agile

---

[17] Burns, Larry. "The Ugly Truth About Data Quality", originally published May 31, 2005 in DMReview Online (http://www.dmreview.com/article_sub.cfm?articleID=1028545).

methods can generate large amounts of "scrap and rework" over the course of a project.

This is not necessarily bad, in and of itself, provided that the "scrap and rework" can be kept to a manageable level, and that each iteration brings the team closer to its goal. What needs to be avoided is what I call "thrashing" – constant changes that don't result in measurable progress for the application. There used to be a popular software magazine that carried a column featuring two programmers who spent inordinate amounts of time tweaking the same code over and over again. They would fix one piece of code, only to introduce errors in another, which would eventually lead to the redesign of a third section, which would break a fourth, and so on. Most of these problems probably could have been forestalled by spending an hour or so reviewing the application design. In this case, the most "Agile" thing to do would have been to *cease* the pointless activity, take a step back, and regroup. However, the activities of these programmers were being held up as an example of how application development should be done!

I can sympathize with the desire of Agile practitioners to avoid what they refer to as "Big Design Up Front" (BDUF). But on every project, I believe there is what Scott Ambler refers to as the "sweet spot", some middle ground between doing too much planning, analysis, and design, and doing too little. The one extreme can lead to just as many problems, and just as much lost time, money, and productivity, as the other. Doing a certain amount of planning, analysis, and design at the beginning of a project or iteration can save the team a lot of time and aggravation later on, and result in a much higher-quality product.

- **Resources**. The Agile approach works best when resources are 100% dedicated to a single project. This is easier to do for application developers, who generally only work on one or two projects at a time, than for people in the rest of the organization. DBAs and other data managers have to support multiple projects concurrently, while helping the rest of the organization with its data needs (e.g., data quality, data analysis and reporting), fixing data problems, and maintaining existing databases and servers. Similarly, business users have to spend their time running the business; their ability to commit time to an application development project is severely constrained. This can often be a source of frustration for Agile developers, when they can't immediately get the support they need for their project.

- **Focus**. Generally speaking, the focus of application development teams is to get a single application up and running, and out the door, on time and under budget. But for those of us in data management, the focus is on designing and building a data delivery infrastructure that meets both the current and future data needs of the entire organization. In that sense, we operate in a manner similar to other infrastructure support groups, such as the server support group and the network support group. Infrastructure work requires a greater adherence to standards and a more rigorous attention to detail and quality, which can sometimes conflict with Agile's more *laissez faire* approach.

One consequence of this infrastructure focus is the requirement to consider future needs, as well as current requirements. For example, our server support group doesn't build a server with only the minimum amount of CPU, memory, and disk space needed for today. Having to "refactor" a server after it's already running in production would be too disruptive to existing operations and users. So they consider the probable growth of usage of the server over its expected life, and build to those specifications. This results in fewer unpleasant surprises later.

- **Maintainability**. One aspect of application development that all too often is overlooked is that somebody is going to have to maintain the application after it is written. In most large organizations, this is a separate group from the development group, so most developers don't have to, as the saying goes, "eat their own dog food". I personally feel that developers should have to maintain their applications for at least a year after deployment; perhaps then we would see a greater emphasis on quality and documentation in software development! We, as DBAs, have to maintain the databases we build, and we realize that maintenance activities don't add much business value to the company, so we try to design and build databases that require as little maintenance as possible.

It also needs to be considered that the cost of maintaining an application over its useful life usually far exceeds the initial cost of development. This is true of database development, as well, which is why, for example, our database group creates a database design document for each database we build (this will be explained in more detail later on). It's important to at least document the requirements and business rules around which the application and database were built, the design decisions that were made, and the reasons for them. This way, support people don't have to spend a lot of time reverse-engineering the requirements out of the code in response to every bug, problem, or change request.

- **Personnel**. Agile projects can involve long hours, frequent requirements changes, intensive collaboration, and lots of stress. This may be a difficult adjustment for data professionals and other enterprise-level people not used to this sort of work environment.

- **ROI**. The emphasis in Agile Development is reducing "time to market": the time it takes to get the application to the business users. However, as pointed out in an excellent article by Susan Kunz in the *Software Development Times,*[18] a more appropriate metric is "time to money", the time it takes for an application to achieve "sustainable positive economic returns" to the company. I have seen applications, rushed into production, that required a year or more of patching and tweaking before they were even usable! In our rush to get application functionality into the hands of our users, we must bear in mind that they must deliver the required functionality *reliably* in order to return value to the company. Ms. Kunz provides some compelling statistics from the National Institute of Standards and Technology (NIST) and the Sustainable Computing Consortium: we spend (world-wide) an estimated 600 billion (U.S.) dollars per year on software development, and an estimated \$300 billion fixing software defects. So, for every dollar spent on software development, we spend 50 cents fixing bugs. What effect do you suppose that has on ROI?

Again, I raise these issues not to argue against an Agile approach *per se,* but to note that they will arise on projects, and will need to be addressed. I don't recall ever seeing these issues acknowledged, let alone addressed, in the literature on Agile Development.

A Building or a Garden?

Agile developer and writer Craig Larman, among others, likes to quote the following passage from a 1986 article by Fredrick Books:[19]

---

[18] Kunz, Susan. "Forget Time-to-Market: It's All About Time-to-Money". Software Development Times; August 15, 2006 (http://www.sdtimes.com/printArticle/column-20060815-01.html).

[19] Brooks, Jr., F.P., "No Silver Bullet—Essence and Accidents of Software Engineering," *Information Processing 86*. H.J. Kugler, ed. Elsevier Science Publishers B.V. (North Holland)

The building metaphor has outlived its usefulness. It is time to change again. If, as I believe, the conceptual structures we construct today are too complicated to be accurately specified in advance, and too complex to be built faultlessly, then we must take a radically different approach

Larman has said, "Architecture is a bad metaphor. We don't construct our software like a building, we grow it like a garden."[20] This seems to be a reaction to the John Zachman approach to Enterprise Architecture, which uses the architecture metaphor to advocate up-front requirements specification, analysis, design, and modeling.[21] Leaving aside questions of accuracy for the moment, the preference of Agile developers for the "garden" metaphor, and the preference of most data practitioners for the "building" metaphor goes straight to the heart of the conflict between these two groups. So let's examine this issue for a moment.

First of all, I think this is a false dichotomy; the way in which these metaphors are used reflects a lack of understanding of both architecture and gardening. As John Zachman makes clear, the purpose of architecture is *not* to define all the requirements up front. Architectural drawings are used to incrementally refine the customer's understanding of the requirements (which are usually hazy at the beginning), and then communicate these requirements to critical project stakeholders (for example, contractors and sub-contractors). As anyone who has ever built a house knows, requirements and specifications do change over the course of construction. Houses and buildings also evolve over time, even after they are built, in response to the changing requirements of their owners/users (as do gardens and parks). And although Craig Larman talks about "ivory tower architects" who don't know how

---

[20] Larman, Craig. "Large-Scale Agile Design and Architecture: Ways of Working". March 18, 2011 (http://www.infoq.com/articles/large-scale-agile-design-and-architecture).

[21] Zachman, John A. "A Framework for Information Systems Architecture". IBM Systems Journal, Vol. 26 No. 3, 1987, pp. 276-292.

to code, real architects need to understand how buildings are built (not to mention the applicable building codes) in order to do their job. Likewise, landscape designers need to know how to do gardening, even if they don't do the actual work.

Anyone who has done landscape gardening (as I do), knows that a certain amount of up-front architecture and design work is essential to a successful landscaping project. A landscaper begins every project by making a sketch of the property involved, noting the position of buildings, streams, large trees, landmarks, and so on. The path of the sun across the property at different seasons of the year will be noted, along with areas of sun and shade, direction of the prevailing wind, high and low elevation areas, direction of water drainage, etc. You don't just go out into the back yard with a shovel and start digging! You don't want to end up, for example, putting a patio or decorative pond in an area that will be covered with six inches of water in the winter. Nor do you want to put shade plants next to a steel-sided building that reflects 105 degree heat in the summer. A building architect takes much the same approach, drawing an initial sketch of the property involved, and adding features of the building to this drawing as they are specified by the customer.

These architectural sketches, at this relatively high level of detail, serve two purposes: first, they capture the *scope* and *constraints* of the project, so that impossible or impractical customer requirements are immediately identified before too much work is put into implementing them. A building architect may have to tell a client, "No, you can't put a six-car garage there; that's where the drain field for the septic system needs to go." Second, they provide the framework in which the customer's requirements can be captured and understood ("Yes, that's right; I want a flagstone path to go between those two cedar trees, and end at a gazebo at the back of the shade garden"); these requirements can then be communicated, via the drawings, to the people who will do the actual construction.

So these metaphors don't really reflect a choice between doing architecture and design, or not doing architecture and design. You *need* to do architecture and design.[22] It's just a question of how much architecture and design is done, when, where, how often, and by whom.

The amount of architecture and design work you do (especially up-front, before construction begins) depends on:

- The expected total cost of the project (if you're putting in a vegetable garden, you'll do less design work up-front; if you're building a skyscraper, you'll do more)

- The cost and difficulty of making changes after construction starts

- The cost and difficulty of maintaining the end product over time

- The cost and risk of project failure

- The number of people involved in the project, their roles, and the degree to which they interact.

One implication of software developers' preference for the "garden" metaphor is that you don't need to be as careful with software projects as with building projects, because software can be more quickly and easily changed after construction starts than a building can. This may be true, to some extent. But don't make the mistake of thinking that the costs and risks of inadequate software design are zero. I once worked for a company that spent two years and five million dollars developing an application, and then discovered that their mainframe environment didn't have enough capacity to support it. The project was scrapped. Asking a few architectural questions up front could have saved that company a lot of grief.

It is also important to consider the cost of maintaining the end product over time. One comment of Craig Larman's that I find

---

[22] As playwright Jean Kerr once said of the modern theater, "I like to feel as though the playwright has done some work before I got there."

especially puzzling is his assertion that the application code is the source of the application architecture and design.[23]   Since application developers, by and large, don't have to maintain the applications they write, and since it's not cost-effective to have to derive the application requirements and design from thousands or millions of lines of source code every time a change needs to be made, this is the same as saying that there *is* no architecture or design. The owner of a building, calling in a contractor to do a major remodel, wouldn't say, "I don't have any blueprints; you'll have to examine the building." Similarly, trying to change an application where all the requirements and design are embedded in the code would be a lengthy and expensive undertaking. I've been an application support person. Believe me, I know.

The Agile approach can help reduce some of the necessity for front-loaded design, especially if the project team is co-located (that is, all or part of the work isn't being outsourced or distributed) and working together. There is less of a need to prepare detailed specifications to be handed from one team member to another, the way a building architect prepares detailed drawings to give to a contractor. The client (customer) is an integral part of the project team, and can answer questions and help refine requirements as the need arises. Also, roles on an Agile team are less segregated; most, if not all, of the team members should be able to handle analysis, architecture, and design activities in addition to coding and testing. Indeed, one of the major reasons developers prefer the "garden" metaphor is to avoid being thought of as nothing more than implementers, people who code to the design and requirements given to them by others.[24] However, landscape

---

[23] Larman, Craig and Bas Vodde. *Practices for Scaling Lean & Agile Development: Large, Multisite, and Offshore Product Development with Large-Scale Scrum.* Addison-Wesley, 2010, page 283.

[24] Per Larman, "What happens…in a group with the following cultural value and message: *'There is the Architecture group over there; your regular programmers are not architects'.*" Ibid, page 286.

designers often contract out the actual implementation work, so again, the analogy is imperfect.

It's important to understand what architecture and design actually are, and what they contribute to a project. Then, and only then, can sensible decisions be made about how much of each to do, and when (and how often) this work should be done.

Agile vs. Software Engineering

Before closing this chapter, I'd like to say a few words about Agile Development as compared to some of the more traditional development methodologies, such as Software Engineering. Although at first glance they may seem incompatible, I view them as more-or-less complementary. Consider the following:

- Agile and Software Engineering both have the same goals – to ensure the success of software projects, and to give customers software that works correctly and meets their needs.

- Agile and Software Engineering are both trying to avoid the same thing – software bugs and requirements deficiencies that aren't surfaced until too late in the project (when the cost of fixing them is high).

- Agile and Software Engineering both embrace the concepts of verification and validation (Boehm, 1981). Verification ensures that the product meets the requirements definition ("Are we building the product right?"). Validation ensures that the product meets the customer's requirements ("Are we building the right product?").

- Agile and Software Engineering are both based on the idea that the longer it takes to detect an error or defect, the more expensive and time-consuming it is to correct.

- Agile and Software Engineering are both group-focused and role-based. The idea of doing software development in teams has always been an essential component of Software Engineering; the concept of "egoless programming" (including peer reviews of code) was first espoused by Gerald Weinberg in 1971!

- Agile and Software Engineering both acknowledge the fact that requirements change over the course of a project, and that developers must be flexible in accommodating change. One Software Engineering textbook states it like this: "It is essential that our software engineering tools be used with an eye toward flexibility. In the past, we as developers assumed that our customers knew from the start what they wanted. That is not usually the case."[25] For this reason, Software Engineering introduced the concept of *phased development*, in which complexity is gradually added to the application over time, and each iteration of the application is tested before proceeding to the next.

It needs to be noted that, contrary to prevailing ideas, Software Engineering has *always* accommodated an iterative approach to software development. The traditional, linear "waterfall" diagram, so maligned by Agile practitioners, was created for *managers*, not developers. The intent was to give management visibility into the various aspects of software development, and to give them a tool for planning and reporting.[26] All Software Engineering texts show the waterfall diagram modified to illustrate iteration and recursion between each of the development activities. Most also show Barry Boehm's "spiral" model (first introduced in 1988), which is the prototype for Agile Development.

Roger Pressman, in his seminal text on Software Engineering, notes that multiple approaches to software development are necessary. Applications whose requirements can be more-or-less fully specified at the beginning can use some variant of the

---

[25] Pfleeger, Shari Lawrence. *Software Engineering: The Production of Quality Software*, 2nd Ed. Macmillan Publishing, 1991, p. 26.

[26] See, for example, Ian Sommerville, *Software Engineering*, 4th Ed. Addison-Wesley, 1992, pp. 5-6.

traditional waterfall approach, while those whose requirements are continually evolving will take the iterative path. In some cases, prototyping will be used as a communication tool to help define the requirements; development may then proceed according to the standard life-cycle, but this process may repeat itself over various iterations of the software. As Pressman puts it, "There is no need to be dogmatic about the choice of paradigms for software engineering. The nature of the application should dictate the approach to be taken. By combining approaches, the whole can be greater than the sum of the parts."[27]

So where do the conflicts between Agile Development and Software Engineering approaches come from? Here are a few of the issues:

- Software Engineering emphasizes the idea of software quality, and tries to eliminate as many bugs (or potential bugs) as early as possible in the development process (preferably before they are introduced into the code). Modern approaches to application development (including Agile) place much less importance on software quality. Software vendors have inured us to the idea of living with (or working around) software defects. I have heard some Agile practitioners argue that only "critical" applications need be concerned about quality. This, however, begs the question of what constitutes a "critical" application – if the application isn't critical to a company's mission and bottom line, why is it being built?

- Software Engineering approaches try to minimize the amount of "scrap and rework" required during development, to help reduce costs and eliminate errors. Agile Development embraces a significant amount of "scrap and rework", often extending to the entire application (i.e., if the application is buggy or doesn't meet the customer's needs, just rewrite it). The critical question here is: what is the

---

[27] Pressman, Roger S. *Software Engineering: A Practitioners Approach*, 3rd Ed. McGraw-Hill, 1992, pp. 33-34.

cost-effectiveness of each of these approaches, in the context of a particular business need? Is it essential to the business to get a working product into customers' hands quickly, even if it's buggy or lacks features? Or will time and money be saved by making sure the product works as intended the first time?

- Some Agile approaches emphasize prototyping over formal requirements definition, a practice that makes Software Engineering practitioners uncomfortable. Roger Pressman notes two problems with this approach:[28]

  1. *The customer sees what appears to be a working version of the software, unaware that the prototype is held together "with chewing gum and baling wire", unaware that in the rush to get it working, we haven't considered overall software quality or long-term maintainability. When informed that the product must be rebuilt, the customer cries foul and demands that "a few fixes" be applied to make the prototype a working product. Too often, software development management relents.*

  2. *The developer often makes implementation compromises in order to get a prototype working quickly. An inappropriate operating system or programming language may be used simply because it is available and known; an inefficient algorithm may be implemented simply to demonstrate capability. After a time, the developer may become familiar with these choices, and forget all the reasons why they were inappropriate. The less-than-ideal choice has now become an integral part of the system.*

- Software Engineering puts importance not only on the delivery of the working product, but also on the cost and effort of maintaining the product over time. Given that most IT shops spend between 50 and 80 percent of their

---

[28] Ibid, p. 28.

time and budget maintaining their existing software inventory, this is not an unimportant consideration, and one which is largely ignored in Agile Development.

- Agile Development regards much of the documentation produced in traditional development approaches as an unnecessary and expensive impediment to the project effort, and there is a certain amount of validity to this assertion. Ian Sommerville, however, notes that much of this documentation is produced for the project's *managers*, not for its developers:

  "Existing software management structures are set up to deal with a software process model which results in regular deliverables which are used to measure progress."[29]

Even in shops like ours, which use the Agile/Scrum methodology, projects still have to follow our company's defined project management process, which requires regular "tollgate" meetings to assess the project's progress and cost-effectiveness. Each of these tollgates requires a significant amount of documentation. It is also worth noting that, even though we develop software using an Agile approach, our project management and reporting is still based on the traditional life-cycle model: requirements, design, build/verify, and implementation/control. This is an aspect of software development that has not, I think, been adequately addressed in the Agile literature.

As Agile methodologies have matured, and as application development toolsets have improved, some of these issues are becoming easier to manage. Increasing support for test-driven development (TDD) in development tools and frameworks, for example, have made it much easier to identify and fix code errors early in each iteration of the software, making it less necessary to over-design up-front in order to eliminate defects. Building tests into application and database code greatly improves the

---

[29] Sommerville, p. 12.

maintainability of the application, and makes it easier to enhance and add functionality over time. And the Agile emphasis on streamlining processes and eliminating unnecessary documentation has had, overall, a positive impact on software development, enabling us to get new products out to our customers in months, not years. Much more remains to be done. But change will come more quickly if Agile advocates and Software Engineering adherents can learn to work together and find common ground, instead of being at odds.

Key Points

- Agile is more than just the latest development fad; it is a reasoned attempt to address the root causes of software project failure.

- The Agile approach is characterized by an emphasis on personal interaction and collaboration, as opposed to formal processes and methodologies.

- Agile emphasizes incremental delivery of value, embracing and managing change, empowering people to solve problems, continuous testing, and continual process improvement.

- The Agile approach implies the ability to reuse both application components and data, automate routine processes, design and build loosely-coupled systems, explore new ways of doing things, and continually evaluate and improve tools and processes in light of past experience.

- Agile is not the best fit for all roles in an organization. In particular, people in enterprise-level or infrastructure roles need to devote more time and attention to long-term business needs.

- Issues of quality, reuse, waste, maintainability, and ROI need to be addressed by all projects, even Agile projects.

- Both the Agile and Software Engineering approaches have similar goals, but different areas of emphasis. Improvements in both process and tools are making it easier to reconcile these two approaches.

In the global Information Economy, a company is only as good as its data. More importantly, it's only as good as its data management practices. But good data management is more than just ensuring the quality, availability, reusability, and business-relevance of data; it must also support effective processes that enable new information flows (i.e., applications) to be created, deployed, and modified quickly in response to changing business conditions and new opportunities. This is the context in which an Agile approach to both application development and data management should be understood.

PRISM: The 5 Principles of Data Management

Now that we have an understanding of Agile Development and what it means, let's take a brief look at what data management entails. There are five basic principles which govern most of the work that we, as data managers, do; I've encapsulated these principles under the acronym PRISM. When developers ask me why I, as a DBA, advise doing things a certain way, I usually come back to one or more of these five principles. If you're a developer reading this, I strongly encourage you *not* to skip this section; it will give you a much better understanding of why DBAs and other data managers do what they do. Similarly, if you're a data manager reading this, it may help you to understand how to better communicate the requirements of data management to your developers.

The five principles of data management are as follows:

Performance and Ease of Use. We want to always ensure quick and easy access of data to approved users in a usable and business-relevant form, so as to maximize the business value of both our applications and our data. If we build an application that enables us to perform a task one hour sooner, but it takes users an hour to use the application, we've spent a lot of money for nothing. Likewise, if we return data to a business user immediately, but it takes an hour to put that data into a usable and business-relevant form, we've accomplished nothing. The proper goal of both application development and data management is to improve the cost-effectiveness of every business process we automate and, in so doing, improve our relationships with our customers and business users.

Reusability. Reusability (also called *application independence*) means that our databases are designed and built around general business subject areas, not specific application requirements, and are designed to support multiple applications and multiple business uses. By designing our data around the real-world entities and attributes of the business, we help ensure that our data always has a valid business meaning and value, regardless of how it is used. Also, by enabling data reuse, instead of always having each application maintain its own set of data, we help increase the potential ROI of our data. As I ask in one of my articles,[30] "Why is it that every application needs its own database, when we haven't finished paying for the data we already have?" Consider that the cost of data encompasses things like the cost of building and maintaining the applications that create and use it, and the cost of building and maintaining the databases and database servers, and the licensing costs of the software and so on. Then compare that cost with the business value derived from application-specific data and you may be forced to conclude, as I have, that our companies are probably *losing* money on every database they own!

As I mentioned earlier, companies expect to have the ability to reuse data for many different business purposes (e.g., quality improvement, business process improvement, inventory control, customer relationship management, strategic planning, and so on). It is vitally important for software developers to understand that

---

[30] Burns, Larry. "The Ugly Truth About Data Quality" (op. cit.).

organizations have data needs that lie outside the data requirements of specific applications. Data that is "stovepiped" (i.e., tightly-coupled to a specific application) is much harder to combine with data in other databases, and the results of doing so may be problematic, since data specific to one application may not *mean* the same thing (in business terms) as data specific to another. This is why data integration efforts at many companies have resulted in expensive and publicly embarrassing failures.

We should also remember that one of the principal objectives of object-oriented development is the ability to reuse objects for multiple applications.[31] And since objects contain data, making it easier to reuse data also makes it easier to reuse objects. This facilitates future application development, and makes all of our applications more Agile.

Integrity. I want to make it clear that when data managers talk about data integrity, we're not talking about some hypothetical, theoretical, abstracted concept of data purity. What we're trying to do is ensure that our data always has a valid business meaning and value, regardless of context, and that our data always reflects a valid state of the business. This is why, for example, all database updates related to a single business transaction must be either committed or rolled back as a single unit of work.

It is also important that data should be, as much as possible, self-monitoring and self-correcting, in the same way that applications

---

[31] I acknowledge that there is a lot of disagreement in the developer community about whether code objects can, or should, be reused. However, the evolution of application development, including service-oriented architecture (SOA), team-oriented application development and collaboration tools, and domain-specific languages are all predicated on the idea of reuse. I personally believe that much of what annoys the business community about IT (lengthy development times, project delays, cost overruns, etc.) will never be satisfactorily resolved without addressing the issue of reuse.

are written to detect, and respond gracefully to, any conceivable error condition or component failure.

Security. My recommendations about data security are centered around Richard O. Mason's four pillars of Information Ethics:[32] **P**rivacy (how can people keep secret what they are not obligated to reveal); **A**ccuracy (who is responsible for preventing or redressing errors in data); **P**roperty (who has the right to control access to information); and **A**ccessibility (what information do people have a right to obtain). Our objective as data managers is to make sure that true and accurate data is always available to authorized persons, but *only* to authorized persons. We also want to make sure that the privacy concerns of all our stakeholders – including our customers, partners, and government regulators – are met. The potential costs of failing to do so (as we observe in almost every daily newspaper) are high.

Maintainability. We also want to make sure that we do all of this work at a *cost that yields value*; i.e., that the cost of creating, using, maintaining, and disposing of data doesn't exceed its value to the business. And we want to ensure the fastest possible response to changes in business processes and new business requirements.

These five principles provide the foundation for any effective approach to data management. Now we want to consider the question: how can we do data management in an Agile fashion?

Agile Data Management

So now that we understand the requirements of Agile Development, and the requirements of data management, the question becomes, "How do we do Agile Data Management?"

---

[32] Mason, Richard O. "Four Ethical Issues of the Information Age."
Available online at
www.misq.org/archivist/vol/no10/issue1/vol10no1mason.html.

Over the years that I've been involved with both traditional and Agile software development projects, I've developed a set of high-level values (in addition to the PRISM data management principles) that guide my approach to database work:

- *Respect the legitimate interests of stakeholders.* Many of the disagreements and conflicts in our IT organizations stem from a failure to recognize that everyone who is committed to the success of the organization has a stake in the outcome of our endeavors. As I pointed out in the Introduction to this book, every group has things that they need to do in order to contribute their value to the organization. It is both pointless and counterproductive for any one group to say to another, "Your concerns don't matter." While it may not be possible to satisfy everyone's interests in all circumstances, the legitimate efforts of all groups to contribute to the success of the organization should be recognized and rewarded, not impeded. If a decision must be made that impacts the work of a group, that group should be involved in the decision, and should understand how that decision contributes to the greater good.

- *Maximize the business value of data.* Many, if not most, approaches to data management focus on maximizing data purity. I believe that a proper approach to data management will focus on increasing the business value of data. This is why, for example, I don't subscribe to the idea that data should only exist in one place (i.e., absolutely no replication of data). I certainly agree that business-critical data related to a particular area of the business should be *managed* in one place, and that there should be one acknowledged source of authority for it. After that, however, I see no objection to replicating that data in as many places, and in as many forms, as will contribute more value to the business than the cost of replicating, storing, and managing it.[33] We're not running data museums here; data exists for the purpose of driving innovation and creating business value.[34]

We also need to understand that one business area's view of "the truth" may necessarily be different from that of a different business area. When I worked in financial accounting, for example, I discovered that the definition of basic accounting entities such as Budget and Account varied depending on the funding source (e.g., government funding vs. grant funding vs. private contract funding).

- *Focus on supporting business areas, not applications.* This goes back to the PRISM principles: design and build databases that are extensible and reusable, and can support multiple applications and uses of the data within the context of a business subject area. This is the surest way to increase the business value of data, and avoid the long-term maintenance headaches that result from tightly-coupling applications and databases.

- *Distinguish between the logical and physical views of data.* As will be explained shortly, the central tenet of Agile database development is understanding and maintaining the critical distinction between the logical and physical views of data, creating one or more virtual data layers above the normalized base schema for application objects to

---

[33] Starbucks, for example, manages master data related to customers, products, locations, and suppliers in a central database, then publishes that data to multiple application databases, as opposed to, say, requiring each application to use web services to access this data at its source.

[34] Granted, there is some point at which managing, or trying to manage, multiple copies of the same data across the organization becomes counterproductive. This can be overcome, in part, by making data in central stores easier to access and use. See, for example, my online article "A Vatican II For Data Governance", at http://www.tdan.com/view-articles/13274.

use, and restricting refactoring to the virtual schema, not the base schema, as much as possible. I'm going to have a lot to say in this book about how to create these virtual data layers, and how to use them effectively in Agile Development. And I'm going to be relating these ideas to some of the core concepts of object-oriented development – cohesion and coupling, abstraction and encapsulation, inheritance and association. And, most important of all, reuse!

- *Properly support enterprise data in all its forms.* The principles of data management, properly understood, pertain to data in all forms and in all locations, not just data residing in relational databases (or in any database). Data managers need to understand and work effectively with non-relational and non-database data, particularly XML, file, and object data. It's high time we realized that all enterprise data, in whatever form it's stored and used, is business-critical, and needs to be managed just as effectively as relational data. By treating non-relational and non-database data as though it was "someone else's responsibility", we lose significant opportunities to benefit our companies, and put significant areas of the business at risk. And if databases go away (as at least one Gartner Group study has suggested)[35], what will all of us "data managers" do for a living?

- *Make the database do the data work.* In other words, take an "N-tier" approach to application development, doing data work on the database server, business processing in the application layer(s), and presentation work in the client layer. Ignore approaches to application development which advocate doing all the data work in the application, or putting all of the application code (including the business

---

[35] Beyer, Mark. "The Death of the Database", originally presented at the Gartner Symposium/Itxpo 2006 in San Francisco, May 14-18 2006. Publication number SPG8_837, 5/06, AE.

logic) in the database. Not only do these approaches result in applications that are inefficient, perform poorly, and are difficult to scale, they also tightly-couple applications and data (or applications and databases), and prevent both application components and data from being reusable. They also result in a lot of unnecessary work. For example, if data validity constraints aren't defined in the database, then *every* application that creates or updates data has to contain code to do the validity checking, and all of this code will need to be tested and maintained over time.[36] And, of course, there are no safeguards whatsoever for data updates that occur outside the context of an application (e.g., by outside hackers or internal users). In the databases our group builds, data integrity, validity, and security constraints are always implemented at the database level, not in the applications. This ensures that our data is always valid, no matter how it is created or used.

- *Automate as much of the database development process as possible.* As I mentioned before, the ability to automate routine processes, and improve them over time based on experience, is essential to developing a truly Agile environment. In our group, we have developed tools and processes that enable us to go from a logical data model to a fully-implemented database in a matter of minutes. We have reusable code to support a number of application database functions, such as support for text in multiple languages, supertype/subtype data structures, and auditing of database updates. We maintain a library of standard

---

[36] I'm not arguing against the idea of "defense in depth"; that is, having some redundant checks in the application. As my colleague Bill Sheboy has noted, defense in depth can help to foster reusability when application functions and services have multiple interfaces (online, batch, or service-oriented). I want to make clear, though, that the primary line of defense for data quality should be in the database, not in the application.

solutions (including data model subject areas) for commonly-referenced entities (such as customer data). And our ability to process schema changes quickly has helped take a lot of the pain out of one of the most difficult aspects of Agile Development.

- *Learn to collaborate.* As Scott Ambler correctly notes, no methodology of any sort will succeed unless people commit themselves to making it succeed. For an Agile approach to be successful, all the members of the team must understand what other members of the team are doing and why; they must educate their fellow team members in the importance of what they themselves do; they must learn to communicate effectively both within and outside the group; and they must commit themselves to working together positively and effectively in pursuit of the common goal.

- *Learn to work iteratively (within reason!).* In the modern business world, we all need to learn to work within shorter time frames. At the same time, we need to make sure our efforts are effective and contribute value to the business. Agile Development is a sort of perpetual high-wire balancing act in which tasks and risks are continually being assessed, and achievable goals must be set within realistic time frames. Trade-offs must constantly be made – against doing too much too quickly, or too little too late; against planning too much or too little. These are skills that nobody gets right the first time.

- *Develop a customer service mindset.* As I've advocated in a series of articles for DMReview.com,[37] it is essential for data professionals to be able to work with, and communicate effectively with, all of the stakeholders who

---

[37] Burns, Larry. "Promoting Data Management", Parts 1 and 2, originally published August 11 and August 18, 2006 in DMReview Online (http://www.dmreview.com/article_sub.cfm?articleId=1060633 and http://www.dmreview.com/article_sub.cfm?articleId=1061188)

depend on us for secure, high-quality, reusable, business-relevant data. We need to stay business-focused, recognizing that our ultimate responsibility is to the success of our companies and the well-being of our customers. We should maintain a "can do" attitude, and be as helpful as possible. If we're perceived as obstructionists, people will simply work around us (or behind our backs); if we don't help them succeed, they may help us fail. We need to recognize that ours is a customer-service profession.

In summary, a truly Agile approach to data management will be:

- Stakeholder-based

- Customer-focused

- Business-centered

- Loosely-coupled

- Multi-tier.

The rest of this book will be devoted to explaining how to satisfy these goals in the context of Agile Development.

What is a Database?

Before we leave this chapter, I would like to acknowledge that the approach to database development that I'm advocating is predicated on some assumptions about what databases are, and what application functionality they should support. So let's ask the central question: what *is* a database?

The answer to this question is neither as easy nor as obvious as you might think. In fact, some textbooks on database systems try to avoid committing themselves to a definition of the word "database". Rob Mattison's book *Understanding Database Management Systems* puts it this way:

The question of what exactly a database is could, in and of itself, spark a lot of debate among data processing professionals. Depending upon what a person's experience is and what they are trying to accomplish, a database can be construed to be many things.[38]

Most textbooks on the subject define a database as nothing more than an organized collection of data, for example:

A database is a collection of interrelated data.[39]

A database is a collection of structured information.[40]

Note that, even in these simplest definitions, assumptions are creeping in. Data is assumed to be both structured (in some form) and interrelated. Other definitions of "database" contain further assumptions:

Database*: A shared collection of logically related data (and a description of this data) designed to meet the information needs of an organization.*[41]

A database is a logically coherent collection of data with some inherent meaning. A random assortment of data cannot be referred to as a database.[42]

A database is a collection of data, organized logically and managed by a unifying set of principles, procedures, and functionalities, that

---

[38] Mattison, Rob. *Understanding Database Management Systems*, 2nd Ed. McGraw-Hill, 1998, page 19.

[39] Kroha, Petr. *Objects and Databases*. McGraw-Hill, 1993, page 6.

[40] Agarwal, Vidya Vrat and James Huddleston. *Beginning VB 2008 Databases: From Novice to Professional*. Apress, 2008, page 25.

[41] Connolly, Thomas, Carolyn Begg and Anne Strachan. *Database Systems*, 2nd Ed. Addison-Wesley, 1999, page 14.

[42] Elmasri, Ramez and Shamkant B. Navathe. *Fundamentals of Database Systems*. The Benjamin/Cummings Publishing Company, Inc., 1989, page 1.

helps guarantee the consistent application and interpretation of that data across the organization.[43]

A database is a fully integrated collection of files brought together to serve multiple applications.[44]

Our definition of "database" has now expanded to include data that is: logically coherent, internally defined (by metadata), organized by a unifying set of principles, managed, and shared by multiple applications across an organization.

The definition of database expands even further when we move into the world of relational databases and relational database theory. According to relational database theory, a database table stores a set of assertions about a thing (an *entity*) that we believe to be true. The relational model allows us to draw conclusions from our data, based on these and related assertions.[45]

In contrast, the literature of Agile Development defines a database as little more than a place to store and retrieve data:

A (relational) database is a persistent storage mechanism that enables you to both store data and optionally implement functionality.[46]

Far too many application developers think of a database as nothing more than a repository for application-specific data (what they call a "persistence engine"). To them, a database is a sort of

---

[43] Mattison, op. cit., page 19.

[44] Smith, Peter D. and G. Michael Barnes. *Files and Databases: An Introduction*. Addison-Wesley, 1987, page 5.

[45] See, for example: Date, C. J. *An Introduction to Database Systems*, 8th Ed. Addison-Wesley, 2003. See also, Pascal, Fabian. *Understanding Relational Databases*. John Wiley & Sons, 1993.

[46] Ambler, Scott W. "Relational Databases 101: Looking at the Whole Picture", at http://www.agiledata.org/essays/relationalDatabases.html.

"Fibber McGee's closet"[47] into which data gets stuffed and then, sometime later, retrieved. We hope that the data, by that time, is correct, timely, business-relevant, and easily consumable, but it probably won't be. Databases built according to this definition of "database" characteristically have few, if any, data integrity constraints, because developers prefer to code all such "intelligence" in the application. I'll have something to say about this in the next section of this chapter.

I advocate a more complete definition of "database". A database, in my view, is not just a repository for business data, it is a repository for the *business rules* that constrain the data. This is why (as we will see) having a complete and accurate logical data model is so critical to database development – the logical data model documents the business data requirements and business rules that need to be implemented, in some fashion, in the database. As this book will explain, it is not necessary, and usually not desirable, to implement the logical data model as though it were the actual database design. Nevertheless, the database, once implemented, *must* encapsulate the business data requirements and business rules that are documented in the logical model. That is, the database will contain both *metadata* (defining characteristics of each data attribute, such as its domain, datatype, and optionality) and *constraints* (internal rules that govern the values that each data attribute is allowed to have).

Having a database that encapsulates – and enforces – the business rules surrounding business data helps ensure that the data in the database will always be complete and correct, and that it will always represent, at any given moment in time, a valid view of the

---

[47] I probably need to explain this reference. "Fibber McGee and Molly" was an old radio comedy program in which McGee (a chronic liar) was always running to the hall closet for some tool or something he needed. Molly (his wife) would shout "Don't open that door, McGee!", and all the contents of the closet would empty themselves onto McGee's head. This is what flashes through my mind when I hear developers refer to databases as "persistence engines".

business. Data that can be trusted to be correct, accurate, and timely, that is easily consumable, and that is business-relevant (and not just application-specific) is data that can be reused, over and over again, in support of multiple applications, multiple business processes, and multiple business initiatives. This, in turn, greatly multiplies the value of the data (and the database) to the business.

As I've often said, data management is the art of turning data into business value. Data that is locked in application-specific databases (especially databases that don't bother to enforce the correctness or business-relevance of their data) is data that is not going to be of much value to the business!

That being said, it must be acknowledged that there are some applications whose data will not be of value outside the boundaries of the application. A CAD/CAM engineering application, for example, manipulates design objects in a graphical framework, and stores them in an object database. Since this data has no relevance outside the application, we need only ensure that it is correct from the standpoint of the application, and safeguarded against loss and harm. We don't need to ensure its reusability or business-relevance across the organization. Therefore, the approach to database development and data management that I am advocating in this book will not, for the most part, be germane to these types of databases.

Be careful, though, in assuming that any given set of data will *not* be useful outside the context of the application that creates it. We have an application, for example, that monitors the health of electronic components within our products, and sends messages in XML that are persisted in an XML repository. I suggested at the time that this data would be useful in identifying sub-standard products and poorly-performing suppliers. Now, our Six Sigma (quality improvement) group has suggested putting this data into a database for this exact purpose!

It is very important, when beginning an application development project (or any IT project in which data will be created) to examine the potential usefulness of the data to other areas of the business, and to design and build the data repository accordingly.

In Defense of the "Intelligent" Database

In the previous sections of this chapter, I've talked about implementing data constraints (business rules that constrain data) at the database level, and advocated an N-Tier approach to application development that "makes the database do the data work". As we have already seen, a database should contain not only data, but the implementation of business data rules and metadata that define what the data should look like, what values it is allowed to have, and how data interrelates with other data in the database.

As we will see later in this book, a database should also encapsulate functionality that allows data to be safely updated (in accordance with the appropriate business rules) and quickly accessed in a business-relevant form.

When I've presented these ideas in online forums and at conferences, I've been criticized for advocating putting "intelligence" into databases. Apparently, intelligence is now a bad thing (this would explain much of our current culture!).

At the risk of getting ahead of myself in this book, I would like to take a moment to address these concerns. As we will see, putting data-related business rules and data update/access functionality into the database has many benefits:

- It improves performance by taking advantage of the database management software's ability to pre-define query plans and table joins, and optimize them for maximum efficiency.

- It improves the scalability of applications, by using the database server's CPU and memory resources, rather than doing all the work on the application server.

- It helps ensure data integrity by enforcing business data rules at the database level, rather than trusting the application code to enforce these constraints over time.

- It reduces application development and maintenance costs by making it unnecessary to replicate and maintain database code across all the applications that use a particular database.

- It reduces network bandwidth (and improves both performance and scalability) by doing data retrieval and filtering on the database server and sending the application only the data it actually needs. Similarly, by putting complex SQL code in stored procedures in the database, this code doesn't have to be sent across the network.

- It helps ensure that database updates are done consistently, and that considerations of concurrency (making sure that two different users can't update the same record at the same time) and transaction management (making sure that all updates related to a single unit of business work are either committed to the database or rolled back in their entirety) are managed correctly.

- It helps ensure data security by restricting access to database objects (views, tables, functions, stored procedures) to defined roles or groups. This also helps defend against hacking and SQL injection attacks by not opening up database tables to direct updating.

- It safeguards both data integrity and data security by preventing improper access and update of data outside of applications.

- It improves the maintainability of applications by making it easier to identify and resolve errors and performance issues related to database code. Most database vendors provide many tools to help quickly and easily resolve such issues.

- It makes it easier to change code and data interfaces "on the fly", in response to problems or changing application requirements. It is much easier to refactor a view, function, or procedure (in most cases) than it is to refactor application code or a database schema.

- Finally, it helps promote a more object-oriented approach to application development by creating a set of easily-modifiable database objects that can be reused across projects, and used to meet other non-project data requirements, as well.

With all these advantages to consider, why would anyone **not** want to put data-related code on the database server? One objection I've heard is that removing all intelligence (code) from the database makes it easier to port it to a different DBMS (vendor). However, I'm not sure that this is really the problem we should be trying to solve! Moving from one database product to another is not that difficult, and the various database vendors are more than happy to provide tools, techniques, and consulting help to assist with moving from a competitor's product.

The real issue, I think, is whether you regard a database as a business asset, or as simply an application "persistence" mechanism. In either case, you have to think about what makes the most sense economically. If you think of a database as a business asset, the economic problem lies in making data easily reusable, and in making databases economically viable. As I've already pointed out, a database that supports only a single application is probably costing the company more money to design, build, and maintain than it is deriving in economic value (i.e., most companies are probably losing money on their databases). The only way to derive significant economic value from data is to continually find ways of reusing it to drive innovation and create value. You can't do that (at least, not economically) when the data is tightly-coupled to a single application, or when you're relying on applications to ensure the quality and business-relevance of the data. Ask anyone who's ever worked on a data warehouse or BI (Business Intelligence) project!

However, if you regard the database as merely a persistence mechanism for an application, you have a different economic problem. Database products (most of them, at least) are quite expensive, and a database that supports only a single application (and whose data isn't, or can't be, reused) will have almost zero ROI. This may be OK for, say, a simple web application using an open-source (i.e., free) database product like MySQL, but one of the groups I've talked to, from a company that was adamant about not putting any "intelligence" into their databases, was using Oracle. That's a lot of money to spend for a simple "persistence engine"!

In our organization, we work hard to maximize the economic value of our databases at the lowest possible cost. For example, we can auto-generate the database schema (including all business rule constraints, indexes, triggers, etc.) and database views directly from our modeling tool. We also have a program that auto-generates CRUD (Create, Read, Update, and Delete) stored procedures from the database schema; these procedures can be used by any application, and ensure both transactional integrity and concurrency with minimal locking. This eliminates the cost of writing, testing, and maintaining application code to perform these functions in every application that uses the database, and helps ensure data integrity and reusability at minimal cost. We have a library of reusable code objects to support many common database functions (such as support for text storage and retrieval in multiple languages, and auditing of database updates).

It makes more sense to do the data work (at least, most of it) in the database. By enabling this work to be done quickly and easily, at low cost, in a way that makes data easy to consume and reuse, DBAs and other data professionals can add significant business value to their organizations, while freeing up development and support resources that can be used to tackle more important business problems.

Key Points

- The five principles of data management are: **P**erformance (and ease of use), **R**eusability, **I**ntegrity, **S**ecurity, and **M**aintainability. We can summarize them under the acronym **PRISM**.

- An Agile approach to data management should be stakeholder-based, customer-focused, business-centered, loosely-coupled, and multi-tier.

- Data that is of value only to a particular application can be "persisted" in any sort of data repository. Data that can be of value across multiple applications and business functions must be designed for reuse, and persisted in a manner that supports reuse.

- Data professionals must learn to manage data in whatever form it is persisted and used within the enterprise. Data can exist in different forms at different times; not all data resides in databases, and not all databases are relational.

- Generally speaking, it makes more economic sense to handle the processing of data within the database, using the resources of the database server and DBMS. This is also the surest way to maintain the integrity and business value of the data.

CHAPTER 4
Data Management Roles and Responsibilities

In the first chapter of this book, I listed many of the stakeholder groups that are involved in any application development effort. In this chapter, I'd like to focus on the various roles and responsibilities involved in data management, and describe their contribution not only to application development, but to the enterprise as well.

The Art of Data Management

Data management, as a profession, dedicates itself to the creation, management, and use of data as an enterprise asset. As mentioned in Chapter 1, data is a special type of circulating asset that can be reused many times, in many different ways, to help a company develop information processes that can create value for the business in numerous ways (i.e., *virtual value chains*). These information processes, if properly managed, are themselves assets, and can be reused to create even more value.

From an enterprise standpoint, the work of data management is to help manage the complex interactions between databases, applications, business processes and people, in a manner that helps create what noted educator and business consultant Thomas Davenport refers to as an "Information Ecology", a network of smoothly-flowing information processes that result in increased innovation, improved decision-making, and knowledge assets that can be used over and over to improve goods and services, increase customer satisfaction, and add value to the enterprise.

But data management is also an art; the art of turning data into business value. Data managers are committed to creating and maintaining data structures that return the maximum amount of value to the organization at the lowest possible cost over time. Although the work of data managers is often thought of as a set of well-defined techniques and processes, there is an art to making data available in usable forms to a variety of different applications, in ways that do not compromise the integrity, security, or reusability of the data. There is also an art (a very political art) involved in satisfying both the short-term needs of multiple constituencies – such as application developers, project managers, and business users – and the long-term data and information needs of the enterprise. It must be kept in mind that in our data management work, we are supporting the creation and use of information systems, which involve complex interactions between (and among) human beings and technology.

Throughout all of our work, the "big picture" of data management must be kept in mind. In the words of my friend and mentor John Dart, the goal of data management is to get:

> The right *data*
>
> To the right *person*
>
> At the right *time*
>
> In the right *form*
>
> At a cost that yields *value*.

Data professionals have always concerned themselves with data as a reusable business asset. This, however, is not enough. As I have already noted, data professionals need to concern themselves with the processes (including software applications) that turn data into flows of information. They must manage not only the quality and reusability of data assets, but the quality and reusability of the information processes that turn data into knowledge, and knowledge into results.

In the following sections of this chapter, we'll examine some of the ways in which data management professionals contribute value to the enterprise.

The Data Manager Role

Data managers oversee the people, processes, and resources involved in carrying out the mission of data management in an organization. They interact with managers of other groups (e.g., the application development, application support, server support, and Operations groups), as well as upper-level management, to ensure that the resources needed to support the work of data management are available when needed. This includes not only budgetary support for the data management organization, but also infrastructure and personnel resources. For example, the data group will need support from the Enterprise Architecture group to set process and technology standards for data management. They will need support from the server, network, and storage groups in setting up the necessary infrastructure for database servers and databases. They will need support from the Operations and application support groups to assist with the day-to-day operational support of database servers, databases, and database applications. And they will need support from the software development group to develop a set of shared tools, processes, and standards for application and database development, and to ensure that these practices and standards are followed.

In particular, the data manager must function as a resource manager for the data group, since there will be numerous demands for the time of everyone in the group. This is true of all departments in an IT organization, but it is especially true of the data group, since it performs so many functions within the organization. As we will see in the following sections, members of the data group are continually involved in setting standards for data management processes and technologies, assessing and evaluating new technologies, meeting with business users and management to determine the data needs of the organization, designing, building, and maintaining databases and database servers, and much more. There are never enough resources to satisfy all these needs, so the data manager must prioritize requests and allocate resources in the most effective way possible.

The Data Analyst Role

Data analysts (as they will be called in this book) perform the work of helping determine and document the data requirements of the business. They meet with business users, business managers, project managers, and application architects to examine a subset of business data and process needs, usually in the context of a project, application, or business function. They also assume a lead role in data quality (DQ), master data management (MDM), and business intelligence (BI) initiatives within the organization.

As part of the process of determining business data requirements, data analysts also document these requirements, usually in the form of one or more data models. Data modeling usually starts with a high-level context diagram called a *conceptual data model*, then progresses to a lower level of detail in the form of a *logical data model*. The logical data model, and its accompanying supporting material, documents the agreed-upon business data requirements, and the business definitions and rules that define and constrain the data.

In some organizations, this work is divided between *Data Architects* (who determine the business data requirements) and *Data Modelers* (who model the requirements).

The Database Developer Role

Database developers (or Development DBAs) perform the work of designing and building databases (or other data structures) to support business data requirements. As we will see, there are two aspects to this work: creation of a physical schema that satisfies the business data requirements of the logical data model, and creation of one or more data layers to support specific applications.

Database developers also participate in the work of writing database code (such as SQL queries, database triggers, functions, views and stored procedures), and may also help with the development of online reports, analytic cubes for data analysis, and similar work.

The Database Administrator Role

Database administrators (or Operational DBAs) are responsible for building and maintaining database servers (each of which supports database management software and one or more databases), and ensuring the performance, security, and recoverability of databases. They also apply changes to databases and database servers in the Certification/QA and Production environments (in accordance with the organization's change management process), perform audits of database and server access, respond to production problems and issues, and so on.

The Data Steward Role

Data stewards are business managers who are responsible for defining the data requirements and business data rules for a particular area of the business. They work with one or more data analysts or data architects, as well as with application architects and project managers, to make sure that new projects and applications satisfy these data requirements.

Note: The roles previously described may be defined differently in different organizations, or allocated across different groups. Not all organizations have a separate Data group to oversee the data management function (although they should!). Even in companies with a data management group, some of the work may be done within the software development, application support, or Operations groups.

The Data Development Cycle

Data professionals participate in an iterative process very similar to the one that application developers follow in their work. There is a continuing cycle of data development that comprises the following steps:

- Working with the business to determine data requirements, business rules, and definitions

- Documenting these requirements in one or more data models

- Designing the appropriate data structure(s) to satisfy these requirements

- Creating the data structure(s) and any supporting infrastructure (e.g., a database and database server)

- Working with application developers to create and test data access objects and any other supporting database code

- Performance tuning the database and database code

- Implementing the database schema (or schema changes) and database code in the Certification (QA) and Production environments

- Repeat as necessary!

The important point here is that the data development process, far from being monolithic, is as iterative as the application development process! An Agile approach to application development does not require us to merge an iterative software development process with a monolithic data development process; it requires us to merge two iterative processes together.

Data Managers as Intermediaries

Although data development work is iterative by nature, data professionals face a challenge in doing their work in an Agile environment. To understand why, we need to look at the very nature of data work itself.

Data managers, by definition, translate business data requirements into data structures that are appropriate; i.e., representing the best choice of technology that meets the needs of the business, secure, well-performing, easily accessible by authorized users, recoverable (in case of lost or damaged data), and easily maintained.

Data professionals essentially act as intermediaries between two groups of people: data *owners* (the people whose requirements for data and information need to be met) and data *consumers* (the people who perform the work of generating the data, and putting it into usable form for the data owners). Data owners are usually higher-level business managers; data consumers are usually application developers and/or lower-level business users or managers. The business data requirements of the data owners are documented in the logical data model and ancillary documentation; the functional requirements of the data consumers are usually documented in a systems requirements document containing use cases, user stories and an application class model.

Data professionals need to balance the short-term vs. long-term interests of both the data owners and the data consumers. Data owners have to get the information they need in a timely fashion to meet short-term business obligations and take advantage of current business opportunities. Data consumers have to meet time and budget constraints for application development. Data professionals do their best to meet these needs. However, the long-term interests of both groups are best met by ensuring that an organization's data resides in data structures that are secure, recoverable, and reusable, and that this data is assured of being as correct, timely, relevant, and usable as possible. Therefore, data professionals must work in ways that meet the short-term needs of both data owners and consumers, while creating data structures that can continue to add value to the organization after these short-term needs are met.

Database Development Tasks

Since much of the rest of this book is going to focus on database development from the viewpoint of a Development DBA, I'd like to describe some of the tasks that DBAs (both Development and Operational) are responsible for.

Database Development:

- Gather and validate physical database requirements

- Choose the most effective target platform (i.e., choice of architecture and technology) to meet the data requirements

- Determine the infrastructure requirements of the data repository (server size and location, disk space requirements, CPU and memory requirements, etc.)

- Design and build physical data structures (databases, XML schemas, analytic cubes)

- Create database server instances (Test, Certification/QA, and Production)

- Review data model and physical database design

- Help develop/review database coding for stored procedures, views, functions, triggers, etc.

- Work with developers to ensure quick and easy movement of data to and from the application data layer

- Ensure integrity and concurrency of database updates (and make sure they are enforced as close to the database as possible!)

- Assist with migration and/or integration of data from existing sources

- Assist with the development of data reporting and analytical applications

- Manage continuing changes to the database based on evolving application and business requirements

- Test and tune application database performance

- Implement database security

- Develop a service-level agreement (SLA) for the database and the database server

- Document physical database design and SLA, to ensure the maintainability of the data repository and its associated objects.

Database Operations Management:

- Implement new databases and database servers into the certification (QA) and production environments

- Implement database operational processes (database backups, transaction log dumps, index rebuilds, statistics updating, data archiving and purging, etc.)

- Implement mechanisms for clustering and failover of the data repository, if continual availability of the data is a requirement

- Implement mechanisms for replication of the data, if network latency, performance, or other concerns make it impractical to service all users from a single data source

- Manage changes to databases in the certification (QA) and production environments

- Create the necessary Operations turnover and support documentation

- Identify performance bottlenecks and tune as needed

- Implement proper error detection and reporting mechanisms

- Design, implement, and document data retention (archiving and purge) policies and processes

- Design, implement, and document database recovery policies and processes

- Monitor database security; implement and review auditing of database accesses and updates, as appropriate

- Monitor database sizes and rates of growth (called *Capacity Management*) to ensure adequate available storage for new data

- Assist with problem analysis and resolution, as needed.

Database Technology Assessment:

- Research and evaluate new database and data access technology

- Pilot, prototype, test, and evaluate the application of new technologies to applications

- Support the implementation of new database and application technologies

- Create and maintain standards for the implementation of new technologies

- Develop and document a long-term strategy (architecture) for the adoption and use of database technologies.

As you can see, DBAs have many responsibilities! Speaking as a DBA who does both Development and Operational DBA work, I enjoy the multi-faceted nature of database work and the feeling that I'm contributing a great deal of value to our IT organization.

The Evolution of Data Management

Before getting into a description of how data management is done in an Agile environment, I'd like to say a few words about how Agile (and similar progressions in the field of software development) is changing traditional roles in data management. Traditionally, most DBAs have performed more of an operational role; building and maintaining databases and database servers, addressing production problems and performance issues, and so on. DBAs have also worked with application developers in the past, but at a remove. They were like the DJs at your local rock-and-roll radio station – if you called them up and caught them at the right time, they might take a request. But several things have happened in recent years to start moving DBAs and other data professionals out of their traditional roles:

- Many of the traditional operational processes that DBAs have done are becoming standardized to a point where they can be done by (or outsourced to) lower-paid workers. Improvements in GUI-based tools, such as Microsoft's SQL Management Studio, are helping to fuel this move. At our company, many of our operational DBA processes are being documented, standardized, scripted, and turned over to our Operations department. The DBA group thus becomes the second-level, rather than the front-line, database support group.

- Alternatives to server-based DBMS (DataBase Management System) products are becoming more widespread. These include XML databases, object databases, cloud-based data persistence, RFID (where objects carry their own data), in-memory data storage, service-oriented architecture (SOA) using web services, and many others. Although, I believe, relational DBMS products still deliver the best "bang for the buck" in terms of performance, scalability, reusability, and data integrity, they are by no means the only player in the game, and other technologies are now making significant inroads into application development and deployment. Unfortunately, most current data management practices and tools are predicated on a database-centric and relational view of data.

- The need to manage and work with unstructured data (something that most DBMS products don't do well) is becoming more and more critical to organizations trying to leverage their information assets.

- Iterative (Agile) software development practices require more direct, continuous involvement in the development process from all participants, including the business users, architects, QA, and the Data group. The days of "maybe we'll have something for you in a year or two" development projects are over; now, business users expect to see tangible solutions in a matter of weeks. This necessitates a deeper commitment from everyone on the project team.

- Agile also requires that all participants be able to assist a project in whatever way is needed to solve a problem, overcome an obstacle, or meet a tough deadline. Agile encourages people to develop skills outside their particular area of specialization, so they can help with whatever is needed at any given stage of a project. In the last project I worked on, I not only did the DBA work (designing and building the database, tuning performance, and making incremental changes as needed); I also wrote a lot of the application SQL code, helped develop a SQL/CLR component used to perform calculations, wrote triggers to send database updates to a web service, wrote SSIS packages to integrate SQL and mainframe data, converted data from existing databases, files, and spreadsheets to populate the database, and assisted with QA testing. This level of involvement is quickly becoming the expected norm for DBAs on Agile projects at our company.

- Another important driver is the desire of companies to leverage and reuse their data assets to provide increased value. Traditional approaches to application (and database) development have produced decades worth of stovepiped, application-specific, "islands of data" that cannot easily be integrated or reused. An entire multi-billion dollar industry (can you say "data warehouse"?) has sprung up to address this problem. Now, with businesses wanting to capitalize quickly on every available business opportunity, and with the advent of easy-to-use software for creating online reports, multi-dimensional analytical "cubes", dashboards, scorecards, and collaboration sites, there is a huge demand for people with the ability to design and create information systems quickly, and populate them with high-quality data from disparate data sources. This is the role that Dan Sutherland, in his excellent TDAN article,[48] refers to as the "information architect". Dan correctly notes that, in the future, the role of data professionals will be much more closely tied to the creation of *information systems* than to the creation of databases, per se.

Data professionals perform at least two roles in an IT organization: They have a *facilitation* role, geared to meeting immediate needs, such as the need of a development team for an application database they can start coding against, or for a stored procedure to perform a critical application function. They also have what might be called a *control* role, which helps ensure that the data generated from a given application is secure, reusable, high-quality, and business-relevant. It is in the intersection (and the constant juggling) of these dual roles that data professionals provide the greatest value to the business.

However, in order to keep their relevance in modern organizations, data professionals will have to develop skill sets outside the ones they currently have. They are going to have to shift their focus from database technology (especially the current relational technology) to information technology, where information can exist, and be transported, persisted, and reused in many different forms. They are going to have to develop skills in the areas of technology architecture, information management, application development, and enterprise application integration (EAI). They are going to have to develop new tools, processes, and modeling constructs. For example, they may need to move beyond the current entity-relational (ERD) modeling techniques, and embrace some of the newer modeling methods such as object-role modeling (ORM). They will need to become more conversant with process modeling and business rules. Most importantly, they will need to

---

[48] Sutherland, Dan. "DBAs Reinvented", published September 1, 2009 in TDAN, The Data Administration Newsletter (http://www.tdan.com/view-special-features/11305)

work in close and continuous association with all other IT stakeholders, including business users and managers, enterprise architects, application architects, and developers. The work of creating reusable and business-relevant information processes will no longer be the exclusive province of the data management group; it will be a collaborative effort involving all affected groups.

In the future, data management professionals will be increasingly asked to contribute to the organization's well-being in ways that greatly expand their current and traditional roles. This will be uncomfortable, at first; however, embracing these changes will help ensure the continuing relevance of data management to the enterprise.

Key Points

- Data management is the art of turning data into business value. Data managers are committed to creating and maintaining data structures that return the maximum amount of value to the organization at the lowest possible cost over time.

- Data management must support effective processes that enable new information flows (i.e., applications) to be created, deployed, and modified quickly in response to changing business conditions and new opportunities.

- Data professionals act as intermediaries between data *owners* (the people whose requirements for data and information need to be met), and data *consumers* (the people who perform the work of generating the data, and putting it into usable form for the data owners).

- Agile processes are changing and expanding many traditional data management roles, requiring data management professionals to learn new skills and to become more involved in all phases of application development.

- In the future, data professionals will need to shift their focus from database technology (especially relational technology) to information technology. They will need to develop tools, processes, and modeling constructs that allow them to effectively work with non-database, non-relational, and unstructured data.

CHAPTER 5
Managing the Logical-Physical Divide

At this point, I would like to move away from the general discussion of Agile Development and Data Management, and examine how databases should be designed and built in the context of an Agile project. I will be basing a lot of this material on my own personal experience working on Agile development projects in my company's IT organization. In our IT organization, we have mostly used the Scrum methodology (an approach to Agile that involves multiple development cycles called Sprints). Most of our applications rely on relational databases, although we make extensive use of XML and web services too. Our relational DBMS of choice is Microsoft SQL Server, although we also use Oracle and IBM's DB2. Our Data Analysts use an ERD-based modeling tool that supports both logical and physical data modeling, and allows the DDL (Database Definition Language) that creates the database and database objects to be generated directly from the modeling tool. Most of our application development is done in Microsoft .NET, using its Visual Studio Team System (VSTS) development tool, which has a built-in source control repository.

I'm telling you all this so that you will be aware of the implicit bias and orientation that will assuredly creep into most of the following chapters. For those readers who use other tools, processes, and methodologies, all I can suggest is that you try to understand the underlying principles behind my approach to Agile database development, and try to find ways of applying them to your own particular situation. In the long run, it is the principles of the approach that are important, not any particular application of them. Technologies and methodologies evolve; tools and processes are continually changing. If Agile teaches us nothing else, it teaches us that we must be willing to continually adapt our processes to newer and more effective ways of doing things, so that everyone in the organization benefits.

First of all, we'll look at one of the most important concepts in this book, the distinction between the logical and physical views of data.

The Object-Relational Impedance Mismatch

The greatest friction between application developers (especially Agile Developers) and data administrators stems from what Scott Ambler has termed the "object-relational impedance mismatch". Put simply, this means that applications and databases (especially relational databases) often see and work with data in different ways. Applications see data as properties of object classes; relational databases see data as attributes of entities.

The irony here is that both views represent correct and accurate depictions of real-world things; they're just not the *same* things! For example, an application might contain an object class called *Invoice*, which contains customer data, shipping and billing data, order and item data, tax data, pricing data, and so on. In the database, or at least in the data model, these are all represented as separate entities. The reason for this, of course, is that most of this data is used for business purposes other than simply creating invoices. Having all of this data thrown together into a single *Invoice* table in the database would make it a lot easier to write the invoicing application, but a lot harder to use that data for anything else!

So what is the answer to this dilemma? To answer this question properly, it's very important to understand and appreciate the difference between *logical* and *physical* views of data. Indeed, most of the difficulties, misunderstandings, arguments, and controversies that exist in the data world originate from confusion in this regard. So, a clear understanding on this point is absolutely essential.

The *logical* view of data is data defined (and modeled) in terms that are business-centered, implementation-independent, and application-neutral. A *logical data model* describes and documents the data requirements of a particular subject area of the business (e.g., Accounts Receivable, Inventory Management, Order Processing, Customer Relations, or Personnel). In a logical data model, there is no prescription (and ideally, no assumption) as to how the data requirements will be implemented, or how the data will be used by a particular application. In any given area of the business, there should be one and only one logical data model describing the data related to that area of the business. This model will, of course, evolve over time as that area of the business grows and changes, but it will change in business-specific (rather than application-specific or technology-specific) ways.

The *physical* view of data is data defined by its implementation in a particular technology (e.g., in a relational or object database, or in XML, or in a file on a file share), and by its relationship to one or more specific applications. It's important to note that a single logical schema can support any number of physical schemas, and that each of these physical schemas can represent different implementation technologies and different application-specific views of the data.

I will be addressing this issue in more detail in the subsequent sections of this book. For now, it's enough to recognize that the logical and physical views of data represent and support two different sets of requirements – one that is more business-centered, and one that is more application-centered. Business managers, data modelers, and enterprise architects work with the logical view; DBAs and application developers work with one or more of the physical views.

The logical view of data is highly normalized (i.e., distinct business entities are kept separated and uniquely identified). This is necessary to ensure that all the business data requirements and relationships have been correctly identified and documented. In the database, particularly relational databases used for online transaction processing [OLTP], this logical view of the data is usually implemented as a *base schema* of normalized tables and relational constraints. The normalized base schema helps to ensure the reusability of the data, increases update performance, and reduces the risk of update anomalies and bad data. But it's important to understand that the base schema, though implemented physically, still represents the *logical* (application-independent) view of the data.

In my opinion, the "object-relational impedance mismatch" comes down to this: application objects need to work with a *physical* view of data that maps directly to the physical properties of those objects. Since the normalized base schema of relational OLTP databases represents a *logical* view of the data, and since there are valid business and performance reasons for keeping the base tables normalized, it follows that application objects should *not* map to the base schema of the database! Instead, these objects should map to some abstracted, virtual, application-specific data layer sitting somewhere above the base schema. It further follows that most, if not all, refactoring of application data requirements should be done at this level; the normalized base schema should be changed only when a business requirement forces a change in the logical data model.

Sources of Confusion

Confusion about the distinction between the logical and physical views of data often results when a logical data model, expressed as an entity-relationship diagram (or ERD), is translated into a set of normalized tables in a relational database to support online transaction processing (OLTP) applications. In these cases, the *base schema* of the database will probably be more-or-less the same as the logical model (I say "more-or-less", because usually not all the artifacts of the logical model are implemented in the database, or as tables in the database). For OLTP databases (as opposed to, say, data warehouses, data marts, and other decision-support, analytical or reporting databases), having a normalized base schema is a good thing. It ensures against duplicate, redundant, and inconsistent data values; increases the performance of updates; and makes the data structures more extensible and reusable. Also, normalized data structures are usually a more accurate representation of the business data requirements. For example, denormalized data structures (in which attributes of different logical/business entities are combined into a single table) often lose critical information about the uniqueness and optionality requirements of key attributes. We will see (later in this chapter) an example of a denormalized database table for an online timesheet and job-assignment application that allows the employee, department, task, and week number to be omitted or changed after the timesheet record has been created (exercise for the reader: define "timesheet").

Still, the normalized base schema represents a logical (application-independent), not physical, view of the data. What I often see on application development projects is some variation on one of two possible errors: either making no distinction at all between the logical and physical views of data, or having a total disconnect between them. In other words, the data is either looked at from a purely logical point of view, or from a purely physical (application) point of view, but the difference between the two is not understood.

For example, in one project involving a third-party contractor, we received regular updates of the logical data model, and changes to business requirements were always accurately reflected in the model. However, the actual database was a denormalized mess, and the business data requirements were very often not implemented correctly. When we pointed this out to the contractors, we were told there were "application requirements" for the poor database implementation. The contractors, evidently, viewed the logical data model as just a useless piece of documentation that the customer required, rather than as a set of business data requirements that needed to be implemented in the database.

I've worked on projects where the thing that was called the "logical data model" was nothing more than the physical database schema, showing the (often denormalized) database tables. In this case, the actual requirements of the business become lost, masked in the implementation details of a specific application. The data model becomes nothing more than an artifact of the application, and ceases to be usable for other business purposes.

Conversely, I've also worked on projects where well-intended DBAs implemented only the completely normalized logical model in the database, and forced application developers to use it, resulting in the object-relational impedance mismatch described in the preceding section. On one project, the DBA also insisted that all changes to the database, even physical-only changes such as the length of a text field, had to be driven through a change to the logical model, which made the changes take longer and was very frustrating to the developers.

Application developers tend to have a "physical only" view of data, regarding databases as nothing more than persistence engines. Data managers, on the other hand, tend to have a "logical only" view of data, focusing on the design artifacts to the exclusion of actual usability. Both of these views are erroneous, and both have serious and often unintended consequences, often leading to increased development costs, schedule impacts, poor product quality, and lots of frustration and personnel issues.

The Virtual Data Layer

The apparent disconnect between the logical and physical views of data can be resolved through the introduction of what I call the Virtual Data Layer (VDL). To visualize this, I use the concept of the "Data Services Stack", which illustrates the way in which business data requirements are delivered to the end user (similar, in a sense, to the TCP/IP stack, with its various layers of network, transport, and application protocols). See Figure 5.1.

At the top of the stack, most applications consist of a *user interface* (screen-based, form-based, or web-based), on top of a *business layer* (which contains the application logic). In the business layer, application objects (instances of object classes) interact with the user, and with each other, via methods (things that the objects know how to do). These objects have properties (characteristics), which are the data that the application needs to work with. Therefore, most applications have an *application data layer*, which usually (but not always) interacts with a database to get the data needed for an object, or to update the database when objects are created or deleted, or when object properties are changed.

Figure 5.1 The Data Services Stack

Application	User Interface
	Business Layer
	App. Data Layer
Database	DB Virtual Data Layer (VDL)
	Database Schema
	DB Physical Design
Requirements	Logical Data Model
	Conceptual Data Model
	Business Data Requirements

At the bottom of the stack, the business data requirements are translated first into a conceptual data model (which shows only the entities and their relationships), and then into a logical data model (in which all the attributes – properties – of the entities are defined). The DBA then translates the business data requirements of the logical model into a physical database design (more on this process later), and creates the base schema for the database.

In all too many cases, the process stops at this point. The DBA says "I'm done", and turns the database, with its normalized base schema, over to the application developers to struggle with. The "object-relational impedance mismatch" occurs when the application data layer (which is object-based) tries to interact with the database (which is usually relational, and usually normalized). Data needed by the application (which may be in several tables) must be joined together before passing it to an application object, which can slow down performance. Data in the application object must be "shredded" (parsed) before it can be updated in the database. How can we resolve this dilemma?

One common approach is to denormalize the database to fit the application class model. This, however, results in an application-specific database, and several of the problems previously described: an application tightly-coupled to the database schema, a database that can't be changed without breaking the application, corrupted and non-reusable data, and (sometimes) performance issues from locating too much of the data in the same place.

Another approach is to accept (and in many cases mandate) the impedance mismatch. This can, however, impede application development (resulting in lost time, work, and money), can introduce errors and performance problems into the application, and often results in conflicts between the development group and the data group.

The solution I propose is the introduction of what I call the *Virtual Data Layer* (VDL), which sits between the database schema (base tables) and the application data layer. The VDL consists of a set of database objects (and possibly application data objects, as well) which serve to mask the complexity of the underlying database schema from the application, and present data in a form that can be easily consumed and updated by the application. This approach has several advantages:

- It eliminates (from the application point of view) the object-relational impedance mismatch by creating virtual data objects that map to application object classes

- It reduces coupling between the application and the database schema

- It simplifies application code, with fewer complex joins to code, and data constraints handled in the database instead of in the application

- It increases application performance, since the database code is optimized for quick execution, and runs on the database server, not the application server

- It increases the scalability and reliability of the application, since database performance and availability issues can be managed separately from those of the application

- It reduces network traffic and bandwidth, since less data has to travel back and forth between the application and the database.

It has been argued that the use of virtual data objects does not actually eliminate the object-relational impedance mismatch; it masks the impedance from the application and moves it from the application to the database. But this is as it should be! One of the primary objectives of database work is to manage data in a way that enables its easy consumption by applications and business processes. It should not be necessary for developers or business users to understand exactly how the data has been implemented in the physical structures of a database (an objective known as *data independence*). And since the impedance is an artifact of the DBMS, it makes sense for it to be managed at the database level, not in the application.

Similarly, it has been argued that virtual data objects don't eliminate coupling, they just transfer the coupling from the application to the database. But again, this is as it should be. All interactions between application components, including the application layer and the database, involve some degree of coupling. The choices you make in application design involve two considerations: what degree of coupling is acceptable, and how easy is it to implement changes (without causing dire consequences).

I am going to argue that the use of virtual data objects reduces coupling between the application (or application data layer) and the database schema to a minimal and acceptable level. The Virtual Data Layer helps insulate the application from changes in the database schema. Most importantly, it increases Agility by making refactoring easier. Objects in the Virtual Data Layer can be created and refined incrementally, and they are much easier to change "on the fly" than application code or the database schema (see, for example, Chapter 12 of Scott Ambler's book *Agile Database Techniques* for an eye-opening look at what's involved in refactoring a database schema). Although the current Agile approach to database development involves continual refactoring of the database schema, this is actually the *least* Agile approach! Changing the database schema can be a lot of work, and can have a "ripple effect" across multiple applications. Regression testing of all affected applications is required whenever the database schema changes. Data conversion and/or cleansing may also be required.

A database object, such as a view, can easily be changed without affecting the underlying schema or data. Often, the object can be changed without affecting any other applications that use it (e.g., when a new column is added to a view). Any necessary cleansing and transformation of data (including assignment of default values for missing data) can be done in the view. If a change is required that may affect other applications, two alternative approaches are possible: either add a new column to the view, and gradually transition other applications from the old column to the new one, or create a new view for the specific application that requires the change. Either way, the amount of work involved is much less than the schema-refactoring approach.

The Virtual Data Layer in Action

Here is a concrete example: for the timesheet and job-assignment application mentioned earlier, the application wanted to define an object that looked something like what appears in Figure 5.2.

Figure 5.2 Application Data Class

EmployeeTasks

EmpName: varchar(120) NULL
Project: varchar(75) NULL
ProjectMgt: varchar(120) NULL
Task: varchar(75) NULL
Account: varchar(75) NULL
OTApproved: char(3) NULL
StartDate: char(10) NULL
EndDate: char(10) NULL
HoursToDate: decimal() NULL
OverTime: decimal() NULL

The developer's solution to the problem of data persistence was to create a single database table for the application that looked like what appears in Figure 5.3.

Figure 5.3 Denormalized Database Table

Tasks

TaskID: int IDENTITY

TaskTitle: varchar(75) NULL
TaskDesc: varchar(255) NULL
ProjectMgr: varchar(75) NULL
EmployeeName: varchar(75) NULL
WeekNo: smallint NULL
Hours1: smallint NULL
Hours2: smallint NULL
Hours3: smallint NULL
Hours4: smallint NULL
Hours5: smallint NULL
Hours6: smallint NULL
Hours7: smallint NULL
OTHours: smallint NULL

You can see the problems this approach creates:

- Data for critical (key) attributes (e.g., the employee name, task, and week) can be omitted, or changed after the record is created (by the way, this table is misnamed; this is actually *timesheet* data, not *task* data!). The missing and incorrectly modified data caused multiple application failures.

- Additional data pertaining to employees, project managers, or tasks can't be captured without changing the structure of this table which, in turn, will break the application, since the application object is tightly-coupled to the table.

- There is no way of ensuring that the employee, project manager, and task data that is entered is actually valid (e.g., you could easily add a record for a non-existent employee).

- The fact that project managers are also employees (with assigned tasks) isn't captured at all.

- Reusing the employee, project manager, and task data for other purposes will be difficult, if not impossible. Do we keep employee data for any purpose other than tracking time? Of course we do!

For these reasons, the conventional (normalized) design for a database of this sort would break out attributes (properties) for distinct entities (business objects) into separate tables, where they could be more easily managed. The normalized database design would then look something like what appears in Figure 5.4.

But this design, of course, makes it more difficult for the application object to access the data (the "object-relational impedance mismatch"). Data in the tables must be joined together before being passed to the application object, which can slow down performance. Data in the application object must be "shredded" (parsed) before it can be updated in the database. How can we resolve this dilemma?

Figure 5.4 Normalized Database Schema

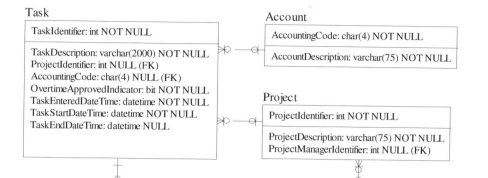

The solution is to use the principle of the Virtual Data Layer by creating a database view (a virtual table) that can join the data from the various tables (often renaming or reformatting it in the process). Figure 5.5 shows the SQL code that would be used to create such a view.

This view of the data (which appears in Figure 5.6) gives the application exactly what it was looking for: data that can be mapped directly to the data properties of the application object class. At the same time, we have satisfied all the necessary data management requirements: data can be stored and updated safely, without being accidentally deleted or corrupted, the data is internally consistent, and performance bottlenecks have been eliminated. By denormalizing virtually (rather than denormalizing the database schema), we've satisfied the application requirement without sacrificing data integrity and performance.

Figure 5.5 SQL Code to Create Database View

```
CREATE VIEW EmployeeTasks (EmpName, Project,
ProjectMgr, Task, Account, OTApproved, StartDate,
EndDate, HoursToDate, OverTime)
AS
SELECT CONVERT(varchar(120), emp.EmployeeFirstName
+ ' ' + emp.EmployeeLastName),
proj.ProjectDescription,
CASE WHEN emp2.EmployeeFirstName IS NULL THEN 'No
Manager' ELSE CONVERT(varchar(120),
emp2.EmployeeFirstName + ' ' +
emp2.EmployeeLastName) END, CONVERT(varchar(75),
task.TaskDescription), acct.AccountDescription,
CASE task.OvertimeApprovedIndicator WHEN 1 THEN
'Yes' ELSE 'No' END, CONVERT(varchar,
ta.AssignmentStartDate, 101),
CONVERT(varchar, ta.AssignmentEndDate, 101),
ta.OTHoursToDate

FROM TaskAssignment ta
INNER JOIN Task task ON ta.TaskIdentifier =
task.TaskIdentifier
INNER JOIN Employee emp ON ta.EmployeeIdentifier =
emp.EmployeeIdentifier
INNER JOIN Project proj ON task.ProjectIdentifier =
proj.ProjectIdentifier
LEFT OUTER JOIN Employee emp2
          ON proj.ProjectManagerIdentifier =
emp2.EmployeeIdentifier
INNER JOIN Account acct ON task.AccountingCode =
acct.AccountingCode
```

Figure 5.6 Database View That Maps to Application Class

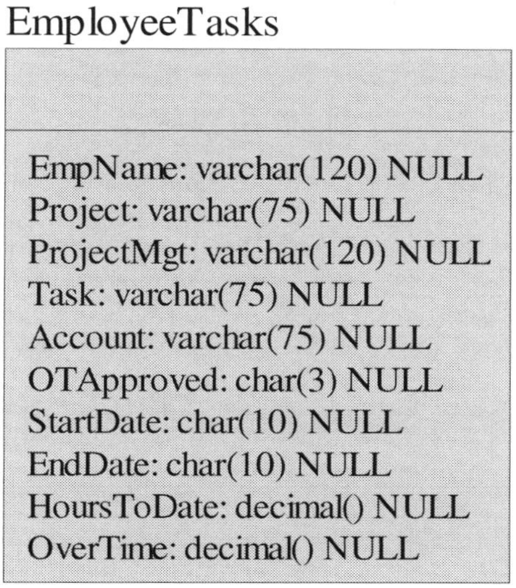

EmployeeTasks

EmpName: varchar(120) NULL
Project: varchar(75) NULL
ProjectMgt: varchar(120) NULL
Task: varchar(75) NULL
Account: varchar(75) NULL
OTApproved: char(3) NULL
StartDate: char(10) NULL
EndDate: char(10) NULL
HoursToDate: decimal() NULL
OverTime: decimal() NULL

Notice some of the things we are able to do in this view:

- We can format the employee name, combining the first and last names

- We can assign a default value of "No Manager" to the ProjectMgr field if the employee does not have a manager

- We can change the binary value of OvertimeApproved Indicator to a more readable "Yes" or "No"

- We can format the date fields to a readable MM/DD/YYYY format

- We can change the names of fields in the view from what they are called in the database

- We can also change the length and data type of the fields.

As we will see later on, updating of the database can also be done through this view, using "Instead-Of" triggers on the view.

Subsequent sections of this book will describe the process of logical and physical design, and the creation and use of the various components of the VDL, and their value in application development.

Key Points

- The logical view of data is business-centered, implementation-independent, and application-neutral. The physical view of data is technology and application specific.

- Confusing the logical and physical views of data results in many common data management problems, including the so-called "object-relational impedance mismatch".

- The apparent disconnect between the logical and physical views of data can be resolved through the use of a Virtual Data Layer (VDL), which maps the database schema to application objects.

- Use of the VDL has many other benefits, including reducing coupling between the application and the database schema, increasing application performance and scalability, and making it easier to change the way the application interacts with the database.

In this chapter, I'm going to talk about the role of data analysis and design in the context of Agile Development. I want to make it clear from the onset that I am NOT going to talk about how to do data modeling and requirements gathering; there are a number of excellent books (many from this publisher) on those topics.

Instead, I'm going to discuss what data design is, and is not, and how and when data design can be done in the context of an Agile project. Also, in this chapter and the next, I'll have something to say about normalization, and the differences between normalization in the logical view of data and normalization in the physical view of data.

The Focus of Data Design

The purpose of data design, which usually manifests itself in the form of a logical data model and some accompanying documentation, is to isolate the business data requirements and business data rules from the general requirements analysis, and ensure that they are *complete* (i.e., that they are sufficient to meet all of the identified requirements), *consistent* (i.e., that they work not only for the current set of requirements, but for all previously identified requirements in this business area), and *correct* (i.e., that the data definitions, relationships, rules, domains and constraints are correctly defined from the point of view of the business).

It is very important to understand the following things about data design:

- The data design represents a *logical* (*not* physical) view of the data. In other words, it describes a business data domain and a set of logical business data requirements; it does not describe or prescribe the way in which these requirements will be implemented.

- The data design encompasses all the data requirements and rules of a particular *business subject area*; that is, an area of interest to the business, such as customer relationships, inventory, personnel, sales, order processing, accounts receivable, etc. You don't have a different data design for each application; you have a single data design for a business subject area. The importance of understanding the business context of data is one of the major differences between data requirements and application (functional) requirements.

- The data design is *implementation-independent*; that is, it does not specify which, if any, of the data requirements will be implemented in a particular form, or using a particular technology.

- The data design is *application-neutral*; that is, it encompasses, but is not constrained by, the requirements of any given application or use of the data.

What this means is that the data design changes only in response to changes in the business data requirements or business data rules, or to the business' understanding of them. It does *not* change in response to changes in application requirements (unless they involve related changes to business data definitions or business rules), or to changes in technology. Also, there is nothing in the data requirements *per se* that dictate what technology will be used to implement them; it would be perfectly reasonable, in certain circumstances, to implement a logical data model as an office filing cabinet or a Rolodex![49]

The Cost of Losing Focus

This critical distinction between the logical (requirements) and physical (implementation) view of data often tends to get blurred or lost in the crush of deadline pressures and resource constraints,

---

[49] Or whatever iPhone app currently serves this function.

to the detriment of both projects and products. For example, we know that in object-oriented development, it's usually important to create both an OOA (analysis) class model, which encompasses the logical view of the application requirements, and an OOD (design) class model, which embodies design decisions specific to the chosen implementation approach. But how often have you heard developers say "I've created a class model for my application"? Similarly, I often hear people say, "I've created a data model", when what they mean is that they've created a database design. The two are *not* synonymous!

So what happens when this distinction is lost? First, blurring the line between the logical and the physical results in tightly-coupling your company's view of its data to a particular set of application requirements or technical constraints, which makes it harder to adapt or extend them in response to changing business needs, technology, or market opportunities.

Second, it puts the cart before the horse, so to speak: It's reasonable to expect changes in business conditions to drive changes to a company's applications and data; it is not reasonable to expect changes in a company's applications to alter the definitions of its data, or the business rules that constrain it.

Third, it makes refactoring during application development much more difficult, labor-intensive, time-consuming, and expensive. Instead of simply changing the *implementation* of a requirement in an application or database, you end up having to drive the change through the refactoring of the logical data model and/or the OOA class model, as well as the database schema.

Our company had a project some years back that illustrates perfectly the dangers of blurring the line between requirements and implementation. This was a diagnostic software application for machine components, and the developers insisted that the logical data model be a mirror image of the actual database implementation (the DBA, making the same mistake, insisted that the database implementation be a mirror image of the logical data model!). The first iteration of the project implemented only a single component; however, the data model was so tightly-coupled to the application design that it couldn't be extended to accommodate additional components! Worse yet, it couldn't even be extended to accommodate a different version of the component that was actually implemented. Still worse, every single database change, right down to changes in the length of a text field, had to be processed via a change to the logical data model, which made even the simplest of changes take much longer than it should have, and resulted in increasing frustration for both the data and development teams.

Moreover, the resulting database could be used only to support that single application, for that one component; there was no way to reuse the database (or the data) for any other purpose. For example, one might reasonably expect to be able to run a defect analysis in the database to identify the suppliers of faulty parts. But there was no way to do this, given the design of the database.

So what we ended up with was a data design and database that couldn't support more than one iteration of the application without expensive re-engineering, that couldn't accommodate even the simplest of changes without unreasonable effort, and that couldn't be used to support any other business need. In addition, the continual refactoring of the both the data model and the database resulted in project delays, extra costs, and lots of frustration and bad feeling between the developers and the data team.

Hopefully, a word to the wise will suffice: eliminating the distinction between requirements and implementation (the logical and physical points of view) may seem, at first glance, like an easy way to cut corners, reduce costs, and shorten development time. But developers will find that they'll pay the price in increased development time for future iterations, increased effort for even minor refactorings, an inability to easily accommodate future requirements, poor product quality, and increasing personnel issues.

How Much Design is "Just Enough"?

One of the more controversial aspects of Agile Development is its rejection of what it calls "Big Design Up Front" (BDUF). Instead of the traditional "waterfall" approach, which makes a clear distinction between the requirements-gathering, analysis, design, and implementation tasks, Agile projects incorporate all of these tasks together in a single effort (called, for example, a "Sprint" in the Scrum approach to Agile). Each iteration of the project includes "just enough" requirements gathering to understand what the users expect out of that particular iteration, just enough analysis to understand what those requirements mean, and just enough design to figure out how to implement them. Also, in contrast to more formal methodologies, Agile activities may or may not result in any actual documentation, only sticky notes on the wall, scribblings on a whiteboard, or text messages sent between team members.

This raises the inevitable question of how much design is "just enough", and in what context? From the standpoint of the Agile developer, "just enough" may mean "just enough to get this iteration of the project finished and into the end users' hands". But, as we pointed out in the first chapter, this view ignores the legitimate interests of other stakeholders, including the people who are paying the bills. So, to answer the question of how much analysis and design activity is "just enough", we need to consider the requirements of all the project stakeholders, and the needs of the company as a whole. From the standpoint of data design, it is important to understand that what is being documented is not merely the data needs of a particular application, but the data domain of an area of the business as that area of the business evolves over time.

From the standpoint of data design activities, I would consider that the end result of "just enough" process and documentation would include the following:

- A conceptual (business-level) model, showing the real-world entities (objects) of the business subject area and the relationships (roles) between them, in some appropriate form. Most people use Entity-Relationship Diagrams (ERDs); others advocate the use of Object-Role modeling or UML. A high-level (OOA) class model may also satisfy this requirement.

- A logical data model, which decomposes the high-level conceptual entities to a set of lower-level constituent entities, each of which is clearly and uniquely identifiable, extensible, reusable, and possessed of distinct characteristic properties (attributes). The logical data model, in whatever form, ensures that all of the entities needed to support the data requirements of the business subject area have been identified, that the relationships (roles) between them are understood, and that the characteristics of the entity properties (attributes) are in the correct form, and associated with the correct entity.

- Any other necessary supporting documentation, which may include the following:

  - Detailed attribute definitions (including data domains, uniqueness, and optionality)

  - Descriptions of entities, attributes, and relationships in business terms

  - Business rules and constraints that apply to attributes, entities (objects), and relationships (roles). This includes the constraints used to identify unique instances of each entity/object

  - Business requirements and/or design decisions that drove development of the logical model in a particular way

  - Sample data to illustrate the characteristics of entities/objects.

An important point needs to be made here: I am *not* suggesting that it is necessary to determine and model *all* of the data requirements for a business subject area in advance of any use of that data. I'm saying that, as project and business requirements drive the need for data in a business area, these requirements should be added to the logical data model for that business area. In other words, the logical data model for a business area provides the context in which new data requirements are understood and implemented.

Each data management group must make its own determination of how much documentation (and in what form) is needed to support a given business area. Bear in mind, though, that this documentation is intended to be reusable. As additional application, reporting, analysis, and other uses of this data are proposed and developed, it should be possible to easily extend the data design to accommodate these new business requirements. This documentation will support both the maintenance of the current version of the application and the development of subsequent versions; it will also be used when new applications or processes that use this data are being proposed or developed. As opposed to many application development artifacts, which may be used once and then discarded, data design artifacts should exist in a form that allows them to be easily maintained and reused over time.

Also, as we'll see later, this documentation can be very beneficial to the project team as a development artifact. I intend to argue (and demonstrate from my experience on Agile projects) that the logical data model is an excellent example of an "Agile Model", and perfectly supports the goals of Model-Driven Development (MDD).

It should also be kept in mind that the data design, at the conceptual and logical level, is (or should be) less susceptible to change than physical database and application objects. The data design should change only in response to new business requirements in a given subject area, or to changes in the business' understanding of those requirements, or to changes in the business rules governing those requirements. The logical data design should *not* be affected by changes in the way that data requirements are implemented in the physical database (or other persistence object), or consumed by applications. If the data design has been properly done, based on a sufficient understanding of the business data requirements in a given subject area, the data model should be relatively isolated from continual refactoring. Moreover, refactoring at the logical level is a relatively quick and painless undertaking, a matter of minutes rather than of hours or days.

As a general rule, it is not a good idea to try to model too far ahead of the work that has actually been defined for the current iteration of the project (i.e., the current set of user stories). However, since the logical data model has (as we'll see) value as an application development artifact and springboard for discussion of requirements, and since changing the logical model is a relatively quick and painless undertaking, there is not much harm, and possibly some good, in modeling at least some of what has been understood and agreed upon as probable requirements of future user stories, provided that this is kept at a relatively high level, with a minimum amount of detail. Knowing when and what to model is something that data analysts on Agile projects will learn from experience.

The data analyst must also make a determination of how much analysis and modeling of a given area of the business should be done to accommodate a particular business requirement (e.g., a request for a new application). Must the entire business subject area be modeled and documented before anything further is done? I would argue that this is necessary only in extreme cases, involving applications that encompass the entire business area, such as a CRM or ERP application. Also, as will be pointed out shortly, the development of the logical model can be done incrementally, during the analysis portion of each Sprint and user story.

The Purpose of Normalization in Logical Design

Now that we have an understanding of what logical data design entails, and why it is done, let's take a look at the somewhat touchy subject of normalization.[50] In logical data design, as opposed to physical database design, normalization serves some very particular purposes:

- Normalization enables the data analyst to identify the constituent entities of business objects (e.g., to determine that an Order contains data elements pertaining to Customer and Product). These constituent entities become candidates for reuse; they can become the components of multiple application objects, reports, analysis objects, etc.

- Normalization provides assurance that the essential characteristics of each entity (including those needed to uniquely identify each instance of an entity) have been identified, and correctly described.

- Normalization also provides assurance that all essential relationships (roles) between entities have been identified. The relationships, in turn, help identify object methods involved in application processes.

Developers often panic when they see a logical data model because it seems overly-complicated. It's important to understand that a logical data model is more of a business requirements document than an application design artifact. When designing the actual physical database (as we'll see in the next chapter), we'll see that normalization and denormalization are done in different ways, on different levels, and for different reasons. It's also important to note that the logical data model is going to be much less subject to change than the actual physical code or design artifacts. For these

---

[50] I don't intend to get into a long-winded discussion of the rules and techniques of normalization in this book; many such references exist elsewhere. For the purpose of this book, normalization can be simply defined as ensuring that each attribute (data item) in a data model:
- Exists only once in the model
- Is associated with the appropriate entity
- Describes some essential characteristic of that entity
- Is uniquely identified by the key of that entity.

reasons (and others we've already noted), it makes more sense to over-normalize on the logical side, to make sure that all the data requirements have been properly captured and understood. This also makes it easier to extend the model as needed in response to future business requirements.

When to do Data Design

The next important question is: when, in the context of Agile, does it make sense (or is it even possible) to do data design? This is an excellent question, as the highly-iterative, fast-paced nature of an Agile project oftentimes leaves little room for design activities. Based on my own experience as an Agile developer, here are my recommendations:

- Application development projects always begin with a series of meetings with the business users/managers and project stakeholders, for the purpose of identifying the business requirements for the application. At these meetings, the data analyst should be developing and refining the conceptual data model (and perhaps a rough draft of the logical data model), along with any necessary supporting documentation, as described in the previous section (definitions for entities and attributes in business terms, business rules, sample data, etc.).

- During (and after) these meetings, a set of user stories will be developed, briefly analyzed, and prioritized. This process often yields additional understanding of the business requirements and the business subject area. The data analyst is cautioned not to try to model all the user stories; many of them will not be done in the current project; some others will be rejected as redundant, unimportant, contradictory, or too expensive. At this point, the focus should be on understanding the general "arena" in which the business – and the current set of requirements – will operate.

- The first iteration of an Agile project usually encompasses the work of defining and designing an overall architecture for the application, and putting into place the processes, tools, and infrastructure (the server environment, application development environment, and so forth) that will be needed for development.[51] The data analyst should take advantage of this part of the project to complete a first-cut of the logical data model, and review it with the development team before actual development starts. The idea here is not to create a comprehensive model that won't need to change; the idea is to agree on a model that is "good enough" to start development with.

- At the beginning of each development Sprint, a set of user stories is selected from the Product Backlog, in support of a general goal for the Sprint. At this point, the data analyst should review the current data model to identify deficiencies, questions that will need to be answered, and issues that should be raised during analysis.

- As the individual user stories are being worked on, there is usually a brief analysis session associated with each story. The data analyst should attend all of these sessions, make sure to ask any necessary questions and resolve any important issues, and make sure the logical data model accurately reflects and supports the requirements of the story.

- At this point, the logical model should be turned over to the DBA, who will take the process through the design and build phases for each story (more on this in the next chapter).

At each point in the development process, the goal of the data analyst is to model enough to meet the immediate requirements of

---

[51] This initial Sprint is sometimes, though not necessarily, referred to as "Sprint 0". I will probably use this term to refer to it, even though on many Agile projects it will simply be Sprint 1.

the Sprint, and all reasonably anticipated future requirements related to the stories being developed.[52] This is something of a judgment call, based on experience and expertise; the data analyst won't have time to do much more work than is needed for the immediate Sprint, but there may very well be, say, attributes of entities that we know will need to be in place to support upcoming stories, and it may be just as easy to do this work now rather than later. Some changes may need to be made when those future stories are analyzed, but again, remember − changing the design at this level is relatively quick and painless; a matter of minutes rather than of hours or days.

---

[52] There is an Agile concept called "rolling planning" which relates to this. The general idea is that in Sprint Planning, a team plans the User Stories for the current Sprint, and they look ahead to discuss what they believe will be the stories in the next two Sprints. This allows the entire team to consider upcoming work and the impacts upon design.

Key Points

- The purpose of data design is to isolate the business data requirements from the general (functional) requirements, and ensure that the understanding of these requirements is complete, consistent, and correct.

- Logical data design is business-area focused, implementation-independent, and application-neutral.

- Blurring the distinction between the design and the implementation of the data usually results in tightly-coupling the data to a particular set of application requirements, making it harder to use this data for other purposes. It also makes changing or extending the data design more difficult.

- The logical data model changes only as a result of new or changed business requirements (or the team's understanding of them), and is thus much less susceptible to change than other application development artifacts. It is also much easier to change.

- Data design artifacts are intended to be reusable, and have value both during and after the project. They will be used to support both current and future versions of the application and all future uses of the data.

- The purpose of normalization in logical design is to make sure that the business data requirements have been fully captured and understood.

- Logical design work on Agile projects is done during requirements-gathering, Sprint planning and estimation, and user story analysis.

Once the data requirements have been understood and modeled, it must be determined how, whether, and to what extent these requirements should be implemented in some sort of physical data structure. As we will see, there are many decisions to be made, and many aspects to be considered. The DBA or database developer will need to work very closely with the development team during this process.

The Focus of Database Design

The goal of database design is to map the business data requirements, as expressed in the logical data model, to an intelligent choice of implementation, architecture, and technology. Let's examine each of these, in turn:

- *Implementation*: It is often simply assumed that a set of business data requirements will be implemented in some sort of database, but that is not necessarily a valid assumption. I once worked on a project in which, after designing and building the database, it turned out that the application didn't need a client-side database at all; data only needed to be sent from the server to the client via XML, and persisted in a read-only form on the client machine. A number of new data-persistence technologies have now become available, and their use is becoming wide-spread enough to lead some people to declare, in the words of one Gartner Group paper, "The Death of the Database".[53] Although I think such claims are over-blown (I don't think Wal-Mart will be giving up its data warehouse any time soon!), I think it's important to ask the question at the outset — does this application actually need a database?

---

[53] Beyer, Mark. "The Death of the Database", op. cit.

133

And if so, why? Some of the reasons for using a database might include better support for transactional updating,[54] performance, security, data protection, support for data reuse (including data analysis, Business Intelligence, and ad-hoc reporting), cross-platform data access, and the need to persist data over long periods of time.

- *Architecture*: It is also necessary to address the question of *where* the data will be accessed and/or persisted: on a central database server, on an application server, on each client machine, or "in the cloud" (i.e., on some external web-based repository). For example, an application might read data from a central database server, persist it in memory on each client machine during use, and then send an XML "updategram" back to the database server when the application is closed. Or an application process, such as a Point-Of-Sale application, might store purchase transactions in an XML repository on the client (or web server); then a back-end process periodically extracts this data and updates the central database. You get the idea – the answer to the question of where the data resides, and in what form, is not mutually-exclusive: data might reside in different places, in different forms, at different points in the application process.

- *Technology*: Most of us who started our IT careers during the client/server era tend to think in terms of relational databases; and to be sure, relational databases have lots of

---

[54] I'm aware that some writers, including Mark Beyer, suggest that database updates and deletes aren't needed (one obtains the current state of an object by examining the history of all transactions affecting it). This approach might be made to work acceptably for some applications (such as Point-Of-Sale and Inventory), but would likely be too cumbersome, poorly-performing, and storage-intensive for most other applications. This sort of "insert only" approach to databases is most likely an attempt to do an "end run" around what are perceived as onerous database standards. This is the real problem that needs to be addressed.

advantages. In particular, the ease and speed with which large sets of records can be read, transformed, merged (with other sets of records from other databases), displayed, and updated makes relational technology a very good fit for many if not most applications. But, relational is not always the best fit for every application; some applications (e.g., document repositories) require a more hierarchical view of data, while others (CAD/CAM comes to mind) require an object-based data repository. Some applications might need nothing more than a flat file; others might only need to access data on an RFID chip. The choice of technology should be governed by the way in which the data is most normally organized for use.

Having chosen a particular target technology, the next task is to map each of the logical data requirements to appropriate artifacts of that technology. For relational databases, for example, an entity in the logical data model might be implemented as a table or a view; a minor entity might be implemented as a code table, a rule, or a constraint; a relationship might be implemented as either a foreign-key constraint or a trigger; and so on.

Of course, the mapping of data requirements to database objects is only part of the work of database design. Most modeling tools will assist with this mapping (some do this work a little too well, masking some of the important decisions that ought to be made by the DBA or Data Analyst[55]), and many of them will also generate

---

[55] One of the great challenges of database design is getting the modeling tools (which are mostly designed to support logical data modeling) to work for physical design, in a way that doesn't involve simply implementing the normalized logical data model as-is in the database schema. In our modeling tool, for example, I'll create separate subject areas in the Physical tab for the base schema and the virtual data objects. I'll give the virtual objects prefixes that indicate how I intend to implement them (as views, functions, work tables, etc.). Also keep in mind that most modeling tools allow you to designate design objects as "logical only" or "physical only".

the DDL (Data Definition Language) code needed to create the database schema. Database design work cannot be done in a vacuum by the DBA; just as logical data modeling depends on interaction with the business users and stakeholders, physical database design depends on interaction with the end users and application developers.

Finally, the DBA creates (or helps create) the virtual database objects needed to satisfy the requirements of the particular application. If these objects are created by the development team, the DBA will review the code to make sure all standards are met (and will, of course, have communicated those standards to the team at the beginning of the project!).

The Physical Design Process

An important part of the physical design process is to schedule a physical design review with the consumers of the database (primarily the application developers[56]) to surface and resolve any potential issues with the database design prior to implementation. The purpose of the physical design review is not to discuss the logical data model or the data requirements, but rather to discuss how best to expose the data for consumption by business users and applications. Among the possible topics for discussion are the following:

1. *Design Decisions.* Review, discussion, and approval of the choices made about implementation, architecture, and technology for data persistence, described above.

2. *Attribute Characteristics.* Review of the data type, size, default, and nullability specifications for each data element. The logical model usually assigns each attribute to a

---

[56] Some discussions, such as reporting, data retention, and ad-hoc query requirements, may involve the business users. Most of the database-level discussions will involve only application developers or application architects.

domain, which then defaults to a specific type and size in the physical model (e.g., a "Code" attribute may always default to a type of "varchar(4)" in the physical model). In some cases, this will need to be changed. Defaults and/or constraints may need to be applied. The nullability (optionality) of each data element should be reviewed and corrected, if necessary, in the logical model.

3. *Attribute Naming.* Review of the element and attribute names as implemented in the physical design. Most companies have some standards in place for the naming of logical and physical data objects. In some cases, physical names may be allowed to differ from the logical (domain) names (e.g., replacing "Identifier" with "ID"). In other cases, more application-friendly or user-friendly names can be implemented in the database using views or functions.

4. *Record Keys.* Data elements used as record keys should be reviewed. Will the key values be system-assigned or user-assigned (based on actual data values)? If system-assigned, will they be implemented as IDENTITY keys, GUIDs (unique identifiers), or be populated from a lookup table? Should multi-attribute natural (business) keys in the logical model be replaced with a single surrogate (system-assigned) key for better performance?[57] Are there any dependent keys (multi-column keys where the lowest-level key is a sequence number which starts from 1 for each unique combination of the other keys)?

---

[57] One thing to keep in mind is that the query optimizer used in most relational DBMSs will work much better if record keys (and their corresponding indexes) are kept as small as possible. As a general rule, I try to keep key lengths to 20 characters or less. Also, numeric (integer) keys will perform better than alphanumeric (character) keys. This does not, however, imply that all keys should be surrogate keys; code values can be used as keys so long as they are short, static (unchanging), and have a clearly defined meaning to the business (i.e., the code values should not be arbitrary).

5. *Minor Entities.* Should minor entities in the logical model be implemented as code tables in the database (so that code descriptions can be displayed in drop-down lists in the application), or simply as rules or constraints?

6. *Subtype/Supertypes.* Are there any minor supertype/subtype entities (consisting of only one subtype) that could be collapsed into a single table?

7. *Concurrency Control.* For tables that can be concurrently updated in an ad-hoc manner by several different users, some mechanism should be implemented for ensuring that two users cannot update the same record at the same time. This usually involves adding a data element of type "timestamp" ("rowversion" in SQL Server) or "datetime" to each of these tables, and making sure that the value of this field is checked before the record is modified, and updated whenever the record is changed. Note: concurrency control is not needed for tables that are read-only, or that will only be updated by a controlled process (e.g., a nightly batch refresh).

8. *Update Approach.* An appropriate mechanism for updating data should be discussed and agreed upon. There are a number of possible choices, but the method chosen must satisfy the following criteria:

   a. Any update should be done as part of a defined application process; no direct, ad-hoc updating of the database should ever be allowed. In other words, you don't directly manipulate data in the database; you invoke an application process, based on carefully defined business rules, which updates the database.

   b. All updates relating to a particular business process must be managed as a single unit of work, and either committed in their entirety or else completely rolled back (transactional integrity). No partial updates of the database should ever be allowed to occur (for example, the two database updates involved in taking money from a bank customer's savings account and moving it to checking should never be allowed to commit independently!). This ensures that the data in the database, at any given moment in time, represents a valid state of the business.

c. Two or more users should not be allowed to update the same record at the same time (concurrency control).

d. Any errors in updating should immediately cause the current database transaction to abort and roll back, and the error should be immediately reported to the calling process or application.

e. The ability to update a particular database table should be restricted to a set of users (i.e., a group or role) authorized to do so.

f. Updates should be restricted to a small number of records at a time, to prevent excessive locking of tables and "hanging" of an application if a large update needs to be rolled back.

Among the possible update mechanisms that could be considered are the following:

- Fundamental stored procedures (FSPs). Each FSP implements one operation (Insert, Update, Delete, or Select) on a limited number of records (usually designated by one or more key values) for a single database table. FSPs, if used, should be automatically generated, either from the physical model or from the database schema (although so-called "alternate" FSPs, involving more complex update logic, can be coded as needed). FSPs can be called from higher-level stored procedures or application code that handles data updating for a particular object class.

- Application data layer. An application component can be written that calls stored procedures in the database to perform updates across multiple tables (or that calls multiple FSPs). Stored procedures are recommended because they perform better (the SQL code is precompiled and pre-optimized), they are more secure (only designated users or roles can execute them, and the tables aren't opened up to SQL injection attacks), they are easier to maintain, and errors or performance problems can be easily detected and corrected.

- Dataset updating. In ADO.NET, records in an application dataset or datatable can be updated through a DataAdapter object, which can, in turn, be associated with a set of stored procedures that perform Insert, Update, Delete, and Select operations. A similar mechanism can be used for objects created in .NET's Entity Framework.

- Updateable views. In some relational DBMSs, such as Microsoft SQL Server, database views can be associated with a set of "Instead Of" triggers that can handle updates of the underlying tables in a controlled manner. As with FSPs, it is preferable to generate this code in an automated fashion, to reduce or eliminate time spent in coding, testing, and maintenance.

9. *Security*. What is the security classification of this data (Public, Company Confidential, Top Secret), and what security constraints need to be applied to the data? Do updates to the data (or certain data elements) need to be captured for audit purposes? What application roles should be defined in the database, and how should permissions on database objects be assigned to those roles? The general rule is that permissions on database objects should never be granted to individual users, only to roles (groups). Users can then be moved into and out of roles as needed; this greatly reduces maintenance and enhances security.

10. *SLA*. Discussion of a service-level agreement (SLA) for the database. What are the performance requirements (e.g., the maximum permissible time for a query to return results, or

for a critical set of updates to occur)? What are the uptime requirements for the database? What is the acceptable error time-out period? What is the dollar cost per hour of downtime? During what window(s) of time can database maintenance operations (such as database and transaction log backups, database consistency checks, re-indexing, and statistics updating) be done? How often should database backups and transaction log backups be done (i.e., what is the longest period of time we can risk non-recoverability of the data)?

11. *Storage Requirements.* What is the expected size of the database? What is the expected rate of growth of the data? At what point can old or unused data be archived or deleted? Are there data retention policies or guidelines that pertain to this data? How many concurrent users are anticipated?

12. *Data Virtualization.* What sorts of virtualization of the data are needed to support application requirements?

13. *Data Reuse.* Will the data in this database need to be made available to other applications or processes? If so, how?

14. *Data Integration.* Will data from other databases or data sources need to be integrated with data in this database? If so, how will this integration be done?

15. *Ad-hoc Usage.* Will users expect to be able to do ad-hoc querying and reporting of the data? If so, how will this requirement be accommodated?

16. *Functional Requirements.* What, if any, business or application processes need to be implemented in the database (e.g., trigger code that does cross-database integrity checking or updating)?

17. *Database Environments.* What database environments will need to be created? Will there be a single Development database instance, or will each developer have a development database environment? How will changes be promoted from the Development database(s) to Test, and

then to the Certification or QA environment? Can existing database servers be used, or will new servers be required? Is any particular version of the DBMS required?

18. *Globalization.* Will any of the text data in the database need to be maintained and accessed in multiple languages? Will monetary data need to be displayed or used in multiple currencies? Will date and time data need to be stored as GMT (UTC) date/times, and converted to local date/times at individual sites?

19. *Developer Concerns.* Are there any other application or developer concerns regarding the database, or the database development process, that need to be addressed?

The information from this discussion should be used for two purposes: first, to produce a revised physical database design suitable for implementation; and second, to produce a physical design document (see the following section) which captures all aspects of the physical design and its implementation. This document will be referenced by future developers and DBAs, who will need to know what design options have been chosen or discarded, and why.

At the end of the database design process, you should be able to produce (ideally, auto-generate) two sets of database objects from your physical model: the *base schema* (consisting of the base tables, indexes, constraints, rules, and defaults) and at least a subset of the *Virtual Data Layer* (for example, a set of Fundamental Stored Procedures, or the equivalent, for updating the base tables, and any joined views, functions, triggers, complex datatypes and work tables needed to support the application).

Database Design Deliverables

As suggested above, the physical database design process should result in the following deliverables:

- A data repository (database) that represents an appropriate choice of architecture, that properly maps the data requirements expressed in the logical data model to the choice of architecture, and that contains appropriate constraints to ensure the integrity and security of the data.

- An instance of the DBMS to support the database, if the chosen architecture requires a DBMS.

- A server environment to support the data repository, of a sufficient size and capacity to ensure adequate performance, configured for the appropriate level of security, reliability, and availability.

- Appropriate mechanisms for ensuring the recoverability of the data to an agreed-upon point in time, in response to all possible circumstances that could result in loss or corruption of data.

- Appropriate mechanisms for abstracting (virtualizing) the data in ways that maximize its availability, usability, and value to the organization.

- Appropriate mechanisms for detecting and reporting any error that occurs in the database, the DBMS, or the data server.

- A service-level agreement (SLA) with the users and owners of the data, which describes the requirements for the availability, security, integrity, and usability of the data. The SLA should also contain information about who should be notified in case of planned or unplanned service interruptions.

- A physical database design document, which documents the translation of the data requirements into the physical data structure. This document should include the following:

  a. A description of the business function of the database design; i.e., what aspect or subset of the business data does this database design encompass?

  b. An explanation of the database architecture chosen, and the reasons for that choice.

  c. Design options considered and not chosen, and the

reasons for rejecting them (to prevent thrashing during future development or enhancement efforts).

d. Any constraints that affected the selection of the DBMS, including cost constraints, policy constraints, performance constraints, reliability or scalability constraints, security constraints, expected volumes of data, etc.

e. A description of the process by which the database design was implemented, including the means used to create the database and its associated objects.

f. A description of the differences between the physical design and the logical model, and the reasons for them.

g. A description of the update mechanism chosen for the database, and how it was implemented.

h. A description of the mechanisms implemented in the database for ensuring the integrity, security, recoverability, and accessibility of the data.

i. Documentation of the expected size and rate of growth of the database, the required longevity of the data (i.e., the length of time data must be kept in the database), and the means by which outdated or unneeded data will be archived and/or purged from the database.

j. A description of the service-level agreement (SLA) for the database, and how it will be met.

k. A description of any user or application requirements for the database, and how they will be met.

Again, the point here is not to produce documentation for documentation's sake; it is to document the agreements between the stakeholders involved in the design and development of the database. Understanding these agreements, and the reasons for them, will be essential to both maintaining the database and to modifying it quickly and effectively over time.

Note, however, that this document is not primarily of value to the current application development effort (that is, it is not really an application development artifact); it is primarily of value to the people who will support, modify, and enhance the application after it has been deployed to Production. For this reason, creation of this document should not be an impediment to the project. If necessary, creation of this document can be deferred until it is time to turn the application over to the Application Support and Operations groups.

How Much Should You Implement?

As with logical design, there is the question of how much of the physical design work can and should be done as a part of each Sprint or user story. Since the work of designing the physical database can't start until the logical data model (or at least the first cut of one) is complete, the DBA is going to have to hit the ground running. The DBA is going to have to spend the initial Sprint(s) of the project performing several tasks:

- Getting familiar with the data requirements. This will involve (initially) reviewing the conceptual data model and whatever there is of the logical data model and supporting documentation, and then (later) reviewing the first-cut logical data model with the data analyst.

- Getting familiar with the user stories and business requirements in order to understand and anticipate the application requirements.

- Setting up the database environment for the development effort. This may mean, for example, setting up Development and Test (QA) database instances on a test database server machine.[58] An appropriate server must be identified for the

---

[58] In some development environments (such as Microsoft's Visual Studio Team System), each developer has a copy of the development database to work with; database changes from multiple developer databases are collated, vetted, and then promoted as a unit to the Test database.

project (or purchased, and then set up and configured), along with the necessary amount of disk storage (which may also need to be purchased). The Dev/Test database infrastructure will need to be in place at the beginning of the development effort; later on, Certification and Production environments will also need to be created.

A first cut of the physical database will probably be required early in the first development Sprint. This means that the following tasks will need to be completed as quickly as possible:

- A review of the first-cut logical data model by the project team (including business users, business analysts, application designers and/or architects, application analysts, the data analyst, and the DBA).

- The physical design review session, as previously described, to establish the essentials of the database design and to surface expectations and issues regarding the database environment.

- Publication of the first-cut logical data model and physical database design (and any subsequent review and modification). These documents help provide the framework for the discussions that will take place during the analysis and design meetings for the various user stories.

- Creation of the first-cut physical database in the Development and Test environments.[59]

---

[59] I should probably explain my use of these terms. In our shop, developers code in a Dev environment that is in constant flux as user stories are developed. When one or more stories have been completed, a build of the application (along with database structures and code) is deployed to the Test environment to be evaluated by our QA team and key business users. When all the user stories have been completed and tested, the application and database are moved into the Certification environment for general user evaluation and performance testing, prior to deployment into the Production environment.

The design and implementation of the physical database is handled a bit differently from the way the logical data modeling is done. Since refactoring the logical model is relatively simple and painless, and since having a comprehensive model to use for discussion and analysis provides benefits in and of itself, there is little harm (and much good) in modeling in advance of the Sprint requirements. At the physical level, however, it's usually best to only design and implement what's needed at any given point. Trying to clean up unused entities and attributes at the end of a project is time-consuming, difficult, and error-prone.

The Purpose of Normalization in Physical Design

One of the biggest areas of confusion in the logical/physical divide is the subject of normalization. Data managers have a tendency to want to implement the normalized logical model in the physical database to ensure data integrity, while developers have a tendency to want a denormalized schema in order to (ostensibly) simplify their coding and improve performance. There are, however, some very important things that need to be kept in mind here:

- Normalization and denormalization are done for different reasons in the logical and physical realms. In logical modeling, normalization is done primarily to ensure that all business data requirements have been accurately captured and understood, while in physical design, the primary purpose is to create data structures that are highly cohesive, loosely coupled, and reusable. For example, you would want to have a single data structure, or set of structures, containing Customer data that contains all data relevant to customers (highly cohesive), that changes only when business or application requirements directly related to customers change (loosely coupled), and can be reused to support any application or business process that involves customers.

- The degree of normalization done in the physical design and base schema also depends on the nature and purpose of the database being created. Relational databases that support transactional processing (OLTP) tend to be more normalized in design; this helps improve performance during updates and reduces the risk of data anomalies. Databases used for reporting and analysis purposes will have a more denormalized design, to improve speed of data retrieval and put the data into a more useable form. Denormalization in these types of databases is acceptable, since data is not updated in an ad-hoc fashion by users, but is updated (or refreshed) by controlled processes.

- It's also important to understand that, in the physical database, denormalization can be done in different ways, and at different levels of the database. Even if the base schema is highly normalized, you can still create denormalized application objects in the Virtual Data Layer. Views, stored procedures, functions, and work tables (or materialized views) can all serve to mask the complexity of the underlying database schema, simplify application coding, and improve performance, without sacrificing the integrity of data in the database.

Two other things to keep in mind: First, denormalizing the base schema incorrectly can lead to both data anomalies and application errors (as we saw in the example of the Timesheet application). Second, denormalizing the base schema doesn't necessarily improve performance (as is often alleged); putting too much data in one place can actually make performance worse, as database locking and blocking results from multiple users trying to access the same table(s) at the same time. Also, denormalizing the base schema can result in SQL code that is more complex and performs more poorly.

As an example, take a look at the following denormalized table (from an actual production database):

Event

EventID	IDENTITY
EventTypeCode	smallint
EventType1Key	int
EventType2Key	int
EventType3Key	int
...etc. etc. etc.	
EventDateTime	datetime
EventDesc	varchar

The problem here is that data for multiple entities is contained in the same table, therefore each query against the table must be coded in such a way that it extracts data for one entity, and ignores the others.

Now, all the stored procedures that access this table must have the following parameter list:

```
CREATE PROCEDURE dbo.csGetEventData (@EventType
smallint, @EventType1Key int = null, @EventType2Key
int = null, @EventType3Key int = null...)
```

And the WHERE clause for the SELECT will have to look something like this:

```
WHERE (@EventType1Key IS NOT NULL AND @EventType1Key =
Event.EventType1Key)
   OR (@EventType2Key IS NOT NULL AND @EventType2Key =
Event.EventType2Key)
   OR (@EventType3Key IS NOT NULL AND @EventType3Key =
Event.EventType3Key)
```

Or perhaps like this:

```
WHERE (@EventTypeCode = 1 AND @EventType1Key =
Event.EventType1Key)
   OR (@EventTypeCode = 2 AND @EventType2Key =
Event.EventType2Key)
   OR (@EventTypeCode = 3 AND @EventType3Key =
Event.EventType3Key)
```

In either case, the presence of the multiple ORs in the WHERE clause will cause the SELECT to become non-optimizable, and the query will have to do multiple scans of the Event table, resulting in very poor performance. In this case, our developers ended up having to code dynamic SQL queries to get around this problem, but still had to take a performance hit (although not as great a one) because dynamic SQL can't be pre-compiled and pre-optimized.

On the other hand, it is also possible to over-normalize the base schema. I can think of two databases in our organization (one is a document database, the other supports a rules engine) where implementing the fully-normalized logical model in the database resulted in tables that had no purpose other than to complicate joins and slow down retrieval of data. So we need to address the question: when should you denormalize the base schema, and when shouldn't you?

When Should You Denormalize?

Generally speaking, denormalization of the physical database design can be considered in areas where there will be no ad-hoc updating by individual users. For example:

- Reporting tables: We often create special work tables (or materialized views) to support the reporting components of an application. We then create background processes to refresh the data on a regular basis.

- History and auditing tables: These tables maintain a history of update transactions and/or user activity, for the purpose of creating an audit trail that can be used to troubleshoot application problems or to ensure compliance with auditing and regulatory requirements.

- Insert-only structures. For example, many retail applications will capture customer order and Point-of-Sale transactions in a denormalized data structure on the front end of the application; a background process then extracts that data, parses it, and updates the back-end database.

- Tables supporting controlled processes: If a table is updated only by a well-defined application process (e.g., the controller for a conveyor belt), and concerns of reusability and ad-hoc updating are not factors, the table can probably be denormalized, if needed.

- Tables supporting third-party software: In the case of third-party software, the schema is defined by, and supported by, the vendor. Updates to the schema are done via scripts supplied by the vendor. In these cases, the DBA usually has no responsibility for this data, other than to ensure it is backed up and recoverable.

Denormalization can also be considered when implementing a logical entity would result in a physical structure that is unneeded or non-reusable. Some entities in the logical model will exist solely for the purpose of documenting a business rule or constraint, or because the nature of the modeling tool forces their creation. It is the responsibility of the DBA to come up with a database design that accurately implements the business data requirements while, at the same time, creating database structures that can be easily mapped to real-world objects and that are reusable. I've seen databases where several tables needed to be joined together to get a single useful and reusable data object; this is wasteful and unnecessary.

When Shouldn't You Denormalize?

Denormalization of the physical design (i.e., the database schema) should NOT be done when:

- The resulting structure does not have a clearly-defined meaning and purpose. In other words, all database structures should represent real-world objects.

- The resulting structure is difficult or expensive to update or reuse.

- There is a significant risk of violating data integrity or security requirements.

- Performance issues will result from putting too much data in the same place.

In our example of the "Tasks" table, we saw several of these recommendations violated. The table, created for the convenience of the application developer, was clearly not designed to represent a real-world object, it is clearly not reusable, it would be difficult to change without breaking one or more applications, and the design ensures that several critical data attributes (employee, task, project, week) will either be missing or become corrupted. Moreover, performance issues would almost certainly arise from putting all the data for the application in a single table. In the case of the Event table mentioned earlier, a better approach would have been to implement it as a supertype with a set of associated subtypes (one for each event type).

Normalization "After the Fact"

The "Tasks" table example also illustrates the danger of another approach that is sometimes advocated: starting with a denormalized physical design, and then trying to normalize tables incrementally "after the fact".[60] When I tried to refactor the denormalized "Tasks" table to fix the application issues caused by the denormalized schema, I discovered that it was impossible to do so. Since the table columns corresponding to key attributes (e.g., the employee name, task name, and week number) were defined as optional, non-key attributes, the data in these columns was either incorrect or missing entirely. The data needed to populate the key columns in a more normalized table structure wasn't available. Fortunately, we caught this problem in testing, so it wasn't a big issue to delete all the data from the database and start over. In a production database, however, this would have been much more of a problem!

When to do Physical Design

As mentioned above, a first-cut of the database will be created at or near the beginning of the first development Sprint, in conjunction with the publication of the first-cut logical data model. Iterative changes to the physical database design and base schema will then occur as the individual user stories are developed, and their requirements better understood.

Usually, as each story is being developed, an analysis session is conducted to make sure the business requirements of the story are understood. The data analyst attends this session. If business requirements are surfaced that result in a change to the logical data model, the data analyst will take care of this.

---

[60] Scott Ambler describes this approach as follows: "Although normalization is often applied within the scope of a near-serial process, the fact is that you can apply the rules of normalization within an evolutionary process as well." *Agile Database Techniques*, page 70.

The analysis session will usually be followed by a design session, which the DBA will attend. The design session will focus on how the application will implement the business requirements of the user story, and the DBA will want to understand what needs to be present in the database to support these requirements. The DBA will update the physical design of the database as needed, implementing just enough of the logical data model to support the story. The necessary changes to the database schema will be made and validated. The DBA will then work with the developers to create or update the necessary virtual objects (views, stored procedures, functions, etc.) to support the application requirements. Data requirements should be implemented as virtual objects whenever possible, as these objects are much easier to refactor than the underlying database schema.

Moving From the Logical to the Physical

To sum up, moving from the logical to the physical involves the following steps:

- Making an intelligent choice of implementation, architecture, and technology. What sort of data repository, if any, is required? What business and/or application processes need to be supported. What is the best choice of architecture? Where should the repository reside? What is the most suitable choice of implementation technology?

- Having a clear understanding of both the logical (business) and physical (application) data requirements.

- Creating a physical design that maps the logical (business) requirements to the choice of implementation, architecture, and technology in a way that satisfies the application requirements.

- Generating the base schema of the repository from the physical design into an instance of the chosen technology.

- Creating any virtual objects necessary to decouple the data and application, making the data easier to consume, transform, and reuse.

- Documenting the physical design, and the decisions and agreements that went into creating it.

I'll state the obvious: this is a *lot* of work! However, a lot of this work is front-loaded (this is also true of the logical design work); there will be a great deal of work involved in the early iterations of the project, while core requirements are being understood and key user stories are being developed. After the first few iterations, though, changes tend to proceed in a much more evolutionary fashion; the later user stories and their data requirements build onto what was developed in the earlier work.

Key Points

- Physical design involves mapping the business data requirements (as expressed in the logical data model) to an intelligent choice of implementation, architecture, and technology.

- Physical design decisions should be discussed with, and approved by, the development team. These decisions should then be documented in a physical design document, for the benefit of anyone working with the database in the future.

- The purpose of normalization in physical design is to create database objects that are highly cohesive, loosely-coupled, and reusable. Denormalization of the physical design is OK in some cases, not OK in others. Remember that denormalization can be done in the Virtual Data Layer!

- Physical design work on Agile projects is done during Sprint planning and estimation, and user story design.

- The database schema and related database objects should be auto-generated, as much as possible, from the physical design model.

- Do only as much of the physical design (and implementation) as is needed to support the current set of user stories.

CHAPTER 8
Agile Modeling and Documentation

As we've seen in the preceding two chapters, a certain amount of documentation needs to be produced as part of the logical and physical data design processes. From an Agile point of view, we need to ask: is this documentation necessary? The Agile methodology is not opposed to all documentation, only to documentation that will not be used, or that will not be kept up-to-date. Most certainly, Agile supports the current trend toward Model-Driven Development (MDD). In this chapter, we'll take a look at the requirements for Agile models and documentation, and see where our data and database design artifacts fit into the Agile framework.

What is an "Agile Model"?

Generally speaking, three types of non-code artifacts are produced during an application development effort: *requirements* (e.g., the user stories that define what the application needs to do), *models* (artifacts that guide the application development effort, such as an object class model), and *documentation* (which describes the application for an outside audience; e.g., the Operations group or the Application Support group). Training materials for end users would also fall into the category of documentation.

We've already described the logical data model as a requirements document (along with use cases, as-is and to-be process flows, and architecture diagrams). The logical data model captures the business data domain, business data requirements, and the business rules that constrain the data. We've also talked about the physical database design document, and how it will be used to help support the database (and the applications that use it) over time, thus reducing support costs and increasing the ROI of both the database and the applications that use it.

The question that arises here is this: can any of the artifacts produced during the database development process (e.g., the logical and physical data models) be construed as models in the context of application development? And, if so, can these models be considered "Agile Models"?

To answer this question, we must first consider two others: What makes an application development artifact a "model", and what makes a model "Agile"?

In answer to the first question, Scott Ambler lists several important distinctions between models and documentation:[61]

- Models involve active participation by multiple project stakeholders; documentation is usually written by a single person for a single target audience.

- Models follow a standard. There are accepted standards for the development of all types of models, including data models and application class models.

- Models support common design patterns. For all types of models, a set of common patterns, representing the application of the model to a set of common problems, is available to aid the modeler. This keeps each modeler from having to "reinvent the wheel" over and over again.

- Models are collectively owned. Anyone on the project team can use any given model, and can have input into changing it.

- Models can be tested. It should be possible, during the development of the application, to test each assertion contained in the model.

- Models promote group communication and collaboration. The essential purpose of a model is to enable the project

---

[61] Ambler, Scott. *Agile Database Techniques*, Chapter 10.

team to quickly reach a common consensus on what needs to be done, and how.

To be considered Agile, a model should meet the following criteria.

- It can be created quickly. To be effective, especially in an Agile context, it should be possible to develop the model quickly. A model that takes six weeks to produce, for example, won't be of very much use in an Agile project!

- It can be created incrementally. Since Agile is an iterative methodology, it follows that all models created during an Agile project will be created and refined iteratively, as requirements evolve or become better understood. Also, it should be possible to do this incremental updating quickly and painlessly.

- It contains only the amount of information required to achieve its purpose. Agile draws a clear distinction between models, which are created to achieve specific purposes during development, and documentation, which is created to provide long-term support for the application. Agile models aren't weighted down with excess verbiage or diagrams better suited to documentation.

- It is simple, clear, and concise. Agile models should communicate their purpose as quickly and painlessly as possible.

- Only important information is captured. An Agile model should never capture trivial, redundant, or obvious information.

- It maximizes stakeholder investment. Agile models are created to maximize stakeholder participation in (and understanding of) the project and its requirements. They are updated only when another iteration of understanding and communication is needed to move the project forward.

Scott Ambler makes the point that many models created during an Agile project may be only temporary artifacts. Use cases may be written down on index cards. User interfaces may be sketched on white boards, or mocked up using an HTML editor. The application design may consist of a sheet of flip-chart paper and some Post-It notes. The essential question is one of reusability: is the model needed only to satisfy some immediate application need, or will it be reused (and updated) over a longer period? The answer to this question will determine the form in which the model (ultimately) will exist and be maintained.

Is the Logical Data Model an "Agile Model"?

The logical data model is often derided as a useless artifact, an unnecessary piece of documentation, and a sterling example of "Big Design Up Front" (BDUF). Not, in other words, an Agile model.

In my experience on Agile projects, however, the logical data model has shown itself to be a very useful development tool, and an important driver of the development effort. I would argue that the logical data model serves several important functions:

- It captures critical information that isn't captured anywhere else. Most application development requirements artifacts, such as use cases and user stories, capture only *functional* requirements (what does the application need to do; how does the user interact with the application, etc.). What often gets lost are the higher-level *business* requirements, especially business data requirements. In the Timesheet application we've been talking about, for example, the developers obviously captured the requirements for being able to enter and update timesheet data. But they didn't capture the requirement that each timesheet must be a unique instance of an employee, a task, a project, and a week number, nor did they capture the requirement that this critical (key) data *must* be entered, and *cannot* be changed after the timesheet is created.

  To see how important it is to capture these non-functional requirements, we need look no further than the vendor databases that support commercial off-the-shelf (COTS) software products. These databases are notorious for being poorly designed and poorly implemented. Currently, I'm wrestling with the database for an application that supports tools in our manufacturing plants that are connected to our company's network (in other words, each tool has an I/P address). We have discovered that the application allows users to assign the same I/P address to multiple tools, but does *not* allow them to fix this error! When we tried to run a script to fix this problem, we discovered that several of the underlying code tables in the database contained duplicate entries, resulting in many more records being updated than intended. Then we had to write another script to fix this problem, etc. The lack of data integrity constraints in the database has become the focal point for several production issues involving this application.

- It serves as a springboard for analysis. Far from being a useless design artifact, or an example of "Big Design Up Front", the logical data model has been used during the analysis sessions on several of our Agile projects as a basis for discussion, to make sure that everyone was talking about the same thing, using the same terms. The logical model provided a general context, an overview, of the business data domain, helping the development team to understand the business-level associations between the user stories. It also became the means to document assumptions and decisions that were made in the course of the analysis sessions. Yes, these assumptions and decisions changed over the course of the project, but the logical data model enabled us to answer questions like: "Why did we think this was needed earlier?", or "Why did we decide to do it this way?"

We used the entity and attribute comment fields in our modeling tool to capture these assumptions and decisions, along with the entity and attribute definitions, which user story (or stories) they applied to, and sample data. We then used a home-grown application to extract this data, put it into document form, and write it to a PDF file. We posted each iteration of this document file (along with a PDF of the current data model) on the project's intranet site, so that people could review them during meetings and discussions. We also made sure that printed copies were always available in the team room. I must admit, it gave me a great deal of satisfaction to see members of the project team carrying copies of the logical data model into analysis and design review sessions, and talking to areas of the model during their discussions!

- It is a driver for the physical database design and schema changes. In most modeling tools, you can easily apply changes in the logical model to the physical model, even when these models differ. Then, you can generate the DDL to apply the database schema changes from the physical model. Thus, these models serve not only as analysis and design artifacts, but also as development tools!

For these reasons, I would argue that the logical data model meets the criteria for a model (certainly standards and design patterns apply to logical modeling, and they are testable during both the design and implementation phases of the project). But is the logical data model an "Agile model"? I believe it can be, provided some caveats are met:

- Development of the logical model must be a collaborative effort. Even if the actual modeling is done by one person (presumably the data analyst), all persons involved in gathering and analyzing business and application requirements should be involved in the development and refinement of the model. Each iteration of the model should be reviewed with these stakeholders to make sure it reflects everyone's understanding of the requirements.

- Development of the logical model should be done iteratively. As described previously, the logical model can be developed and refined during all of the requirements-gathering and user story analysis tasks that comprise each iteration of an Agile project. Data Analysts must learn to work within the iterative context of Agile.

- Only business-level data requirements should be captured in the logical model. Application-specific data requirements (e.g., database tables or columns used only to support a specific application function) should be captured in the physical database model, and refactored there, if necessary. Driving all the application-specific physical database changes (such as the length of text fields) through the logical model diminishes the application-independent nature of the logical model, and increases the complexity and time of the refactoring process.

Each iteration of the logical data model reflects the current understanding of the business area's data domain and business rules, applied to the requirements of the current project. This understanding will not be complete at any given point in the project, and there will be a temptation to want to stop work until more of the requirements are known. But, for Agile projects, there has to come a point in each iteration where the team as a whole says, "We don't understand everything, but we understand enough to be able to begin the current set of user stories." As I said earlier, there are two ways to do anything – do nothing until you completely understand the problem, or do something with the understanding you have, and let your understanding of the problem develop as you solve it. Those of you who do carpentry or landscaping (as I do) will understand what I'm talking about. You plan as well as you can, but you never know everything you need to know at the beginning of a project.

It's also important to understand that the logical data model (as opposed to the database or the application code) is comparatively easy to change. It doesn't take much time (using a decent modeling tool) to add or delete entities, move or copy attributes, redraw relationship lines, etc. This makes it easy and relatively painless to treat the logical data model as a living document, and increases its usability as an application development artifact.

By being willing to develop the data model iteratively, instead of entirely up-front, it reduces the risk of having the application design get out in front of the data design (i.e., getting the cart before the horse). The data model, as a living and iteratively developing artifact, becomes much more useful to the project team as a basis for discussion, analysis, design, decision-making, and implementation. This reduces the risk that data requirements won't be captured in the rush to develop application functionality.

By approaching data modeling in an Agile fashion, and by demonstrating the value of the data model as an application development artifact to the project team, data analysts can greatly increase their value to the development effort, and help ensure that the data design drives the application design, not the other way around.

Is the Physical Database Model an "Agile Model"?

I would use similar arguments to make the case that the physical database model (as opposed to the database design document, which is a documentation artifact) should also be considered an Agile model. It serves many of the same functions as the logical data model, but works at the design level, rather than the analysis level. It gives project team members a common point of reference during design discussions, shows team members what is currently implemented in the database (so it can easily be determined what new database objects are needed to support the current iteration), allows assumptions and design decisions to be documented, and can be used to generate the DDL needed to update the database schema.

I would emphasize, though, that the physical model should document not only the base schema, but also the virtualization objects that have been created to support the application. For example, the modeling tool we use allows the designer to create what are called "views" in the physical design (these "views" might be implemented in the database as views, functions, stored procedures, or work tables/materialized views). Since we want developers to code to these virtual objects rather than to the normalized base tables, it's important to show them what virtual objects have been created, and are available for use. During design discussions, requirements for new virtual objects might surface, and these requirements can be captured in the physical database model.

Agile Documentation

In addition to requirements and models, an application development project will also create at least some measure of documentation. Documentation serves at least three purposes: it communicates important information to external stakeholders (e.g., Operations and Application Support personnel), it facilitates the process of deploying an application to Production, and it helps minimize the cost and effort involved in supporting the application (and database) over time, thus increasing ROI.

In the context of Agile, there are several questions that need to be considered when documentation is being produced:

- What specific documents need to be produced, in order to satisfy external stakeholders at each phase of the project?

- What information does each document need to contain?

- When do these documents need to be produced? For example, some documentation may be required to satisfy a defined approval process for each phase of the project. Other documentation is required only when the application is implemented in Production and turned over to support staff.

- What is the audience for each document, and what will it be used for?

- Who will own and maintain each document?

Agile documentation should satisfy the following requirements:

- No documentation should be produced that will not be used.

- No documentation should be produced that will not be kept up-to-date and maintained over time (unless the document is intended only to satisfy an immediate project requirement, such as funding or governance approval).

- Documentation should focus on information that is unlikely (or less likely) to change. The more stable the information is, the more likely it is to be actually used, and the easier it will be to maintain it over time.

- Documentation should be produced in a "just in time" fashion. Avoid writing documentation while the information it contains is still in a state of flux. Produce a document only after the information it contains has stabilized, and at the point where this information needs to be communicated to its target audience.

- Do not document information that is obvious, trivial, redundant, or easily obtainable from other sources (e.g., you can create a model of your physical database design, but don't bother to document the actual schema of your database).

- Documentation should be available in a form that is quickly and easily accessible. For example, documents that are available online in a collaboration site will more likely be referenced than documentation stored away in a binder somewhere.

As much care should be taken in the design and implementation of the application development artifacts (such as models and documentation) as in the design and implementation of the application itself. Make sure these artifacts serve their intended purpose, satisfy the needs of their intended audience, and maximize the investment of the project stakeholders.

Key Points

- Models are collectively owned and created collaboratively. They follow a standard, support common patterns, and are testable. They enable the team to quickly reach a consensus on what should be done, and how.

- Agile models are created quickly and incrementally. They are simple, clear, and concise, and contain only the information needed to achieve their purpose.

- Models created to satisfy only immediate project needs may be temporary (such as white board drawings or Post-It notes). Models that are intended to satisfy longer-term needs must be kept in a maintainable form.

- The logical data model can be considered an Agile model. It captures information that is not available anywhere else, promotes analysis and discussion of requirements, fosters collaboration, and drives the physical database design.

- It is important for data analysts to be willing (and able) to develop the data model iteratively and collaboratively.

- The physical data model can also be considered an Agile model. Like the logical model, it is useful for analysis and discussion of design issues, it fosters collaboration, and it drives changes to the database schema and the Virtual Data Layer.

- Documentation (like the physical design document) can be considered Agile if has a clear benefit and target audience (such as Operations and Support staff), is kept up-to-date, focuses on information that is unlikely to change, is quickly and easily accessible, and does not contain trivial or redundant information.

CHAPTER 9
Building the Agile Database

Now we come to the meat of this book — an explanation with examples of how to implement virtual data objects in a database. A couple of caveats here: most of these examples are going to be drawn from my experience working with relational DBMSs (specifically Microsoft SQL Server, although some examples from Oracle will also be shown). I'll be mentioning some non-relational (and non-database) approaches, as well, but most of the work I've done in this area has been done using relational databases. The other caveat is that the DBMS vendors have not done as good a job as they might have in implementing virtualization into their products. For example, it should be possible to update data directly through a joined view, and have the updates apply automatically to the underlying database tables, but the DBMS vendors haven't supported this. It is necessary to use other techniques (such as creating "Instead-Of" triggers on the view) to achieve this functionality.

In spite of the limitations of the available technology, data virtualization is still a useful approach that can deliver a great deal of benefit to application development projects, especially Agile projects. What we try to accomplish in our database work, especially in database coding, is to reduce or eliminate the "object-relational impedance mismatch" in a way that still safeguards the security and integrity of our data. Using the techniques described in this chapter, we can create virtual data objects that can map more readily to application objects, without tightly-coupling the application to the database schema, or denormalizing the database in a way that makes it unusable for other purposes.

Abstraction and Encapsulation

A truly Agile approach to database design is based on the Object-Oriented principles of Abstraction and Encapsulation. Abstraction means identifying the critical functionality that needs to be made available to the user (the "what"). Encapsulation means packaging this functionality in a way that hides the manner of implementation (the "how") from the user. The idea is to present an easy-to-use interface that enables the "what", and hides the "how". You don't have to know anything about electricity in order to turn on a light switch; you don't have to know anything about mechanics to operate a car. In fact, we use these interfaces every day without even being aware of them!

Developers working with databases are often frustrated because the design of these databases requires them to have an in-depth knowledge of how the data is structured and stored before they can access it. They also have to know exactly where the data is located (sometimes down to the level of which specific disk volume the data is on). When the structure or location of the data changes, the application breaks. Developers think this is stupid. They are right.

The answer, as you know by now, is to create one or more layers of abstraction between the application and the database, to hide from the application as much as possible the details of the physical implementation of the data. This serves at least two purposes: it makes database applications much easier to write, and it enables the structure, implementation, and location of the data to be changed without breaking the applications that use it. In this chapter, I'm going to describe a number of different ways of "virtualizing" data. The idea is to make data as easy to use as possible, without sacrificing data quality.

This approach extends to the database server, as well. We define DNS (Domain Name Service) alias names for our database servers. Applications reference the server alias name in the database connection strings (in the application config files), rather than the actual server name. This way, if a database needs to be moved from one server to another, the application doesn't break.

It is important to abstract and virtualize, as much as possible, an application's access to its data. The goal is to maximize the reusability of our data structures, while minimizing the impact on applications of any changes to those structures.

Cohesion and Coupling

Two other important Object-Oriented concepts affecting database issues are Cohesion and Coupling. We've talked about Coupling before; the goal is to keep applications and databases "loosely coupled" so that changes to the database schema have a minimum impact on applications, and databases can support multiple applications and multiple uses of data. Cohesion is the other side of the coin: all data needed to support the properties of an application object should be available in one place.

On the surface, these two goals appear to be mutually exclusive. As we've seen, we help achieve "loose coupling" by keeping the base schema of the database more-or-less normalized (for OLTP databases) and application-independent. But this scatters data needed by application objects throughout the database, making it harder to achieve cohesion. How do we reconcile these two goals? You know the answer: we achieve the cohesion we need by reconciling data virtually, creating database objects that bring data together from the base schema to be consumed by application objects.

Virtualizing the Database

Some of the most effective techniques for virtualizing data are as follows:

- Views
- Stored Procedures (including Fundamental Stored Procedures)
- Triggers
- Functions
- Work Tables and Materialized Views
- Application Data Objects
- Complex datatypes.

The implementation and use (along with the pros and cons) of each of these techniques will be described in detail in the following sections.

Views

Database views are, in my opinion, the single most important virtualization tool the DBA has, and many of my previous writings[62] extol the importance and value of using views in the database. Among the many benefits of views are the following:

- They can support multiple application-specific views of data, without having to modify the underlying database schema.

- They enable the decoupling of application code (and application objects) from the database schema. Changes can be made to the schema without breaking existing applications; views can also be used to transition applications from one view of the data to another.

- They can be given application-specific data names, lengths and datatypes, which can map directly to the properties of application data classes. Applications no longer need to be constrained by database naming standards and conventions.

- They can be used to enforce data security. Different views of the data can be set up for different groups of users, so that each user sees only the data that he/she is entitled to see.

- They can join together data from multiple tables and databases, hiding the complexity of these joins from the user and making queries easier to write. Table joins in a view are precompiled and pre-optimized for optimum performance, which can significantly improve query

---

[62] Burns, Larry. "Views: The Key to Database Agility", originally published May 31, 2005 in The Data Administration Newsletter (TDAN) (http://www.tdan.com/i034ht03.htm).

performance. Views will make use of any indexes that have been created on the underlying tables.

- Support for data encryption is improved (since most commercial data encryption tools work through columns on views, not base tables).

- They can be used to do on-the-fly conversion, cleansing, and reformatting of data from remote sources without having to modify the data at the source. This prevents development projects from having to be held up while data problems are fixed.

- They can be used to join relational and XML data, or to give users an XML (hierarchical) view of relational data, or vice-versa.

- They can be made updatable (using Instead-Of triggers that map updates on the view to updates on the underlying database tables).

To illustrate the usefulness of views, take the refactoring example from Chapter 12 of Scott Ambler's book, "Agile Database Techniques". In this example, we want to change a numeric USA zip code to an alphanumeric international postal code. Ambler spends several pages describing the steps involved in refactoring the database schema, converting the data, deprecating the original schema, running regression tests, etc.

But what happens if the application is referencing a view instead of a table? Then it's simple: you add the new postal code column to the table, copying data as needed from the old zip code column. Applications using the existing view don't break. Modify the stored procedure that updates the old zip code column to also update the new postal code column. Create a new view that references the postal code column instead of the zip code column, and then transition your applications from the old view to the new one at your leisure. No mess, no muss, no fuss.

Alternatively, add the new postal code to the existing view; as long as SELECTs from the view are being done using column references (i.e., no SELECT *), no harm is done. Transition your applications at leisure to reference the new column; then, delete the old column. All of this work can be done on the fly, in seconds, without impacting any existing applications.

Most importantly, from an Agile Development perspective, views are easily modifiable, and can be developed incrementally, in response to evolving application needs. Data can be added, changed, or removed from views without having to modify the database schema. Developers can use views to experiment with new configurations of data before requesting changes to the schema. And developers can make these changes themselves, instead of having to go through the DBA.

Use Views When...

- You want to define a view of the data that maps more directly to an application object

- You want to mask or predefine table joins in order to simplify coding or improve performance

- You want to reuse a particular view of the data to support multiple consumers

- You want to limit users' view of the data, impose security constraints, or support encryption

- You want to decouple the application view of data from the base schema.

Advice on Views

- Keep views small and focused, rather than large and general. It is better to have a larger number of views, each of which returns a small number of rows and columns, than a smaller number of generalized views that return everything under the sun. Large views tend to perform poorly, so you may need to trade off some reusability for performance.

- Views should directly reference base tables. Avoid referencing views within views, especially not to more than 2 or 3 levels, as this will adversely affect performance. In particular, avoid views that jump back and forth across database or server boundaries (e.g., a view on Server A references a view on Server B, which references another view on Server A, etc.).

- Don't worry about having a lot of views in the database – they require little or no maintenance.

- Identify opportunities for views early in the development process, ideally during design; get the necessary views created before other database coding starts. Ideally, there should be at least one view in the database for each object class defined in the application class model.

- Make sure that appropriate indexes exist for the underlying tables and table joins.

- If SELECTs from a view will return a large number of rows, use a wrapper procedure or function to access it. The wrapper procedure or function should be parameterized, so that only rows corresponding to particular parameter values will be returned.

- Never use "SELECT *" in views; always define each individual column. This keeps the view (and the applications that use it) from breaking if the schema of the underlying table(s) changes.

- Avoid using table hints in views; use them only as a last resort.[63]

---

[63] Table hints force the SELECT in a view to use a particular index that exists for a table. In some cases, this may improve performance. In other cases, especially when the number of records in the table changes drastically, table hints can force the SQL query optimizer to use a non-optimal query plan, resulting in much poorer performance.

- Consider using SELECT WITH NOLOCK in views. Since NOLOCK permits what are called "dirty reads" (i.e., you can see records that someone else is in the process of changing), it is not appropriate to use in all cases. However, in cases where it doesn't matter, using NOLOCK prevents the holding of locks on the underlying table(s), and will improve performance.

- Be sure to document views with comments explaining the purpose of the view, the type of data that is being returned from the view, and the use of the view in applications.

- Use standard version-control processes when changing view code.

Standards for Views

- Views (and all other database objects) should have descriptive names in mixed-case format (e.g., HourlyEmployees). The view name should describe the type of data contained in the view (for convenience, the view name can be the same as an application class name).

- In our organization, we normally prefix the view name with 'vw' (e.g., vwHourlyEmployees). For foreign views (views that contain references to remote databases), we use the designation 'vf' instead of 'vw'. Since these views will contain hard-coded database and server references (not all organizations take this approach, but we find it preferable to coding dynamic SQL), this makes it easier to identify views whose code must be modified when deploying across environments.

- SELECT permission on views can be granted to one or more database roles that have authority to view that data. These roles, in turn, are associated with security groups containing individual application and user accounts. In this way, an individual user's database permissions can be changed simply by moving that user's account to a different security group, which is associated with a different role in the database. You never want to define database permissions at the user account level!

Example of View[64]

```
-- View to display products and product
descriptions by language:

CREATE VIEW Production.vwProductAndDescription
AS
SELECT
     p.ProductID
     ,p.Name
     ,pm.Name AS ProductModel
     ,pmx.CultureID
     ,pd.Description

FROM Production.Product p
    INNER JOIN Production.ProductModel pm
     ON p.ProductModelID = pm.ProductModelID
    INNER JOIN
Production.ProductModelProductDescriptionCulture
pmx
     ON pm.ProductModelID = pmx.ProductModelID
    INNER JOIN Production.ProductDescription pd
     ON pmx.ProductDescriptionID =
pd.ProductDescriptionID
GO


GRANT SELECT ON Production.vwProductAndDescription
TO roReadOnly, roReadWrite
GO
```

---

[64] Note: all examples shown in this section are from Microsoft SQL Server's sample "AdventureWorks" database. Note that many of Microsoft's naming conventions for database objects are different from the ones our organization uses; for example, 'v' instead of 'vw' for views, and 'ufn' instead of 'fn' for functions.

Stored Procedures

Most people are familiar with stored procedures as a way of implementing data-specific business or application processes, but they serve an important role in data virtualization, as well. Stored procedures can return data to a calling application either as individual values (OUTPUT variables) or as a collection of rows (called a result set, or rowset). Stored procedures that return rowsets are similar in nature to views, with two important differences: they can be parameterized (i.e., they can accept values for one or more input variables), and they can perform complex logic. This allows them to serve as a useful wrapper for views; the amount of data returned to the requestor can be controlled via the input parameter values.

You can also use wrapper procedures to return a specific number of rows of data (say, one screen page's worth). For example, the following procedure will return the next 20 rows of data for a specified customer name, starting from a specified order date/time:

```
CREATE PROCEDURE dbo.csReturnOrderData
        @CustomerName     varchar(120),
        @OrderDate        datetime = '01/01/1900'
AS
SELECT TOP 20 CustomerName, OrderNumber, OrderDate,
OrderAmount, ShippingDate

FROM vwOrderData

WHERE CustomerName = @CustomerName
     AND OrderDate >= @OrderDate
ORDER BY OrderDate DESC
RETURN
```

If your DBMS does not support the SELECT TOP N construct, you can achieve the same results using SET ROWCOUNT N or its equivalent in your DBMS.

Encapsulating data-specific processes with stored procedures provides a number of advantages:

- The amount of data and SQL code sent across the network is kept to a minimum, increasing the performance and scalability of the application.

- Stored procedure code is precompiled and pre-optimized on the database server for maximum efficiency.

- Processing of data is done using the resources of the database server, not the application server or client machine.

- SQL code in stored procedures is easier to test, debug, performance-tune, and maintain than embedded SQL in application code.

- Execute permissions on stored procedures can be used to restrict processes to designated groups/roles for increased security.

- Transaction management in stored procedures can be used to encapsulate a particular "unit of work" in the database; this prevents partial updates of data from occurring. For example, a stored procedure for an ATM application can perform the work of taking money out of a user's savings account and transferring it into his checking account, making sure that both updates occur successfully before committing them (or rolling them both back if an error occurs, or if the ATM machine goes down in the middle of the transaction!).

Use Stored Procedures When...

- Encapsulating any complex data-oriented procedural logic that should be executed on the database server.

- Doing any sort of update to the database (see the following section on Fundamental Stored Procedures).

- Restricting the amount of data returned from a SELECT against a table or view.

- Performing a complex SELECT involving joins of multiple tables (to support analysis and optimization of the joins).

Advice on Stored Procedures

- Treat procedures like all other application code: they should be testable, debuggable, well-documented, well-structured, and reusable.

- Use standard version-control processes when changing procedure code.

- Test all input parameters at the beginning of the procedure to make sure they are present and correct; otherwise, exit the procedure immediately with an error.

- Stored procedures should always send a return value (which should be checked) to the calling procedure or process. If an error is encountered, an error code and clear error message should be returned.

- Comment stored procedure code thoroughly; include a record of changes made at the beginning of the procedure.

- Do code walk-throughs of complex procedures.

- Do performance testing and tuning of procedures prior to implementation. Most major DBMSs provide tools that allow you to examine the execution plan of stored procedures and identify potential performance issues, such as not having adequate indexes in place to support queries or table joins.

- Pay attention to things that can cause stored procedures to be recompiled each time they are executed, as this impacts performance. For example, the use of non-ANSI SET statements, such as SET CONCAT_NULL_YIELDS_NULL, will force a recompile. Also, creating and deleting temp tables in the middle of your procedure can force a recompile; create all temp tables at the beginning of your procedure, and drop them at the end.

- Avoid putting optional parameters in stored procedures; this forces you to put a lot of inefficient "OR" code in your queries. If necessary, combine separate queries using the UNION operator, or use separate procedures for each application condition.

- Extract complex table joins into views; then reference the views in the procedure.

- Beware of dynamic SQL. Dynamic SQL queries (where the query statement is created in the stored procedure and then executed) are useful in situations where the search conditions aren't known until execution time; however, these queries can't be pre-optimized. Also, dynamic SQL code that creates or uses temp tables can cause a stored procedure to be recompiled each time it is executed.

- Encapsulate the smallest possible unit of work in a given procedure. If necessary, use nested procedure calls to break up work into manageable units.

Standards for Stored Procedures

- Stored Procedures (and all other database objects) should have descriptive names in mixed-case format (e.g., GetOrderData or UpdateOrderData). The procedure name should accurately reflect the action that the procedure is taking on the data.

- In our organization, we normally prefix the procedure name with the prefix 'cs' (e.g., csGetOrderData). You can use whatever prefix works best for you, but avoid using the prefix 'sp'; this prefix is usually reserved for DBMS system stored procedures.

- EXECUTE permission on stored procedures can be granted to one or more database roles that have authority to view the data (for read-only procedures) or update it (for update procedures).

Example of Data Conversion Stored Procedure

```
CREATE PROCEDURE
dbo.csReformatXMLProductDescription
 (@XMLDoc xml)
AS
BEGIN

-- Convert Product and Description XML document
into
-- relational form, using OPENXML.

SET NOCOUNT ON

DECLARE @idoc int, @_error int, @_errdesc
varchar(200)

EXEC sp_xml_preparedocument @idoc OUTPUT, @XMLDoc

SELECT ProductID, Name, ProductModel, CultureID,
Description
FROM OPENXML (@idoc,
'/ProductAndDescription/Product',2)
WITH (ProductID int, Name nvarchar(50),
ProductModel nvarchar(50), CultureID nchar(6),
Description nvarchar(400))

select @_error = @@error

if @_error <> 0
begin
   SELECT @_errdesc = 'Error in procedure
csReformatXMLProductDescription: OPENXML returned
error code: ' + convert(varchar, abs(@_error))
   RAISERROR (@_errdesc, 16, 1)
end
EXEC sp_xml_removedocument @idoc
RETURN
END
```

Example of Wrapper Stored Procedure

```
-- Wrapper procedure for Product and Description
view
-- Data can be extracted by Product Model and/or
Culture ID.

CREATE PROCEDURE
Production.csGetProductAndDescription (
     @ProductModel    varchar(50) = null,
     @CultureID       nchar(6) = null
)
AS

-- Check input parameters
IF @ProductModel is null RETURN -999
IF @CultureID is null RETURN -999

SELECT  ProductID, Name, ProductModel, CultureID,
Description

FROM  Production.vwProductAndDescription

WHERE @ProductModel = ProductModel
  AND @CultureID = CultureID

RETURN
GO

GRANT EXECUTE ON
Production.csGetProductAndDescription
TO roReadOnly, roReadWrite
GO

-- Output from wrapper procedure:
-- exec Production.csGetProductAndDescription
'Mountain-100', 'en'
```

ProductID	Name	ProductModel	CultureID	Description
771	Mountain-100 Silver, 38	Mountain-100	en	Top-of-the-line competition mountain bike. Performance-enhancing options include the innovative HL Frame, super-smooth front suspension, and traction for all terrain.
772	Mountain-100 Silver, 42	Mountain-100	en	Top-of-the-line competition mountain bike, etc.
773	Mountain-100 Silver, 44	Mountain-100	en	Top-of-the-line competition mountain bike, etc.
774	Mountain-100 Silver, 48	Mountain-100	en	Top-of-the-line competition mountain bike, etc.
775	Mountain-100 Black, 38	Mountain-100	en	Top-of-the-line competition mountain bike, etc.
776	Mountain-100 Black, 42	Mountain-100	en	Top-of-the-line competition mountain bike, etc.
777	Mountain-100 Black, 44	Mountain-100	en	Top-of-the-line competition mountain bike, etc.
778	Mountain-100 Black, 48	Mountain-100	en	Top-of-the-line competition mountain bike, etc.

(8 row(s) affected)

Fundamental Stored Procedures

Fundamental Stored Procedures are special stored procedures that handle updating of data in the database. More specifically, each fundamental stored procedure (or FSP) performs one type of update (add, change, or delete) on one or more rows of data in a single database table. Fundamental stored procedures have the following characteristics:

- *Restricted updates.* An FSP should update only one, or at most a small number, of records in a single database table, based on the value(s) of one or more key columns. If, for example, a table has a three-part key, it is permissible to create FSPs that operate on the subset of records defined by the values of one or two of those keys, as long as the possible number of updates remains small. Restricting the number of updates ensures adequate update performance, and minimizes problems with locking, concurrency, and rollback of updates if an error occurs.

- *Single operation.* Each FSP should perform one and only one operation on a single database table (Insert, Update, Delete, or Select).

- *Transaction control.* FSPs should ensure that all updates are committed, or rolled back, as a single unit of work. If a higher-level stored procedure is calling multiple FSPs, or multiple lower-level stored procedures that call multiple FSPs, all updates performed as a result of this procedure should be regarded as a single unit of work, and be either committed or rolled back as a group by the higher-level procedure.

- *Concurrency control.* FSPs should use timestamp checking (or some similar mechanism) to ensure that two or more users cannot update the same record at the same time. This supports an optimistic approach to database updating, in which multiple users are allowed to access and update tables simultaneously, rather than being locked out when a table is being updated by another user. Support of optimistic updating is critical to ensuring good application performance.

- *Key support.* FSPs should support whatever key types are used in the database, including programmatically generated keys, user-assigned keys, IDENTITY keys, and GUIDs (Global Unique Identifiers).

- *Error handling.* FSPs should detect any error that occurs during access or update of the database, and return that error immediately to the calling application or procedure.

- *Auto-generation.* FSPs should be automatically generated from the existing database schema. This enables FSPs to be easily created or modified in response to database changes, without adversely impacting application development timelines.

FSPs can also encapsulate additional functionality, including the following:

- *Auditing.* FSPs can check table updates against a configuration table containing information about which tables and columns and update types should be audited. Audit information can then be written to a separate auditing table.[65]

- *Optional column support.* Insert FSPs can be written to allow users to omit specification of columns that are nullable, or that have default values associated with them. Similarly, Update FSPs can be written in a way that allows users to specify only the columns that they want to change. This saves the user the bother of having to specify input values for every column in the table record being updated. This approach also makes using FSPs less susceptible to changes in the underlying tables. If a column that is

---

[65] Our group uses a general-purpose database trigger for this purpose, but other shops will build an optional auditing capability into their fundamental stored procedures.

nullable or has a default is added to a table, existing applications can continue to use the regenerated FSPs without needing to be modified in any way.

- *Subtype/supertype (inheritance) support.* FSPs can treat supertype/subtype relations as a single virtual table. Update operations are performed on the subtype table, and the FSP automatically updates the supertype table, as well. This masks the complexity of these relations from the developers, and lends support to inheritance associations in the database.

- *Multi-language text support.* Our group has built support for multi-language text into our FSPs (since, as a global company, our users want to work with data in their own language). A language (locale) identifier is passed from the application to the FSP, and storage and retrieval of text data in the requested language is handled behind the scenes.

As you can see, FSPs can provide significant functionality and value. The use of FSPs save developers the trouble of writing, testing and maintaining application-level code to handle database updating, and reduces the risk of data corruption or loss due to incorrectly coded updates. Since FSPs are auto-generated, there is no coding effort, and minimal testing effort, involved with their use. Database updates are handled as close to the data as possible, and critical data integrity considerations (such as transaction management, concurrency control, and error detection) are taken care of. The use of FSPs also provides an additional layer of data security: only authorized users (user roles) can execute them, and no direct updating of the database tables should be allowed. This protects the data against accidental or deliberate corruption or loss of data, both by internal users and by outside hackers.

Also, since FSPs are generated from the database schema, it becomes much easier to handle schema changes. After changing, say, a table definition, the FSPs for that table can be regenerated and updated in the database, quickly and easily.

An issue arises, though, in using FSPs in conjunction with virtual objects, such as joined views, in the Virtual Data Layer. Since virtual objects can consist of elements from multiple tables, but FSPs update only a single table, how is updating to be done at the virtual level using FSPs?

One approach is to define a set of complex stored procedures that handle inserts, update, and deletes at the virtual object level. These procedures, in turn, can call the appropriate FSP for each of the underlying database tables. These procedures can be called from components in the VDL (e.g., from an ADO.NET data adapter object) to update the object.

Note, however, that these complex stored procedures must contain the same mechanism for transaction control and concurrency control as the FSPs. For example, if a call to an underlying FSP fails, all of the updates that have been made by the stored procedure should be rolled back. Make sure to check the execution of each FSP to ensure that each update was successful.

Advice on Fundamental Stored Procedures

- Always use fundamental stored procedures to do database updating. Do not allow any direct updating of database tables; this helps protect against accidental or intentional corruption or loss of data.

- For updates on individual tables that are more complex (or updates not involving key values), you can create "alternate" FSPs. For example, you could create an alternate FSP to update the Employee table based on EmployeeName, rather than EmployeeID. In some cases, you can generate alternate FSPs based on an analysis of alternate indexes; in other cases, they can be copied from generated FSPs and modified by hand.

- FSPs can also be created for SELECT as well as update operations (for example, to select records from a table based on one or more key values, or to select all records from a table).

- In development environments where the database schema is maintained in source control, changes to the schema can automatically trigger generation of the FSPs using Continuous Integration (CI).

Standards for Fundamental Stored Procedures

- Our standard naming convention for FSPs is *fsTableName_x*, where x = i (Insert), u (Update), d (Delete) or s (Select)

- Naming convention for alternate FSPs is *fsTableName_xN*, where N = 1, 2, 3, etc.

- Standard FSPs are auto-generated. Alternate FSPs can be created by developers (with assistance as needed from the DBAs). Make sure all FSPs are owned by the DBO schema

- Execute permissions on FSPs should be granted only to groups/roles with update authority on the corresponding tables.

Triggers

A trigger is a special type of database code that is associated with a particular database table; the trigger code is executed when the table is updated. A trigger is associated with one or more update operations (Insert, Update, or Delete). Multiple triggers can be associated with the same update operation, but it can be difficult to control the order in which triggers are fired.[66]

Triggers have a variety of uses:

- *Validation*: Triggers can do complex data validation checking at update time, and fail updates for which the validation is unsuccessful. They are especially useful for

---

[66] Some DBMSs allow you to specify which trigger should be fired first, and which should be fired last; otherwise, the order of trigger execution is random.

cross-database validation (checking data against data in other databases), since standard database constraints won't work across database boundaries.

- *Auditing*: In our organization, we use a general-purpose trigger to do auditing of database updates. The trigger checks a table that contains information about the tables, columns, and update types (insert, update, or delete) we want to audit. If an auditable update event is detected, the trigger creates an audit record with information about the updated record, including its primary key values and the before and after values of the column being audited, the updating userid and server name, and the date and time of the update. This information is then written to an audit table in the database. The audit data can be queried by application processes that need to make decisions based on update (state) events; e.g., the updating of a status code.

- *Event Processing*: Triggers are one way that a database can be programmed to respond to events. For example, we have a transaction table in one of our databases; a web service inserts records into this table in response to updates occurring on the mainframe. A trigger associated with the transaction table then applies those updates to tables in the database.

- *Cross-database Updating*: Triggers can be used when an update in one database needs to cause an update to occur in another database. For example, the processing of a customer order in the Order Processing database may fire off an adjustment to part quantities in the Inventory database. If the quantity-on-hand for a given part falls below the reorder level, a trigger on that table may invoke a process in the Supplier database to order additional quantities of that part from the appropriate supplier.

- *Calculations*: If derived or computed values are being kept in the database, triggers can be used to make sure these values are recalculated whenever records are updated.

- *Data Retention and Archiving*: In response to a Delete operation on a table, a trigger can decide whether to archive all or part of that data, or related data. In one of our databases, deleting an order fires a trigger which archives certain data in a related table, so that it isn't lost when the order disappears.

Standard database triggers execute either just before an update (if the DBMS supports this option) or just after the update. In the former case, you can decide whether to allow the update to occur, based on the trigger logic. In the latter case, you can decide to roll back the update that has occurred, if some error condition (e.g., failure of a complex validation constraint) is detected.

Another type of trigger is the "Instead-Of" trigger. In triggers of this type, the trigger code is executed in place of the table update that would normally occur. For this reason, the trigger code must contain the INSERT, UPDATE, or DELETE statement that updates the table. In the timesheet application we've been using as an example throughout this book, we created a denormalized view over a set of normalized base tables. We could create a set of Instead-Of triggers on this view, so that updates to the view would be automatically applied to the underlying tables. However, this approach (as opposed to the use of FSPs) requires more manual coding and testing, plus it opens up the underlying tables to direct updating (including SQL injection attacks). For these reasons, we tend to avoid this approach in our databases.

Use Triggers When...

- You need to implement a process that automatically invokes whenever a database update occurs

- You need to validate that a database update is correct before allowing it to commit

- You need to update derived or computed values in response to a table update

- You need to synchronize updates across multiple tables or databases

- You need to apply updates of a joined view to the underlying database tables.

Advice on Triggers

- Make sure that any use of triggers in a database is well documented. The management tools provided by most DBMS vendors tend to conceal the existence of triggers, and it can be easy to forget they exist.

- Do not put any complex logic into the triggers themselves, as they are difficult to debug. Instead, put any complex logic in a stored procedure, and call the stored procedure from the trigger. Keep the actual trigger code as simple as possible.

- Do not attempt to start or end a database transaction from inside a trigger.

- Make sure that any trigger processing does not unduly affect database updating, unless you are intentionally preventing or rolling back a database update. For example, you don't want the insert of a single record to fire off a trigger process that takes 30 seconds! Trigger processes should be as unobtrusive as possible.

- Try to avoid having multiple triggers associated with the same update type on a given table, as it can be difficult to control the behavior of these triggers at execution time. If possible, select certain triggers to execute either first or last; for example, I always set my database audit triggers to execute last, after all other processing associated with an update has completed.

- Remember that a trigger will always fire in response to the processing of an INSERT, UPDATE, or DELETE statement, even if no updating actually occurs! For example, if there is an Update trigger on table *TestTable*, then the following statement:

```
UPDATE TestTable
SET col1 = 'SomeValue'
WHERE @UpdateInd = 1
```

will cause the trigger to fire, even if the value of @UpdateInd is 0.

This statement should be recoded as follows:

```
IF @UpdateInd = 1
UPDATE TestTable
SET col1 = 'SomeValue'
```

Standards for Triggers

- Our standard naming convention for triggers is *tgTableName_<FunctionalDescription>_I|U|D.* For example, a validation trigger might have a name like tgCustomer_ValidateCustomerName_IU. An audit trigger might have a name like tgCustomerOrder_Audit_IUD.

Example of Trigger

```
-- This trigger updates the ModifiedDate column in the
ProductCategory table after the record is updated.

CREATE TRIGGER Production.uProductCategory
ON Production.ProductCategory
AFTER UPDATE NOT FOR REPLICATION AS
BEGIN
    SET NOCOUNT ON;

    UPDATE Production.ProductCategory
    SET Production.ProductCategory.ModifiedDate =
GETDATE()
    FROM inserted
    WHERE inserted.ProductCategoryID =
Production.ProductCategory.ProductCategoryID;

END;
```

Functions

Functions (also called user-defined functions) are a special type of database object. Like stored procedures, they can accept parameter values, execute procedural code, and return either single values or rowsets. However, functions that return rowsets (called "table-valued" functions) can be treated just like views, and can even be included in table joins.

There are two types of functions: table-valued, which return rowsets, and scalar-valued, which return a single atomic value (such as an integer or a character string). Aggregate functions, such as the *min, max, sum,* and *count* SQL functions, are a special class of scalar-valued functions.

Scalar-valued functions are useful for doing on-the-fly data conversions and lookups, such as converting a date from Universal (UTC or GMT) time to local time (or vice-versa), or looking up the Employee ID Number for a specified employee name. They can also be used for computations, such as computing the discount on a list price.

Table-valued functions are useful as wrappers for selects from tables (or table joins) or views. You can use them, in cases where a normal SELECT would return too many rows or columns of data, to create a more restricted result set based on some specified criteria.

Table-valued functions have other uses, as well: one of my favorite and most-used functions accepts a delimited string of values (such as a string of customer numbers, separated by commas), and returns a table with each individual value in its own row. As mentioned above, the output from the function can be used directly in a view or table join, so as to restrict the output to those values specified in the string. I could use this function, for example, to query customer orders for a specific set of customer numbers.

Functions do have some limitations: they aren't as well-optimized as procedures and views, and they are very difficult to debug, since you can't use SELECT or PRINT statements to display values from the execution of a function. For this reason, never put any complex code (including complex table joins) inside a function. If necessary, put complex table joins into a view, and reference the view from the function.

You also cannot update tables or views, create temp tables, or call stored procedures from inside functions (you can execute other functions). Generally speaking, functions should only be used for quick and simple data conversion, formatting, and filtering.

Use Functions When...

- You want to do simple parsing, reformatting, or conversion of data on-the-fly (e.g., as part of a SQL query or table join)

- You want to restrict the amount of data returned from a SELECT against a table or view.

Advice on Functions

- Use functions only for simple processes; use procedures for anything complex

- Avoid excessive table joins or complex SQL queries in functions; if necessary, create a view and reference the view in the function.

Standards for Functions

- Functions should have descriptive names in mixed-case format (e.g., ConvertUTCDateToLocal). The function name should accurately reflect the action that the function is taking on the data.

- In our group, we normally prefix the procedure name with the prefix 'fn' (e.g., *fnGetOrderByCustomerID*).

- EXECUTE permission on functions can be granted to one or more database roles that have authority to view the data. Permissions on general-purpose formatting or conversion functions can be granted to 'public'.

- All function references must include the owner/schema name. Parameter arguments for functions must be enclosed in parentheses:

```
SELECT * FROM dbo.fnGetOrderByCustomerID (@CustID)
```

Example of Scalar-Valued Function

```
CREATE FUNCTION dbo.fnGetProductDealerPrice
(@ProductID int, @OrderDate datetime)
RETURNS money
AS
-- Returns the dealer price for the product on a specific date.
BEGIN
    DECLARE @DealerPrice money;
    DECLARE @DealerDiscount money;

    SET @DealerDiscount = 0.60  -- 60% of list price

    SELECT @DealerPrice = plph.[ListPrice] * @DealerDiscount
    FROM [Production].[Product] p
    INNER JOIN [Production].[ProductListPriceHistory] plph
        ON  p.[ProductID] = plph.[ProductID]
        AND p.[ProductID] = @ProductID
    WHERE @OrderDate BETWEEN plph.[StartDate]
AND COALESCE(plph.[EndDate], '12-31-9999');
    RETURN @DealerPrice
END

CREATE FUNCTION dbo.fnGetProductAndDescriptionAsXML (@ProductID
  int)
RETURNS xml
AS
BEGIN
-- Returns the data for a Product ID as XML
DECLARE @XML xml

SELECT @XML = (
  SELECT ProductID, Name, ProductModel, CultureID,
  Description
FROM Production.vwProductAndDescription
WHERE ProductID = @ProductID
FOR XML PATH ('Product'), root ('ProductAndDescription'))
RETURN @XML
END
```

Example of Table-Valued Function

```
CREATE FUNCTION dbo.fnGetProductAndDescription (
     @ProductModel    nvarchar(50),
     @CultureID       nchar(6)
)
RETURNS @ProductTable TABLE (ProductID int, Name
nvarchar(50), ProductModel nvarchar(50), CultureID
nchar(6))
AS
BEGIN

    INSERT INTO @ProductTable
(ProductID, Name, ProductModel, CultureID)
    SELECT ProductID, Name, ProductModel, CultureID
    FROM   Production.vProductAndDescription
    WHERE  ProductModel = @ProductModel
      AND CultureID = @CultureID

RETURN
END
```

Example of Data Conversion Function

```
CREATE FUNCTION dbo.fnGetSizeMap
      (@Name nvarchar(50))
RETURNS varchar(20)
AS
BEGIN
/*
This function finds all the distinct size values that exist
in the table for the specified product name, and returns a
value that concatenates these values (using '|' as a
delimiter).
*/

DECLARE @SizeMap     varchar(20)
DECLARE @SizeCode    char(2)
DECLARE @FirstCode   bit

SET @FirstCode  = 1
SELECT @Name = @Name + '%'

DECLARE name_crsr CURSOR FOR
SELECT DISTINCT Name
FROM Production.vProductAndDescription
WHERE Name like @Name
  AND CultureID = 'en'
OPEN name_crsr
FETCH name_crsr INTO @Name
WHILE (@@FETCH_STATUS = 0)
BEGIN
      SELECT @SizeCode = substring(@Name, charindex(',',
@Name) + 2, 2)

      IF @FirstCode = 1
          SELECT @SizeMap = rtrim(@SizeCode)
      ELSE
          SELECT @SizeMap = @SizeMap + '|' +
 rtrim(@SizeCode)

      SET @FirstCode = 0
      FETCH name_crsr INTO @Name
END
CLOSE name_crsr
DEALLOCATE name_crsr
RETURN @SizeMap
END
```

Example of Wrapper Function

```
/*
This function displays all the information for a
specified Product Model. If there are multiple Product
records for different sizes, a single record will be
returned, with the sizes displayed in a single field,
delimited by '|' (using the fnGetSizeMap function shown
above).
*/

CREATE FUNCTION dbo.fnGetProductAndDescription_2 (
      @ProductModel       nvarchar(50),
      @CultureID          nchar(6)
)
RETURNS @ProductTable TABLE (Name nvarchar(50), SizeMap
nvarchar(20), ProductModel nvarchar(50))
AS
BEGIN

INSERT INTO @ProductTable (Name, SizeMap, ProductModel)
SELECT DISTINCT
      CASE WHEN charindex(',', Name) > 0 THEN
            substring(Name, 1, charindex(',', Name) - 1)
      ELSE Name END as 'Name',
      CASE WHEN charindex(',', Name) > 0 THEN
      dbo.fnGetSizeMap(substring(Name, 1, charindex(',',
Name) - 1))
      ELSE NULL END as 'SizeMap',
      ProductModel
FROM  Production.vwProductAndDescription
WHERE @ProductModel = ProductModel
  AND CultureID = @CultureID

RETURN
END
GO
-- Output from the first function
-- select * from dbo.fnGetProductAndDescription
('Mountain-100', 'en')
-- Note that there is a separate record for each wheel
size.
```

ProductID	Name	ProductModel	CultureID
771	Mountain-100 Silver, 38	Mountain-100	en
772	Mountain-100 Silver, 42	Mountain-100	en
773	Mountain-100 Silver, 44	Mountain-100	en
774	Mountain-100 Silver, 48	Mountain-100	en
775	Mountain-100 Black, 38	Mountain-100	en
776	Mountain-100 Black, 42	Mountain-100	en
777	Mountain-100 Black, 44	Mountain-100	en
778	Mountain-100 Black, 48	Mountain-100	en

(8 row(s) affected)

```
-- Output from the second function
-- select * from dbo.fnGetProductAndDescription_2
('Mountain-100', 'en')
-- Note that there is now only one record for each
product.
```

Name	SizeMap	ProductModel
Mountain-100 Silver	38|42|44|48	Mountain-100
Mountain-100 Black	38|42|44|48	Mountain-100

(2 row(s) affected)

Work Tables and Materialized Views

As we've already pointed out, it's not usually a good idea to try to denormalize the base schema of the database (that is, to merge individual tables together to form larger tables), although this is often suggested as a way to (ostensibly) simplify SQL coding and improve application performance. Tightly-coupling an application to a denormalized database schema adversely affects the extensibility and reusability of the database, increases the risk of data corruption and loss, and can actually *increase* the complexity of SQL queries and *reduce* performance.[67]

Nevertheless, even though denormalizing the base schema is usually ill-advised, it is still possible to create application-specific, read-only, denormalized data objects in the database for specific purposes, and populate them from data in the base tables (or from views or stored procedures referencing them). Note that I emphasize the read-only nature of these objects; creating duplicate or redundant data in the database would also be wrong, if the data was going to be updated.

In the Oracle DBMS, these objects are referred to as *materialized views*. They are similar to normal views, except that the rowset of the view is persisted as an actual physical table in the database. In the definition of the materialized view, you can specify how often you want the data to be refreshed – after every update of one of the underlying tables; after a specified interval of time; or in response to a REFRESH command issued by the user.

In non-Oracle DBMSs, the same functionality can be achieved by creating a work table in the database, and then scheduling

---

[67] Burns, Larry. "Too Simple, Too Soon", originally published November 1, 2007 in TDAN (http://www.tdan.com/view-articles/6121).

periodic updates of the data using a stored procedure or data transfer job.[68]

There are several advantages to using these objects in the database. For one thing, the data is immediately available to the application; it does not have to be read from the base tables, joined together, and reformatted. For views of data involving several tables, complex joins, and hundreds of thousands (or millions) of rows, this could represent a significant saving of time. Also, indexes can be built on these objects for additional performance enhancement, as opposed to views, which can only use the indexes that exist on the underlying tables.[69]

They are also very useful as input to reporting and data analysis tools, which often require the data to be presented in a particular form. We often use work tables in our SQL Server databases to satisfy the input data requirements of SQL Reporting Services reports. They are also useful for "unpacking" recursive data (in tables where one record may reference another record as a "parent" or "child").

There are also a few disadvantages to using these objects, including the additional disk space requirements in the database (and larger backup and transaction log sizes), and some additional maintenance overhead. All of these objects, along with the code required to refresh the data in them, need to be maintained. However, in many cases the additional functionality and

---

[68] For example, in Microsoft SQL Server this could be done using DTS (Data Transformation Services) in SQL Server 2000, or SSIS (SQL Server Integration Services) in SQL Server 2005 and beyond.

[69] Some DBMSs support, at least in theory, the ability to build indexes directly on views. However, my experience has been that this functionality is so limited as to be virtually useless. Moreover, it requires the view to be tightly bound to the schema of the underlying tables, which in my opinion obviates the whole point of using views (which is to decouple the application from the database schema).

performance they provide are well worth the relatively small amount of bother. They should be considered an additional tool in the workbox of the Agile DBA.

Use Work Tables and Materialized Views When...

- An application-specific, denormalized (joined) or aggregated view of data is needed, and regular views cannot provide the required functionality or performance.

- Data must be persisted in a non-normalized or aggregated form as input to an application or application process (e.g., a reporting or BI application).

Advice on Work Tables and Materialized Views

- Try not to use them excessively, especially when views will provide adequate functionality and performance. Remember that these objects take up space and require maintenance. Also remember that the refreshes of these tables will increase the size of your database transaction log. In some cases, I've worked around this by persisting the work table in the tempdb database (which has no associated log segment).

- Also remember that data refreshes on these objects may not be instantaneous; in some cases, for a period of time, the data may not reflect what is actually stored in the base tables.

- When doing refreshes of work tables, I update the data into a temp table first; then, I rename the current work table to another name, rename the temp table to the work table name, and delete the old table. This ensures that the work table is unavailable for only the briefest period of time.

- Have a mechanism in place to detect and immediately report any failure of the process(es) that update data in these objects. It's very embarrassing when you discover that the data refresh hasn't actually occurred for several weeks!

Standards for Work Tables and Materialized Views

- Use the same sort of naming conventions as would be used for views, except for a distinctive prefix to distinguish these objects from other database tables and views (e.g., 'mv' or 'WRK_').

Application Data Objects

Application data objects (such as, for example, ADO.NET datasets and datatables, and objects created using .NET's new Entity Framework) can be used to create an additional layer of data abstraction in the application. Data can be read from the database to create data structures that the application can use. Since these data structures are memory-resident, the data can be accessed very quickly. This provides a means to not only insulate the application from database changes, but also to improve performance.

A few caveats are necessary, though: First, make sure to do any necessary elimination and aggregation of data on the database server using stored procedures before populating the application data structures. This will help avoid unnecessary processing and consumption of resources on the application server, reduce the load on the network, and make the application more scalable. Avoid situations where you're sending lots of complex SQL across the network to the database server (which then has to be parsed, compiled, and executed), and sending lots of data back across the network to be filtered out by the application server. Let the database server and query optimizer do the heavy data lifting!

Second, application data objects should reference views in the database, rather than the normalized base tables. This eliminates the "object-relational impedance mismatch", and helps insulate the application from changes in the database schema.

Third, application data objects should use stored procedures in the database for updating, rather than updating tables directly. Again, you don't want to tightly-couple the application objects to the normalized database schema, nor do you want to open up the tables to direct updating (exposing the data to both accidental loss and corruption, and to outside attack).

The best object frameworks are those that allow you to update application data objects using stored procedures. For example, both ADO.NET and Microsoft's new Entity Framework technology allow developers to create abstracted data objects that can be associated with a set of Insert, Update, Delete, and Select stored procedures. Updating of the data object will automatically execute the required procedures to update the database. This improves update performance, reduces the chance of data corruption and anomalies, and removes the need to open the database tables to direct updating.

A special case of application data objects are those created by OR/M (object-relational mapping) technologies. These tools create a set of application data objects with CRUD (Create, Read, Update, and Delete) methods that map directly to database tables. All database access and updating is done using these objects. I have a couple of problems with this approach: first, it tightly-couples the application data layer to the normalized database schema; as we've seen, this results in the "object-relational impedance mismatch" and will cause the app to break if the database schema changes. Second, this approach opens the tables to direct updating, exposing the data to both accidental loss and corruption and to outside attack. However, some OR/M products, such as NHibernate, do support the use of stored procedures.

To sum up, application objects will perform much better, and be much more Agile, if they operate against views in the database rather than the normalized base tables, and if they use stored procedures and functions in the database for complex data retrieval, data filtering, and updating.

Complex Datatypes

All DBMSs support simple (scalar) datatypes; that is, datatypes such as integer, character, floating point, and the like. Some

DBMSs, such as relational and object-relational, also provide at least limited support for more complex datatypes, which can be useful in creating more sophisticated data definitions that can be more easily mapped to objects in the real world. Complex datatypes can be separated into the following categories:

- *Modified Scalar*: These datatypes are used to define scalar objects constrained by rules that hold a particular type of data. For example, say that you always want to store telephone numbers in your database in the form (NNN)NNN-NNNN. You can create a user-defined scalar datatype for this as follows:

```
-- Create the user-defined datatype "type_phoneNumber":

exec sp_addtype typPhoneNumber, 'char(13)', 'NOT NULL'
go

-- Create a default for this datatype:

create default dbo.dfPhoneNumber as 'Unknown Phone'
go

-- Create a rule that constrains this datatype:
create rule dbo.ruPhoneNumber as
 (@phone = 'Unknown Phone') or
 (len(@phone) = 13 and
substring(@phone, 1, 1) = '(' and
      substring(@phone, 5, 1) = ')' and
      substring(@phone, 9, 1) = '-' and
      isnumeric(substring(@phone, 2, 3)) = 1 and
      isnumeric(substring(@phone, 6, 3)) = 1 and
      isnumeric(substring(@phone, 10, 4)) = 1)
go

-- Bind the default to the user-defined datatype:
exec sp_bindefault 'dfPhoneNumber', 'typPhoneNumber'
go

-- Bind the rule to the user-defined datatype:
exec sp_bindrule 'ruPhoneNumber', 'typPhoneNumber'
go
```

Now you can use this datatype anywhere that you would use any of the standard scalar datatypes:

```
CREATE TABLE CustomerPhoneTable (
CustomerID int IDENTITY,
HomePhone typPhoneNumber,
WorkPhone typPhoneNumber,
CellPhone typPhoneNumber,
FAXNumber typPhoneNumber)
DECLARE @Phone typPhoneNumber
```

- *Table-Valued*: In newer versions of some DBMSs (e.g., SQL Server 2008), you can create table-valued user-defined datatypes, which are very useful for passing multiple rows of data to stored procedures and functions:

```
CREATE TYPE dbo.udtCustomerOrderItem AS TABLE
(
        CustomerID       int        NOT NULL,
        OrderID          int        NOT NULL,
        ItemNumber       varchar(20) NOT NULL,
        ItemQuanity      int        NOT NULL,
        UnitPrice        money      NOT NULL
)
GO


GRANT EXECUTE ON TYPE::dbo.udtCustomerOrderItem
TO public AS dbo
GRANT REFERENCES ON
TYPE::dbo.udtCustomerOrderItem
TO public AS dbo
GO
```

A pointer to a read-only copy of the table in memory (not the actual data itself) can then be passed to a stored procedure or user-defined function:

```
CREATE PROCEDURE [dbo].[csUpdateOrderItemData]
        @udtCustomerOrderItem
udtCustomerOrderItem READONLY
        ,@DBTimestamp varbinary(8)
```

- *Structure:* Some DBMSs (e.g., Oracle) will let you define datatypes that are complex structures composed of multiple scalar types (including scalar UDTs):

```
CREATE OR REPLACE TYPE person_type AS OBJECT (
ssn NUMBER(9), name VARCHAR2(30), address
VARCHAR2(100), phone typPhoneNumber)
NOT FINAL;
```

You can define objects that are subtypes of previously defined objects:

```
CREATE OR REPLACE TYPE student_type UNDER
person_type (
deptid NUMBER, major VARCHAR2(30))
NOT FINAL;
```

You can then define tables as multi-valued instances of these types:

```
CREATE OR REPLACE TYPE student_tab_type
AS TABLE OF student_type;
```

Judicious use of user-defined datatypes will make it much easier to map application object (class) properties to the data in your database.

Standards for Database Coding

For database coding, as with application coding, it's important to agree up-front on a set of coding standards before development starts, in order to ensure the highest possible degree of quality, consistency, and maintainability. Coding standards should be discussed, agreed-to, and published at the very beginning of the development effort. The reason for this is that a lot of new code is copied from previously written code, so that both good code and bad code tends to become replicated throughout a project. Getting off to a good start, code-wise, is very important!

I advocate the use of code templates. For our SQL Server projects, for example, I've created a set of database code templates for things like stored procedures (both read-only and update), functions (both scalar- and table-valued), views, triggers, etc. These templates can be added to SQL Server Management Studio, and referenced when needed using the Template Explorer. Double clicking on a template name will copy the template into a query window, where the developer can work with it.

Here are some of the standards I suggest adopting for database coding:

- Treat database code like all other application code – it should be testable, understandable, and maintainable!

- Code should be neat, easily readable, consistently formatted, and generally uncluttered.

- Code should be well-commented. There should, at least, be comments at the beginning of each procedure, view, function, etc. explaining the purpose of the code, the name of the developer, the creation date, and the name of the application(s) the code is supporting. There should be a change log after the initial comments, with the developer's name, date, and reason for change. There should be a comment preceding each major section of code, explaining its purpose. There should also be explanatory comments for any complex computation or formula, and for any piece of code whose purpose is not intuitively obvious.

- Object and variable names should be non-cryptic and self-explanatory.

- Validate all input parameters and check all assertions. Never assume that parameters or data elements will contain valid or expected values.

- All database updates must be done in the context of an explicit database transaction (i.e., no implicit updates).

- All database updating should be done via stored procedures, not from application code.

- Check for errors after all SQL update statements, and check return codes from all executed stored procedures.

- Return meaningful messages from all errors.

- Use the lowest possible isolation level (e.g., SELECT WITH NOLOCK). When locking is necessary, try to lock at the row level; lock tables only when absolutely necessary.

- Reference tables (in JOINs) in the same order across multiple views, functions, or stored procedures, to avoid deadlocks.

- Use ANSI-standard syntax for table joins (i.e., INNER JOIN, LEFT JOIN, etc.).

- Do not use SELECT * in SQL code, EVER! When coding a SELECT or INSERT statement, specify each individual column. This will keep the code from breaking if a new column is added to a database table.

- For large and complex procedures, embed test code and diagnostic displays, triggered by an optional input parameter, into the procedure code. This will help in debugging logic errors and adding future functionality. If possible, also set up unit tests in your Continuous Integration (CI) environment to unit test each procedure when a build of the application is done.

- Grant permissions on all objects to database roles, not individual users.

- Permissions on objects that do updates (e.g., FSPs) should be granted only to roles that have update authority.

- Database objects can be developed (in the Development environment) by application developers with 'dbo' (database owner) authority, by DBAs, or by developers and DBAs in collaboration. All database objects should be owned by 'dbo' (Note: if you use schemas in your database, make sure that the schemas are owned by 'dbo').

- Qualify all references to database objects with the owner/schema name (e.g., dbo.vw<*ViewName*>). This will enable the SQL Query Optimizer to find and process these objects more efficiently.

- All database objects and code should be reviewed and migrated to the certification and production environments by the DBA, following established change control procedures.

- When in doubt, ask a DBA!

Of course, any standard is worthless if it's not enforced. For this reason, I advocate doing frequent peer reviews of database code (at least once per Sprint), in the same way that application code reviews are done. The DBA should be involved in these reviews. In our organization, we document all issues found in code reviews in a code review spreadsheet for that Sprint. Defects are prioritized and assigned to someone on the team to fix. We do not migrate any database code to the Certification environment until it has been reviewed, and any identified issues have been corrected.

What Should Go Where?

One important issue that needs to be addressed during database implementation is the question of what functionality should go into the database, and what functionality should go into the application's business layer or data layer. Here are some suggested guidelines:

Implement in the database:

- Data integrity constraints, including *entity integrity* (primary key), *referential integrity* (foreign key), and *domain integrity* (check or rule) constraints. These constraints should always be enforced in the database, as close to the data as possible, rather than in the application. This helps ensure that data corruption will not occur if there is an error in application coding, or if updates are made to the data outside an application.

- Simple data validation of the sort that can be easily enforced using triggers, rule or check constraints, or user-defined datatypes.

- Any cross-server data validation.

- Transaction management. This should be controlled at the database level (using stored procedure templates), to ensure that all database updates are either committed or rolled back as a single unit of work. Note: if the application uses a transaction manager, the transaction manager will initiate the highest-level transaction.

- Complex SELECTs. Data retrievals that involve complex table joins, filtering, or ordering should be done on the database server, making use of the query optimizer and the database server's CPU and memory resources. This will take some of the load off of the application server, improve performance, and minimize the amount of data sent over the network.

- Database security. Access to database objects (tables, views, functions, and stored procedures) should be secured using database roles. These roles can then be associated with one or more users or groups in the database.

Implement in the application:

- Complex validation logic. Validation that involves complex logic can probably be implemented more efficiently in application code than in database code.

- Business logic. All business logic (unless it relates specifically to data) should go in the application, not in the database.

- Simple SELECTs. Simple database retrievals (especially if they do not involve complex table joins, and do not return a large number of rows and/or columns of data) can be done from the application, using either embedded SQL or a Framework language such as Microsoft's Entity Framework.

- Application security. Access to application functionality should be handled by the application.

Testing and Diagnostics

You should make sure that all of the components of the VDL are testable, so that changes to an object do not result in unintended consequences to applications. In accordance with the principles of Test-Driven Development (TDD), you should write your tests in conjunction with the development of each database object (view, function, stored procedure, etc.).

There are a couple ways to do this: one is to create a separate set of scripts or stored procedures that invoke your VDL objects, using different combinations of input parameter values, and testing for expected outcomes. You should make sure to test both positive and negative conditions (i.e., make sure that the objects behave as expected when both valid and invalid input values are specified). Make the execution of these scripts or procedures part of the standard deployment process when a new build of the application is created. There are many application development products that support Continuous Integration (CI), in which a defined set of unit tests are executed whenever new code is integrated into a build of the application. The database code that supports objects in the VDL should definitely be a part of the test/build/deploy process.[70]

The other approach is to build test code directly into your VDL object. I use this approach mostly for stored procedures, especially procedures that encapsulate complex functionality and may therefore be challenging to test, debug, and maintain over time.

You can add an optional parameter to the procedure called, say, @TestNumber (integer, default = 0). Then pass non-zero values to

---

[70] Some developers suggest that the DDL for the database schema should also be maintained and updated in the development environment. I have two issues with this approach: first, my preference is to have database changes driven from updates to the physical model; it is much easier (and less error-prone) to change the model and then generate the DDL than it is to type the DDL. Second, this approach presumes an application-specific, physical-only view of data. If you've read this far, you already know my thoughts about that!

this parameter; each value will execute a test of a particular assertion in your procedure and exit with a pass/fail value.

For debugging purposes, I use another optional parameter, @DebugIndicator (boolean, default = 0). When a non-zero value is passed to this parameter, the execution of the stored procedure will result in the display of numerous diagnostics, showing the values of intermediate variables and temp tables. For very complex procedure code, a debugging framework of this sort is invaluable for reducing the amount of time spent resolving a production problem!

In conjunction with the Test and Debug parameters, I use a third optional parameter, @UpdateIndicator (boolean, default = 1). I can pass a value of zero to this parameter during testing and debugging if I don't want to update the database; the parameter will force a rollback of all updating done during execution of the procedure.

You can use these methods in conjunction with the unit test facility built into your application development environment to ensure that your database objects are always tested as part of each new application build.

Your test process should also include a script or scripts for generating the necessary data for the tests. This may include code that deletes existing data from the database and creates a fresh set of data at the start of the testing process. Some developer tools (e.g., Microsoft's Visual Studio Team System for Database Developers) can help with the generation of test data.

Optimizing Performance

Being able to diagnose and resolve performance issues is a DBA's stock in trade, and a good DBA has many tools available to do this. One thing a DBA will rarely do, however, is denormalize the base schema to improve performance. There are several reasons for this:

- It usually isn't necessary. The vast majority of performance issues in the database are usually related to poor SQL or application coding. Other performance issues (see below) can be addressed by creating or modifying indexes, using views or work tables, identifying locking and concurrency issues, creating and/or updating database statistics, or redesigning the process.

- It diminishes the reusability of the data. Remember, that the primary objective in physical database design is to create reusable data objects. Denormalizing the base schema may improve the performance of one application, but may keep the data from being easily reused for other applications and business purposes.

- It may impact other applications. Denormalizing the base schema to help one application may result in performance issues for other applications using that data. Remember, you can always denormalize virtually, using views, functions, stored procedures, and work tables, to support the needs of a particular application.

- It may cause more performance problems! Denormalizing puts more data onto fewer database and index pages in the database. This can cause contention when multiple users (and applications) are trying to access or update this data, producing locking or deadlock problems.

- It can cause data corruption. As we saw with the Timesheet example, denormalizing the base schema can leave critical data unprotected. Data that isn't normalized (at the base schema level) usually isn't identified as critical (key attribute) data, and can contain anything (or nothing) that an application chooses to dump into it.

Denormalizing the base schema is always a DBA's *last* resort (not the first) for dealing with performance problems.

Many books have been written about resolving database performance issues, and I'm not going to attempt to recapitulate them here. In general, though, here are some things to do when investigating a performance problem:

- Capture a snapshot of performance in the database. Most database management system (DBMS) vendors provide tools to do this (e.g., Microsoft SQL Server's Profiler). Pay particular attentions to lock timeouts, deadlocks, and any query or procedure that takes longer than 5 seconds to execute.

- Automate periodic capture and analysis of application database performance in production systems, watching for changes in the top 10 resource consumers.

- Look at poorly-performing SQL code. Start with your performance snapshot (above). Look at individual SQL queries or stored procedure statements that have large execution times, I/O, or CPU usage. Look at the query plan for these queries or statements (e.g., in SQL Server Query Analyzer). Look for table scans, index scans, or a large number of intermediate values being passed from one step to another.

- Also look for frequently-executed SQL code. An individual query, stored procedure, or function may take only a short time to execute, but may be invoked hundreds or thousands of times, creating bottlenecks. This may indicate the need for redesign.

- Check for missing or incomplete indexes. The analysis of the SQL code should make this clear. A table scan (particularly of a large table) probably indicates the need for an index. An index scan may suggest that an additional column or columns be added to an existing index to create a "covering" index. A step in the query plan that produces an exceptionally large number of intermediate values may indicate an incomplete table join.

- Check for locking or deadlock issues. Your performance snapshot should be able to identify lock timeouts and deadlocks. Be sure to distinguish between deadlocks (where one of two transactions contending for database resources is chosen as the "victim", and rolled back) and "live" locks (where one transaction simply waits for another transaction to release resources, and may just time out). These are two different problems, which require different solutions. Also, it is rarely possible to entirely eliminate them, so applications should be coded in such a way as to be able to detect these conditions, wait for a designated period of time for the database resources to become available, and then retry the query. If resources do not become available, the application should be coded to exit gracefully, with an appropriate user-friendly error message.

- Add and/or update database statistics. These statistics keep track of the distribution of data across table columns and index pages in the database. They must be kept up-to-date in order for the query optimizer to function effectively. In particular, large numbers of insert and/or delete operations in a table will skew the statistics for that table, and will make it difficult for the query optimizer to construct an efficient query plan for it. Most DBMS vendors will tell you that their product updates these statistics automatically, but they don't. The DBMS only selectively updates those statistics that it *thinks* need to be updated in order to process a particular query plan. It's a good idea to perform regular updates of database statistics via a scheduled (nightly or weekly) process. In addition, most DBMSs provide tools (e.g., SQL Server's Database Tuning Advisor) that will analyze a snapshot of work in the database and suggest additional indexes and/or database statistics to help improve performance.

- See if virtualization will help. In particular, encapsulating complex table joins into a view will usually help performance. This is particularly true when data is being accessed via user-defined functions, as these joins may not be optimized in functions. In the worst case, creating a denormalized application-specific work table or materialized view may be necessary.

Key Points

- The purpose of coding virtual database objects is to reduce or eliminate the "object-relational impedance mismatch" in a way that still safeguards the security and integrity of data. The virtual data objects can be mapped more easily to application objects, without tightly-coupling the application to the database schema, or denormalizing the database in a way that makes it unusable for other purposes.

- Agile database development is based on the Object-Oriented (O-O) principles of Abstraction and Encapsulation. The necessary database functionality is packaged in a way that hides the manner of its implementation from the user.

- Views, stored procedures, functions, triggers, work tables, materialized views, application data objects, and complex datatypes are different ways of abstracting and encapsulating database functionality in an easily-consumable form.

- Fundamental Stored Procedures (FSPs) are a special type of stored procedure used for updating tables at the schema level. They can be called from higher-level stored procedures or data objects.

- Avoid object/data mapping techniques that tightly-couple application objects to the database schema. Use views and stored procedures to move object/data mapping into the Virtual Data Layer.

- Treat database code objects like all other application code. Make sure this code is well-written, testable, version-controlled, and peer-reviewed.

- Have standards and templates in place for database objects, and make sure these are given to all developers at the beginning of the project.

- Make sure that all complex SQL code is implemented in the database, tested, and optimized for performance.

CHAPTER 10
Refactoring Made Easier

Change is an inevitable part of any application development project. This is particularly true with Agile, as requirements are discovered and developed incrementally throughout the project. This means that change management – always a requirement for any project – becomes a critical necessity for Agile.

There are two basic types of changes: changes that improve the design or implementation of a process without actually changing its behavior, and changes that add or modify functionality (or that support such a change). The term "refactor", technically, applies to the first type of change – a change that results in incremental improvement to a component, but does not alter its behavior. However, the term is often used colloquially to refer to any type of change needed to create, modify, or improve a component or process. I tend to use this term more loosely than an Agile developer would, because at the database level, the work involved in supporting both types of changes is identical.[71] Also, the number of database changes that are true refactorings is very small in comparison to the number of database changes that add or modify functionality. So I'm going to focus on the issue of change generally, not just one kind of change.

One of the complaints that is sometimes directed at DBAs and other data managers is that the process of implementing database changes takes too long. Over the years, our group has worked hard to develop processes and tools that enable us to respond more

---

[71] Although Scott Ambler, in *Agile Database Techniques* (Chapter 13), makes a distinction between database refactorings that "retain the behavioral and informational semantics" of the database (page 177) and those that don't, I've never found this to be a particularly useful distinction. To me, these are simply additional requirements of a change, not a different type of change.

quickly to requests for changes. An essential part of this process is understanding at what level changes need to be made, followed by implementing the necessary tools and processes to enable changes at each level to be made as quickly and easily as possible.

In this chapter, I am going to talk about how both types of changes are managed at the various levels of the database and data model.

Managing Change

Since accepting change is one of the central tenets of Agile Development, it follows that one of Agile's biggest challenges is managing change. I've always felt that one of a project manager's most important responsibilities is to establish a workable process for managing changes and making sure that everyone involved in the project agrees to this process and adheres to it. This needs to be done up-front, at the very inception of the project, because the differing stakeholders involved will all have different ideas of what sort of change is acceptable, and how changes need to be decided upon, prioritized, implemented, and documented. This is particularly true of Agile projects, where numerous changes must be processed quickly and continually.

Here is what you need to know from each group involved in the project:

- How will you determine when something affecting your area needs to be changed (i.e., what are your criteria for defining necessary changes)?

- What number or frequency of change requests will you or your group be able to manage?

- What is your preferred method of requesting changes (service request, change request, email, phone call, etc.)?

- What method do you prefer others to use when requesting changes from you?

- What is your group's process for approving and documenting changes?

- How much of this process can be done asynchronously (i.e., after the fact)? For example, if a change needs to be formally documented, can that documentation be created after the change has been made?

Once you have this information, the project manager or Scrum Master[72] can put together a change management process that satisfies (or rather, minimally dissatisfies) each of the stakeholder groups. It's important to keep in mind, and make provision for, those things that are considered vitally important to each group, while trying to negotiate compromises in areas that are less important. For example, a group may agree to allow changes to be requested via email as opposed to a formal change control process, at least during development, or to do formal documentation after the change has been made, so as not to impede development efforts.

In particular, it is important to have a well-understood process in place for identifying defects, prioritizing them, assigning them to be worked on, and testing them to be sure they really have been resolved.

In our group, we have had to make many adjustments in the way we handle change requests during development.[73] This has been due not only to the increased pace and iterative nature of Agile Development, but also to the fact that more of our development work is being done by outside contractors, who have their own way of working. The challenge has been to determine which of our existing processes we can safely change, and how, while still delivering a high-quality product that's easy to maintain.

---

[72] The Scrum Master oversees the work of the development team during the project Sprints, to make sure the project stays on track, and that Agile processes are being properly followed.

[73] We have a formal, organization-wide process for handling changes after an application has been formally turned over to production support.

For example, where there are a large number of changes, or when changes are being made frequently, or when the developers are off-site, it may be necessary to agree to process changes in batches, rather than one at a time. When the pace of application development was slower, and all the developers were on-site, we could process any given change in an hour or less without having any impact on the project. But where this approach is impractical, it becomes necessary for us to reach an agreement with the development team as to the number of times per day or per week that change requests will be processed, to keep the number of changes per batch at a manageable level and allow us to schedule resources. Single changes are still accepted, and processed as time and resources are available.

Since we use the Scrum methodology for our development projects, there is a team stand-up meeting each morning, during which each member of the team reports:

- What work was accomplished the previous day.

- What work is going to be done today.

- What impediments are preventing necessary work from being done.

The morning stand-up is the opportunity for each team member (including the DBA) to understand what work he or she needs to finish by the end of the day, in time for the next day's stand-up. While interruptions and requests for additional help are almost sure to occur, the primary focus should be on making sure the work that was identified during the stand-up gets done that day.

It's important to make sure there is enough process in place to ensure that necessary work is done correctly, but make sure the process itself is not keeping necessary work from being done!

Determining Where and How to Change

Once it has been determined that a change needs to be made, the next step is to determine where the change needs to be made, and how it can best be accomplished. We are going to see that change can occur at one or more of the following levels:

- The logical data model

- The physical database design

- The database schema

- The Virtual Data Layer (VDL)

- The data itself.

A change in business data requirements or data-related business rules should always result in a change to the logical data model, and this should be the *only* thing that results in a change to the logical data model. If the business requirement is being implemented in the database, then a change must be made in the physical database design. If the change involves, say, the creation of a new table, or the addition of one or more columns to an existing table, then the database schema will need to be modified. This, in turn, may require additions or modifications to the Virtual Data Layer (e.g., the creation of fundamental stored procedures for the new table or regeneration of the FSPs for a modified table, and modifications to the application Data Access Layer).

But not all changes will involve refactoring at all levels. Physical-only changes, such as the creation of an application work table or changing the length of a text field, will not affect the logical model. Logical-only changes (changes to business requirements or rules not implemented in the database) will affect only the logical model. Some logical model changes, such as the creation or modification of a business rule that will be enforced by a trigger in the database or the redesign of a stored procedure, will result in a refactoring of the VDL, but not of the database schema itself. Some physical design changes, such as changes to the way the database integrates with remote data sources, may also involve only refactoring of the VDL.

Here's an example: suppose you have a business constraint on a code attribute that restricts its permissible values to the set {'A', 'B', 'C', 'D'}. The business requirement changes to allow the value 'E'. What do you do? First of all, the description of the constraint in both the logical and physical model must be changed. If it has been implemented in the database as a rule or check constraint, then DDL must be created to modify the database schema accordingly. If it has been implemented as, say, a view or table-valued function (with the constraint values coded in the WHERE clause of a SQL query), then this object must be changed in the VDL. If the constraint has been implemented as records in a code table in the database (so they can be displayed in a drop-down list in the application), then all that is needed is to add a record to the table.

Once it has been determined where the change needs to occur, consideration must also be given as to how the change should be done, in a manner that reduces the impact of the change on customers as much as possible.

Let's take a more detailed look at how refactoring is done at each of these levels.

Refactoring the Logical Model

Refactoring the logical data model is relatively easy, inexpensive, and painless, especially if you have a good modeling tool. It doesn't take very much time to add or delete an entity; to add, delete, or modify entity attributes; or to redraw relationship lines in a model.

The important task for the data analyst is to make sure the business requirements are correctly understood and agreed upon by all affected stakeholders during the requirements analysis session for the user story or stories involved, and that these requirements have been correctly captured in the model. This includes definitions of the entities and attributes involved.

The data analyst should also conduct a review of the changed portion of the model. This helps ensure that the analyst's understanding of the requirements is correct (and correctly modeled), that the model's definitions of the business entities, attributes, and relationships are correct, and that no further change in the requirements has occurred in the minds of any of the stakeholders. The review can usually be accomplished in a short meeting.

Once the data model change has been made and agreed to, the data model can be turned over to the DBA, who will determine what refactoring if any needs to be done on the physical side. A PDF image of the updated logical model should be sent to the team or posted on the team's collaboration site. The model, itself, should be kept in some sort of source control repository.

There are a number of refactorings (called "transforms") that can be done at the logical model level, including:

- Many-to-many resolution. In this transform, a many-to-many association between two entities is resolved to a set of one-to-many associations by creating an intermediate (association) entity between the two.

- Supertype/subtype identity. This transform replaces a single supertype/subtype structure with a set of identifying associations between a parent entity and one or more child entities.

- Supertype/subtype rollup. This transform merges the attributes of the subtypes in a supertype/subtype relationship back into the supertype entity, resulting in a single entity (and the elimination of the previously existing subtypes).

- Supertype/subtype rolldown. This transform merges the attributes of the supertype entity into each of the associated subtypes, after which the supertype (and the supertype/subtype relationship) is removed.

Refactoring the Physical Design

Refactoring the physical database design is also usually an easy thing to do, especially if you have a modeling tool that lets you maintain both the logical and physical models in a single model file. In most good modeling tools, changes to one model will automatically be reflected in the other, unless the change is marked as "logical only" or "physical only". In this case, the DBA only needs to verify that the physical model is correct, making any necessary changes to datatypes and lengths from the domain defaults in the logical model. For example, an attribute denoted as a "Code" in the logical model may default to, say, varchar(4) in the physical model; this may need to be changed by the DBA to something like, say, varchar(6) or char(2), depending on the actual data values that will be stored.

For physical design changes that stem from logical model changes, it is usually not necessary to review the physical design change, since the logical model change has already been reviewed. The only exception would be if the physical implementation of the business requirement involved an unusual degree of complexity that needed to be discussed, or if a choice between multiple options for implementing the requirement needed to be made.

For physical design changes not driven by a change to the logical model, the DBA will make the necessary changes to the physical design model. If a new application table is being added to the model (e.g., a work table, audit table, or reporting table), it will be marked as "physical only" in the model. Similarly, any columns added that don't relate to attributes in the logical model (e.g., a column that exists only to support a piece of application functionality) will also be marked as "physical only". These changes should be reviewed by the development team prior to being implemented in the database.

There are a number of refactorings ("transforms") that can be done at the physical model level, including:

- Many-to-many resolution. When resolving a many-to-many relationship at this level, an association table is created in the physical model, and one-to-many relationships are created. However, the association table exists only in the physical model; the many-to-many relationship is left unresolved in the logical model.

- Supertype/subtype identity. In the physical model, this transform creates the set of identifying associations between a parent entity and one or more child entities, while leaving the supertype/subtype structure intact in the logical model.

- Supertype/subtype rollup. In the physical model, this transform merges the attributes of the subtype tables back into the supertype table, eliminating the subtypes. However, the supertype/subtype relationship is left intact in the logical model.

- Supertype/subtype rolldown. In the physical model, this transform merges the attributes of the supertype table into each of the associated subtype tables, and eliminates the supertype. However, the supertype/subtype relationship is left intact in the logical model.

- Vertical partitioning. This transform allows a single table to be split into multiple tables, all having the same key attributes but different non-key columns. This can help improve performance by putting frequently-accessed data in multiple locations, thus reducing contention for data.

- Horizontal partitioning. This transform allows rows of data to be partitioned between multiple copies of the same table. In this way, current and frequently-accessed data can be kept in one table (on a faster storage device), while older and less-frequently accessed data can be archived off to slower and cheaper storage devices.

- Rollup denormalization. This transform is similar to the supertype/subtype rollup, but can be applied to any parent/child relationship (where the child table contains the key(s) of the parent table, along with an additional identifying key).

- Rolldown denormalization. This transform is similar to the supertype/subtype rolldown, but can be applied to any parent/child relationship (where the child table contains the key(s) of the parent table, along with an additional identifying key).

- Column denormalization. This transform allows a column that is needed in several different tables (e.g., *LastUpdateDateTime*) to be replicated.

In almost all cases, changes made to the physical database design affect only the physical model[74]. For example, if a decision is made to (carefully) collapse a supertype/subtype relationship in the physical design, the supertype/subtype should be left intact in the logical model, since it communicates information about the business data domain.

Another, more complicated, case is when a complex natural key in the logical model (involving several attributes) is going to be replaced by a surrogate (system-assigned) key in the database. In this case, you may be forced to create the surrogate key in the logical model as well, and define the natural key attributes as an alternate key. In the database, the alternate key will become a unique index.

Once the physical model has been updated and reviewed, a PDF image of the updated model should be sent to the team, or posted on the team's collaboration site. The model itself should be kept in some sort of source control repository.

---

[74] In CA ERwin Data Modeler r8, however, horizontal or vertical partitioning and rollup/rolldown denormalization that is done in the physical model will be automatically reflected in the logical model as well. I don't know why; quite honestly, this doesn't make any sense to me.

If the DBA is maintaining a physical design document for the database, that document should be updated as necessary to reflect the change. However, this can be done after the change has been implemented, and should not be an impediment to the project.

One important note: if the change involves refactoring of the database schema, there may be a requirement or pressure to do that refactoring in advance of any changes to the physical database design. If this is a simple change (for example, changing the length of a text field), this is probably acceptable. For more extensive changes (adding tables, for instance), you're probably better off updating the model first, and then generating the DDL code to create the tables from the model. This saves having to type everything twice. In any event, if you make any database changes "asynchronously" (i.e., without changing the model first), make sure you have some sort of tool or process in place to validate the database schema against the model, to make sure they don't get out of synch!

Refactoring the Database Schema

Note that refactoring at the design level is relatively easy and painless, and does not impact other development work. It is at the point that changes are being applied to the database schema and/or the VDL that careful consideration and communication is required to ensure that the refactoring does not adversely impact other members of the team (in particular, developers and testers).

One way to do this is to maintain separate Development and Test database environments. Application development is done in the Development database, either in a single database instance or in individual development databases on each developer's machine. Application testing is done in the Test environment and the Test database. At periodic intervals (when approved by the testers), a stable Development build is then deployed to Test so that another round of testing can be done.

Once the database changes have been agreed on, and permission has been given to proceed with the implementation, the DBA must decide how best to make the change. For simple changes, the GUI environment provided by the DBMS vendor (for example, Microsoft's SQL Management Studio) can be used to make the change. For more extensive changes, the DDL to implement the change can be generated from the physical model, using the modeling tool. One important consideration is whether the change is being made in the development environment only, or must be repeated across multiple database environments (for example, if the application has already been deployed to the Certification environment, the change would also need to be made to the Certification database). In this latter case, a script must be created (or generated) that can be executed in the different database environments, and saved in source control.

Refactoring the Virtual Data Layer

Depending on the type of change, some sort of refactoring will very likely be needed in the Virtual Data Layer. Oftentimes, changes can be made in the VDL without affecting the underlying database schema. In other cases, a change to the database schema may affect one or more virtual objects.

For example, a new application or data requirement may be satisfied by the creation of a new view, function, stored procedure, or work table in the database. The integration of data from a new data source may be accomplished by creating a new foreign (cross-database) view or integration web service. A complex business data rule may be implemented using a database trigger, and so on. These are all virtual changes that don't impact the underlying database schema.

On the other hand, a change to a database table will probably necessitate at least a regeneration of the fundamental stored procedures associated with the table. If this is a new table, these objects will need to be created. If new columns are being added to existing tables, it is advised that these columns either be nullable (optional) or have default values assigned to them. That way, the addition of the columns and the regeneration of the FSPs won't break existing applications.

If one or more columns have been added to an existing table, it may be determined that these columns need to be added to one or more of the existing views, or that new views should be created to accommodate them.

The major advantage to refactoring in the VDL is that virtual objects such as views, functions, stored procedures, and triggers can easily be modified and recompiled in the database, without the effort and impact of changes to the database schema. It is, of course, necessary to first determine the impact of the change on any application objects that reference the database objects (for example, objects in the application Data Layer), and make sure those objects are changed, as necessary. Also make sure that any necessary unit testing of the modified objects is done, as well as any necessary regression testing of the application.

It is even possible to use the VDL to mitigate the impact of changes to the database schema. Columns can be added to views, stored procedures, and table-valued functions to simulate table changes before the schema refactoring has been done; this can keep the development effort from becoming stalled while schema changes are in flux.

Also, in cases where an existing field is being deprecated and replaced by a new one, objects in the VDL can be modified to accommodate both fields during the deprecation period, and then modified again to remove the deprecated field. This sort of refactoring can be done very easily and quickly in the Virtual Data Layer, with minimal impact to applications (see the example at the end of this chapter).

Refactoring Data

One type of refactoring that is often overlooked is the refactoring of data in the database. This primarily occurs during application development, resulting from the refactoring of the database schema, and as part of the process of migrating existing data to a new database environment. However, refactoring of production data is sometimes necessary, as well. This must be done carefully, after consideration of the possible impacts to existing applications and users of the data, and after evaluating possible consequences of a failure to update the data correctly. A data refactoring usually involves the following steps:

- Creation and testing of an update script (unless the change is a simple one, and will be done only in the Development and/or Test databases). Changes to Certification or Production data must always be done using a tested script.

- Notification of and coordination with any affected users of the data. For development data, this will probably be just the members of the development team. For the Test and Certification databases, members of the QA team and user testers will need to approve the change. For existing production data, it will involve business users, the Change Control group, Operations Support, and Application Support, depending on the possible impact to existing production applications.

- Development of a validation plan, to determine whether the update is correct. For development data, validation by one or more members of the development team should be sufficient. For Test and Certification data, the QA team (or QA resource) should validate the change, executing regression tests, as necessary. For production data, validation queries should be developed and run after the update. I usually start a database transaction, run the update script without committing, and then run my validation queries. If everything looks good, I commit the update; otherwise, I roll the update back. It may also be necessary to have the update validated by one or more business users or application support people.

- Development of a backout or recovery plan, in case the update either fails or is found to be incorrect later. This may include a pre-update backup of the database, copying of the affected data to a database table or flat file, and/or development of a script to restore the data to its original state.

- Documentation of the change. Data change scripts created during application development or data conversion efforts will often need to be run multiple times. Make sure the scripts are easily available (preferably in source control) and can be quickly found. Also make sure that sufficient documentation exists, even if it's just a README text file, so that you or someone else will know how to run the scripts next time. If the data change will need to be run each time a new build of the application is deployed, make sure the change scripts have been integrated into the build process. For production data changes, make sure there's a clear record of the change, including when it was made, why it was made, who approved it, and who validated it. Make sure there is a link or pointer to the location of the change and backout scripts. Also record whether the change resulted in any production issues or downtime, and whether it needed to be backed out.

It's important, during any sort of refactoring, to:

- Make sure the change is done at the proper level(s)
- Make sure affected stakeholders are informed and involved
- Make sure the impact of the change is understood
- Make sure the change is tested and validated
- Automate the change and validation process as much as possible
- Make sure the change is documented (as necessary)
- Make sure the change is repeatable (if necessary)
- Make sure the change is reversible (if necessary).

An Example of Multi-Level Refactoring

Here's an example of database refactoring applied at multiple levels: we have an application that manages configuration data for some of our electronic components.

The database for this application contains a table called Parameter, that looks like this:

```
CREATE TABLE [dbo].[Parameter](
  [ParameterIdentifier] [int] IDENTITY(1,1) NOT NULL,
  [ParameterDescription] [varchar](255) NOT NULL,
  [TIMESTAMP] [timestamp] NOT NULL,
```

The application doesn't reference the database tables directly; instead, it was coded to reference views in the database. Here is the auto-generated base view for the Parameter table:

```
CREATE VIEW [dbo].[vwParameter]
(
 ParameterIdentifier
,ParameterDescription
,TIMESTAMP
)

AS SELECT
 Parameter.ParameterIdentifier
,Parameter.ParameterDescription
,Parameter.TIMESTAMP

FROM Parameter
```

A new requirement surfaced in the second round of development for this application: the ParameterDescription data needed to be maintained and displayed in multiple languages, depending on the location of the user. This would appear, on the surface, to be a fairly significant change, but we were up to the challenge.

First, we implemented our standard multi-language support solution, which included adding a new subject area (obtained from our standard solutions library) to both the logical and physical data models. We ran a script (also from the library) to add the necessary tables, views and stored procedures that support multi-language text to the database.

The primary table used in our solution looks like this:

```
CREATE TABLE [dbo].[LanguageText](
  [LocaleIdentifier] [int] NOT NULL,
  [TextIdentifier] [int] NOT NULL,
  [TextData] [varchar](2000) NOT NULL,
  [timestamp] [timestamp] NULL,
```

In this solution, the *ParameterDescription* column of the Parameter table is replaced by *ParameterDescriptionTextIdentifier*, which maps to the *TextIdentifier* column of the LanguageText table. Text data is stored and retrieved based on the input value of *LocaleIdentifier*, a code value that indicates which language is being used. I then performed the following schema and data refactorings:

- I added the column *ParameterDescriptionTextIdentifier* to the Parameter table

- I ran an update script to copy the existing (English) values of *ParameterDescription* into the LanguageText table

- I updated the values of *ParameterDescriptionTextIdentifier* in the Parameter table to the correct values of *TextIdentifier* in the LanguageText table

- I deleted the *ParameterDescription* column from the Parameter table.

I also ran a script to add the corresponding parameter text values in other languages (from a spreadsheet) into the LanguageText table.

The Parameter table now looks like this:

```
CREATE TABLE [dbo].[Parameter](
  [ParameterIdentifier] [int] IDENTITY(1,1) NOT NULL,
  [ParameterDescriptionTextIdentifier] int NOT NULL,
  [TIMESTAMP] [timestamp] NOT NULL,
```

Here's the good part: After refactoring the schema, I auto-generated both the FSPs and base view for the Parameter table. The FSPs handle all the work of updating the multi-language text tables behind the scenes; the only difference from the existing FSPs is the addition of the *LocaleIdentifier* parameter to the argument list of the Input and Update FSPs. Here, for example, is the argument list for the Input FSP for the Parameter table:

```
CREATE PROCEDURE [dbo].[fsParameter_i]
 @ParameterDescription varchar(255)
,@LocaleIdentifier int
```

The generated base view for the Parameter table handles the join to the LanguageText table, and renames the text column to match the original name of the ParameterDescription column:

```
CREATE VIEW [dbo].[vwParameter]
(
 ParameterIdentifier
,ParameterDescription
,TIMESTAMP
,MicrosoftLocaleIdentifier
)

AS SELECT
 Parameter.ParameterIdentifier
,TXT.TextData ParameterDescription
,Parameter.TIMESTAMP
,TXT.LocaleIdentifier

FROM Parameter
LEFT OUTER JOIN LanguageText TXT
  ON TXT.TextIdentifier =
Parameter.ParameterDescriptionTextIdentifier
```

This means that the application code, which was referencing the original vwParameter view, doesn't need to be changed at all! The only change needed to the application is to determine which *LocaleIdentifier* value to pass to the FSPs. The actual work of implementing this new requirement in the database was done in less than an hour.

Key Points

- Make sure that everyone on the project team understands how defects will be reported and prioritized, and how changes will be managed.

- A database refactoring may involve changes at several levels – the logical design (if the change is driven by a business requirement or rule change), the physical database design, the database schema, and the Virtual Data Layer (VDL). Be sure to understand what level(s) a given change affects.

- Make use of the VDL, as much as possible, to mitigate the impact of changes. Remember, changes at this level can be done more quickly than changes to the database schema or application code.

- Make sure that changes are coordinated with, and negotiated with, all affected stakeholders.

- Make sure to test, validate, and document (as necessary) all changes.

- For production changes, be sure to have a backout plan ready to execute if things go awry.

CHAPTER 11
Developing an Agile Attitude

One of the most important and often-overlooked things about Agile Development is that it's not so much about a particular methodology as it is about a particular attitude. There are any number of ways to do application development in an iterative fashion, but none of them will be successful unless the individual members of the project team have the right attitude, and a commitment to work together to do whatever is necessary to ensure the success of the project. In this chapter, I'd like to take a look at the attitudes required to make an Agile project (indeed, any project!) successful, and then examine how these attitudes can be applied across the organization.

The Three Agile Attitudes

Commitment. Agile is a distinctive approach to application development in that it requires a personal commitment from each team member. This is exemplified by the Agile concept of "pigs and chickens". A chicken may contribute her eggs to a breakfast, but is otherwise unaffected; a pig gives her all. This level of commitment is par for the course for application developers, who are used to working long hours at great personal sacrifice to ensure the success of a project. However, it's much less common for DBAs and other data professionals to have this same level of commitment to a single project, primarily because they have to support a number of different projects (along with maintenance and support work) and have many mouths to feed.

Nevertheless, it's important for data professionals working on an Agile project to make this attitudinal transition from being a "chicken" (someone who performs occasional tasks on a project as required) to being a "pig" (someone who is willing to do whatever it takes to ensure that the project goals and schedules are met). Just as a chain is only as strong as its weakest link, a project team is only as strong as its least-committed member. Agile projects are very intense and fast-paced, and issues and problems that arise in the course of development must be addressed quickly and effectively by the team.

Cooperation. Another important Agile attitude is cooperation. Project team members must be willing to work effectively with one another to get problems solved and work done, and should not let personal feelings (or philosophical convictions) impede the progress of the team. Data professionals have a tendency to (I'll try to be as delicate as possible here) stick to a philosophical conviction long past the point that it does any good. While I don't object to having principles (on principle), I do like to point out that the only people who actually get paid for having principles are priests and rabbis. The rest of us get paid for creating business value for the companies that pay our salaries. There's nothing wrong with stating an argument for the value of doing something a certain way. But if that approach doesn't work for the team, and is impacting the project, then it's incumbent on you to either: a) find an acceptable and workable alternative that accomplishes the same goal, or b) accept the fact that it's not going to be done the way you like (at this time), and move on. Better to lose a battle (and if you learn something from it, it's never a lost battle) than to lose the war (i.e., have the project fail with your name on it). Never burn bridges with team members or project managers for the sake of winning an argument. Remember, you will have to work with these same people on your next assigned project!

Communication. The third Agile attitude is communication. Agile projects are distinctive in that they involve nearly-constant communication and interaction with every member of the team. You should do everything possible to facilitate this communication, including attending the daily stand-up meetings (at which the status of work on tasks is reported), the Sprint planning and retrospective meetings, and any meetings involving tasks on which you are working.

If you are not able to make a meeting due to other commitments, give the meeting organizer as much advance notice as possible, communicate your status and input via email, and follow up with a phone call or personal visit as soon afterward as possible.

Proactive communication is a must for data professionals. If there are requirements or standards that must be followed by the developers, they need to be communicated to the project team at the beginning of the project (or earlier, if possible), and those requirements and standards need to be agreed to by the team. Absolutely do not drop a previously uncommunicated requirement or standard on the project team in the middle of the project! If you didn't communicate the requirement at the beginning of the project, this is your fault, not the team's, and you'll simply have to live with it (unless the team wants to be nice enough to accommodate you). Don't jeopardize the success of the project, and your working relationships with team members, by blind-siding them.

Commitment, Cooperation, and Communication are the watchwords for Agile Development. Make them your personal watchwords as well.

Agile in the Organization

It must also be acknowledged that there are often serious organizational and cultural impediments to the work of the data professional, and that data professionals haven't always recognized this fact, or done much to counter it. People in the field of data management generally haven't done a very good job of promoting the value of their work to the organization, recognizing the legitimate concerns of data owners and data consumers, balancing short-term and long-term data needs, educating others in the organization about the importance of good data management practices, and optimizing data development practices to ensure maximum benefit to the organization and minimal impact on data consumers. By regarding data work as an abstract set of principles and practices, and disregarding the human elements involved, data professionals risk propagating an "us versus them" mentality, and being regarded as dogmatic, impractical, unhelpful, and obstructionist.

There are a number of disconnects, clashes in frames of reference, that contribute to this problem. Organizations generally regard information technology in terms of specific applications, not data, and data is usually seen from an application-centric point of view. The long-term value to organizations of secure, reusable, high-quality data (i.e., of data as a corporate *resource*) is not as easily recognized or appreciated. Data management is oftentimes seen as an impediment to application development, as something that makes development projects take longer and cost more without providing additional benefit. Data professionals have been slow to adapt to changes in technology (e.g., XML, objects, and service-oriented architectures), and new methods of application development (e.g., Agile Development). Developers, on the other hand, often fail to recognize how good data management practices can help them achieve their long-term goals of object and application reuse, robust and easily maintainable applications, and a truly service-oriented application architecture.

There are several things that data management practitioners can do to help overcome these organizational and cultural obstacles, and promote a more helpful and collaborative approach to meeting the organization's data and information needs:

- Automate database development processes as much as possible, by developing tools and processes that shorten each development cycle reduce errors and rework, and minimize the impact of data changes on the development team. In this way, data professionals can adapt to more iterative and incremental (Agile) approaches to application development without having to sacrifice data quality or reusability.

- Develop, and promote the use of, abstracted and reusable data objects that free applications from being tightly-coupled to database schemas. The DBA should be familiar with all available means of virtualizing data and be able to recommend the best approach for any situation. The end goal is to make using the database as quick, easy, and painless as possible.

- Promote database standards and best practices as recommendations, rather than requirements, and be prepared to always give reasons for these recommendations. Database standards should never be a threat to the success of a project.

- Link database standards to various levels of support in a service-level agreement (SLA). For example, if recommended methods of ensuring data integrity and data security are accepted by the developers, this can be reflected in the SLA (i.e., the Data group will assume responsibility for the integrity and security of the data). If the development team will be coding their own database update procedures or data access layer, then the SLA should reflect the transfer of responsibility from the Data group to the development (or support) group. This prevents an "all or nothing" approach to standards.

- Establish project needs and support requirements up-front, to reduce misunderstandings about what the project team wants and doesn't want from the Data group. Make sure that everyone is clear about what work the Data group will (and won't) be doing, the way in which the work will be done, the standards that will (or won't) be followed, the timeline for the project, the number of hours and resources involved, and the level of support that will be required during development and after implementation. This will help forestall unpleasant surprises midway through the development process.

- Be a committed member of the project team, and communicate constantly to detect and resolve any issues as early as possible. This includes reviewing data access code, stored procedures, views, and database functions written by the development team; this will help surface any problems with the database design (or their understanding of it).

- Stay business-focused; the objective is meeting the business requirements and deriving the maximum business value from the project.

- Adopt a "can do" attitude, and be as helpful as possible. If you're always telling people "no", don't be surprised when they choose to ignore you and go behind your back. Recognize that people need to do whatever they need to do, and if you don't help them succeed, they may help you fail.

- Accept any defeats and failures encountered during a project as "lessons learned", that can be applied to future projects. You don't have to win every argument. If problems arise from having done things wrong, you can always point to them later as reasons for doing things right in the future.[75] Focus on continuous and incremental improvement.

- Communicate with people on their level, and in their terms. It is better to talk with business people in terms of business needs and ROI, and with developers in terms of object-orientation, loose coupling, and ease of development. Nobody is interested in relational database theory.

- Concentrate on solving other people's problems, not your own.

To sum up, we need to understand who our stakeholders are, and what their needs and concerns are. We need to develop a set of clear, concise, practical, business-focused guidelines and standards for doing the best possible work in the best possible way. And we need to teach and implement those standards in a way that provides maximum value to our stakeholders, and earns their respect for us as facilitators, contributors, and solution providers.

---

[75] Without, of course, saying "I told you so!"

Key Points

- Strive to develop the three Agile Attitudes of commitment, cooperation, and communication.

- Committed project team members make sure to communicate early and continuously. Avoid blind-siding your team with previously uncommunicated standards or requirements.

- Use a gradual process of education to make others in your organization aware of the needs of your group (as regards standards, best practices, etc.), as well as the value that your group contributes to the organization as a whole. This is especially important for data professionals, as the value to the organization of secure, reusable, high-quality data is not always readily apparent.

- Work continually to develop and refine Agile processes that enable your group to deliver maximum value as quickly as possible.

- Promote standards and best practices as recommendations, rather than requirements, and link them to various levels of support in a Service-Level Agreement (SLA).

- Accept any defeats and failures encountered during a project as "lessons learned" that can be applied to future projects. Focus on continuous and incremental improvement.

- Stay focused on what is best for the business.

- Always maintain a "can do" attitude and be as helpful as possible. Never be an obstructionist.

CHAPTER 12
Case Study: Sales Option Management Application

To illustrate the application of the concepts in this book, I've created a fictional company called "Blue Moon Guitar Company". The company designs and builds custom guitars and other wooden stringed instruments to order; that is, it does not mass-manufacture instruments. When ordering an instrument, the customer can specify a number of customization options, such as size, finish, type of tuning pegs and bridge, pick guard design, size and location of the sound hole, type(s) of wood used, type and placement of electronics (if any), and so on. Each model of instrument is associated with a set of these customization options, and each option specified contributes to the total list price of the instrument.

The Sales Option Management (SOM) application will enable the company to input and manage these options, and their relationship to the models of instruments offered by the company. The application will also enable Blue Moon's sales representatives to help customers design their dream instrument, and give them an accurate price quote when all of the options have been chosen.

Description of the Problem

The company has different manufacturing divisions, each of which makes instruments under a particular brand name. The divisions are more-or-less autonomous, and are allowed to set their own prices. Each division has its own factories, and costs of parts (components of each instrument) and labor (for assembly) vary by location for each factory. Part and labor cost data for each factory is maintained in databases on the company's central mainframe computer.

The application will enable Pricing Managers at its divisions to input and manage the customization options for each model of instrument made by that division. Each option/model combination can be associated with an assembly of parts (either individual parts or part structures) called a *configuration*. The aggregate of parts and labor data for each configuration is factored into a set of calculations that determines the base price of the instrument before any discounting is applied. Option, option/model, configuration, and pricing data is kept separate by division, and the data for a division can only be viewed and updated by that division's Pricing Managers.

Each model of instrument has a standard configuration, consisting of a set of standard options. Each standard option is associated with a standard assembly of parts; these assemblies can be shared by more than one standard option. Options are added to or removed from the standard configuration to create a custom instrument. The application must be able to do mass replacements of standard options across all the models that use them. Pricing managers can use the application to create and modify the assembly (configuration) data associated with each option/model.

Each sales option is associated with a hierarchy of categories, which is used to organize and report options by instrument type and function (e.g., options for guitar pickups are associated with the "Guitar/Electronics/Pickups" category hierarchy).

Pricing data is revised quarterly, and pricing amounts entered for an option/model are maintained by price period. At the beginning of each new pricing period, the cost workups for option/models are copied from the current period into the next period.

At any point, updated option, option/model, configuration, and pricing data can be selected to be sent back to the mainframe (via a web service). Updated data is not sent to the mainframe automatically; updates must be reviewed and approved before being published. This data updates the mainframe database that supports the company's Sales and Order Processing applications.

Pre-Development Activities

The first thing the Data Analyst and DBA will do is sit down with the project manager and Scrum Master (and/or the lead developer), and quickly go through a checklist, to get an idea of the scope of the project and the amount of work that will be involved. They will use this information to come up with an initial estimate of hours for the work that will be involved on the data side. Depending on this estimate, the Data Services manager may decide to add more resources to the project (if any are available), or reallocate resources, based on their availability.

The Data Services checklist contains questions such as these:

- What is the estimated duration of the project?

- What type of database(s) is/are needed (OLTP, Analytic, Reporting, etc.)?

- Will any outside (contract) labor be involved in the data analysis, modeling, or database development work? These external resources will have to be managed, as well as educated regarding the company's standards for database development.

- Will data need to be migrated from existing sources into the new database? If so, how many data sources are involved, and who will do this work?

- Will the new database need to be integrated with data from other sources or databases? If so, how many such integrations are needed, and how will the integrations be done? Who will do this work?

- Will any exceptions to the Data Services group's standards be required? If so, what exceptions are needed, and why?

- Will any training of the development team (e.g., in SQL coding or database performance issues) be needed?

The purpose for doing this is two-fold: first, to clarify the roles and responsibilities of the Data Analyst and DBA (so that there are no misunderstandings about who will be doing what); second, to ensure that the resources assigned to the project are adequate for the amount of work that needs to be done. Based on the answers to these and similar questions, the Data Analyst and the DBA come up with an initial estimate of hours for the project. Based on this estimate, it is decided that the current resources are sufficient for the project.

Also, as soon as possible during the project, the Data Analyst and DBA will try to get answers to the following questions:

- What is the security classification of the data for this application (e.g., General Public, Company Confidential, Top Secret). This will determine what mechanism(s) must be put in place for securing the data.

- What is the expected retention period of the data; that is, for how long must the data be kept immediately available, when can it be archived, and when can it be deleted?

- What is the expected volume of the data? That is, are we talking about a roughly 1-2 GB operational database, or a 1+ Terabyte data warehouse? We will need to have some understanding of the data storage requirements, so that additional storage (if needed) can be purchased and deployed.

- What is the required availability of the data, from a Service-Level Agreement standpoint? In other words, when can the database(s) be off-line for maintenance purposes?

- Can the database(s) be deployed on existing servers, or will new servers need to be purchased and deployed?

One of the first project activities is a series of requirements-gathering workshops involving the business users, the project sponsor, the business product owner,[76] the project manager, the

---

[76] By "business product owner", I mean the business user primarily responsible for making sure that the end result of the application

Scrum Master, the Data Analyst, an application developer architect, and a Business Analyst. The requirements (for a Scrum project) are captured as a series of User Stories, in the following form:

"As a [*Business Role*], I would like to [*Description of Business Function*], so that [*Description of Expected Business Benefit*]"

After the user stories have been captured, a very quick and rough analysis of each story is done, for the purpose of identifying dependencies between the stories, performing a rough "order of magnitude" estimate of both the complexity and the work involved for each story, and then prioritizing them in order of importance (to the business), keeping the dependencies and difficulty of each story in mind. The sorted, prioritized set of user stories is called the Product Backlog.

The Data Analyst attends the requirements workshops with the business users and the development team, and creates a conceptual data model of the major entities that have been identified (e.g., *Division, Sales Option, Instrument Model, Option/Model, Option/Model Configuration, Category, Option/Category, Part, Standard Option,* etc.). Key attributes and relationships are added to this model. Later, as the user stories are being (briefly) analyzed, sized, estimated, and prioritized to create the Product Backlog, more information will surface. The Data Analyst will extend the conceptual model into a first-cut logical model containing the major entities, key attributes, relationships, any obvious non-key attributes (*Division Name, Sales Option Description, Category Name,* etc.), and any business data rules and requirements captured during the sessions. The Data Analyst, at this point, is beginning the process of understanding and modeling the business subject area affected by the proposed application, and determining if all or part of it has been previously modeled in

---

development effort satisfies the needs and requirements of the business. "Product Owner" is a designated role in a Scrum project.

conjunction with one or more current business processes or applications. The Data Analyst must also understand whether (and where) the data model for this project will interface or overlap with any existing data model(s).

Note that, even this early in the project, it is possible to create a workable first-cut model. This model will evolve as user stories are worked, and requirements are clarified, but that's OK. As we've already seen, refactoring the logical model is not a lot of effort. Also note that it is not possible to create this first-cut model in a timely fashion unless the Data Analyst participates in the requirements-gathering sessions!

While the developers are setting up the application development environment, the DBA will create an initial physical model and database based on the first-cut logical model. The DBA will do little, if any, physical design at this point; the purpose here is just to have a database (either Development, or Test, or both) for the application development environment (including the build and deployment tool) to connect to. At this point, we've done just enough work to enable the project team to begin development of the application.

The DBA has one additional task: if data conversion work has been identified, a data conversion plan should be drafted, including a statement of the data conversion requirements, a description of the work that will need to be done, the tools and processes that will be needed, identification of the resources who will do this work, and an estimate of the hours required. This should be done as early as possible in the project, as the scope and magnitude of data conversion work is almost always seriously underestimated. The DBA may also, at this point, create the framework for the physical database design document, which will be filled out as the database design and development work proceeds during the project.

Development Activities

The Data Analyst and DBA attend the planning session for each Sprint (or at least a portion of it, as their time permits) to help identify the necessary data-related tasks for each user story being worked on during the Sprint, and provide an estimate of hours for each task.

One or both will probably also attend the Daily Scrum, a 15-minute stand-up meeting in which each member of the project team who is actively working on development tasks (including the Data Analyst and DBA) will answer three questions:

1) What did you work on (and accomplish) yesterday?

2) What are you going to work on (and accomplish) today?

3) What obstacles or impediments are you facing?

The stand-up meeting provides a focus for the day's project activities. At the end of the meeting, the Scrum Master and the Product Owner will have a clear idea of what progress has been made, what is being worked on, and what problems or issues the team is facing.

The Data Analyst and the DBA work with the project team to help identify, model, design, and implement the data requirements associated with each user story. As mentioned earlier, the Data Analyst will attend the analysis session for each user story, to make sure that the data requirements for that story are captured and added to the logical data model. Each iteration of the data model can be used as input to the analysis (i.e., as a reference document for discussion of the requirements of each user story) that produces the next iteration of the data model.

The DBA will attend the design session for each user story, checking the data that will be produced and consumed by each piece of functionality against the logical data model for any inconsistencies (i.e., making sure that everyone's understanding of the data is consistent with the requirements that have been captured in the data model). The DBA will then update the physical model with this data, and apply the necessary updates to the data. The DBA will then continue to work with the development team to address and resolve any database-related issues, create (or help create) virtual data objects, assist with database coding and testing, help create test data, perform (or assist with) data conversion, integration, and reporting, and other work as needed.

If new data requirements surface during development, they will be handled by the Data Analyst (if a change to the logical model is needed) and the DBA.

The following are just a few of the many issues that need to be addressed during the project:

- A decision must be made about how the part and labor cost data on the mainframe will be accessed. The only way to access this data directly is via web services, and this will be too slow for the number of calculations involved. Although the Data Services group wishes to avoid replicating data, it acquiesces in the decision to store the part and labor cost for each component in the database. This data must be stored by factory (plant location) code and part number. A web service is written to update this data in the SOM database as part and labor data are changed on the mainframe. Data from the web service is inserted into a receiving table, and a trigger on that table calls a stored procedure which applies insert, update, and delete operations on the underlying tables, as appropriate. Note: even though this data is being replicated, it will not be changed in the SOM database; this data will be read-only. Also note: the receiving table is a physical-only table.

- Analysis of some of the user stories result in the realization that a batch processing component is needed for the application. For example, the mass replacement of standard options across models is too processing-intensive to be done online. There is also a new user story that says that new models of instruments can be created ("cloned") from existing models, with a specified subset of that model's sales options, and then modified in the application. To support the batch processing, it is necessary to create physical-only tables in the database to hold the input data for the batch processing. These tables are populated by database triggers that execute when certain updates are made to other tables (such as the *Model* and *SalesOption* tables) via the application. The DBA updates the physical database design with the physical-only tables (the logical data model is not affected, since these are not business entities), and auto-generates the schema for the new tables from the physical model. The DBA then creates the triggers to populate the tables and tests them. Finally, the application is tested to make sure the batch processing records are properly created from the online application updates. Note: since these tables are only updated from the database triggers, it is not necessary to create fundamental stored procedures (FSPs) for these tables. A stored procedure is created to perform each of the individual batch update processes. A master procedure is created that invokes each of the individual update procedures. Finally, a scheduled database job is created to execute the batch process each night.

- The application needs to be able to analyze the part and labor costs associated with the components of each model of instrument, and come up with a list price for each model. Unfortunately, since there is a batch processing component to the application, this logic also needs to be present in the database. Since the team doesn't want to maintain two sets of code that perform the same function, it is decided to use a SQL/CLR approach. An application module is coded (using the application's programming language) to perform the calculations. The DBA then takes this code module and encapsulates it in CLR (Common Language Runtime) stored procedures, creating one stored procedure for each method in the code module. This allows the same code module to be used in both the application and the database.

The DBA partitions memory on the database server, so that both the DBMS and the CLR component will have sufficient memory.

- In order to not have to recalculate the list price every time an option/model is viewed in the application, the computed list price for each option/model is stored in another physical-only table in the database. A database trigger calls the pricing module whenever sales options for a model of instrument are changed, and the pricing table is then updated for that option/model. The DBA updates the physical database design with the new table, generates the schema, updates the database, and creates the new trigger.

- A physical-only table is also created to hold an unpacked form of the hierarchical category table (since recursive SELECTs from a hierarchical structure don't perform well in SQL). The DBA codes a stored procedure to unpack the hierarchy and update the table, and a background process to run the update at specified intervals. This helps improve application performance at minimal cost. Note: the denormalization is acceptable because only the original hierarchical table is updated by users via the application.

- There is a requirement that the descriptions for sales options be maintained in the database in multiple languages, since the company does business in many different countries. Fortunately, a solution to do this has already been developed by the Data Services group, and is easily implemented. A data model for the multi-language entities already exists, and is added to the data model for the application as a separate subject area in the modeling tool. Scripts to create the multi-language tables and associated stored procedures are run in the application database. The fundamental stored procedures for the *SalesOption* table are regenerated, and code is automatically inserted into the FSPs that call the multi-language stored procedures whenever insert or update operations are performed on this table. The only application change that is needed is the specification of a language dialect code when the FSPs are called from the application.

- During development, it is discovered that the application must track the changes in state of a sales option (Option Status), and take particular actions when an option changes from one state to another. Again, this is a common requirement for which the Data Services group has a solution: a data auditing component that can easily be implemented in the database. As with the multi-language component, a data model subject area exists, and is added to the data model for the application. Scripts are run to create the auditing tables and a trigger, which is added to the *SalesOption* table. When the status of a sales option is changed, the trigger will cause a record to be inserted into the Audit table; the application then queries the Audit table to determine when and how the status has changed, and takes the appropriate action.

- Late in the project, a new requirement surfaces: business users at the company's various divisions want to be able to do ad-hoc querying and reporting of the option and pricing data for instruments that are manufactured by their division. This presents two problems: first, these activities may interfere with, and impede the performance of, the Sales Option Management application. Second, no division must be allowed to see the pricing data for any other division. The DBA solves these problems by: 1) creating a read-only reporting copy of the database on a separate server, using transactional replication to update the reporting database in real time, and 2) creating a set of reporting views in this database that only allow data for a particular division to be viewed. Each set of reporting views (for a single division) are associated with a division-specific role in the database, and each role is associated with a security group into which business users from that division are placed. A user placed into a security group will have access only to the views associated with a particular division-specific role, and will be able to see only the data for that division. All access permissions are removed from the underlying database tables.

- A mechanism for publishing data changes to the mainframe must also be created. Data selected for publishing is held in a queuing table until it is approved; a trigger on the table then invokes a database process that calls the web service that updates the data on the mainframe.

- One of the major pieces of work in the project for the DBA is the conversion of data for the instrument models, sales options, and prices into the application database. One challenge is that the source data exists in many different forms, including flat files, Microsoft Excel spreadsheets, and Access databases. One of the company's divisions is entering its data using a prototyped version of the new application (and a copy of the application database). The DBA has to develop and test conversion processes for all of the different data sources, and the data conversions are run repeatedly as new data becomes available. Test scripts are developed to validate the converted data in the application database.

At the end of each Sprint, the Data Analyst and DBA participate in the Sprint retrospective, during which the work of the Sprint is reviewed. The team discusses which things went well during the Sprint, and what issues and problems were encountered. The team then agrees on a set of process improvements that will be taken into the next Sprint. In this way, each Sprint represents an ongoing process of learning and improvement for the team.

Post-Development Activities

After development, the DBA participates in the work of performance (load) testing of the application and database, final review of the database code, and deployment of the database to the Production environment. This will include making sure that backup jobs are set up, and making sure that monitoring and reporting of database and database server errors is being done. The DBA will also help resolve any database-related application issues that may surface after deployment. The DBA will finish the database design document (if this hasn't already been done), and will make sure to provide to the Operations and Application Support groups any necessary information about the database implementation.

The DBA will make sure that the physical database model, the database design document, and all database code objects are stored in the appropriate repository(ies) for future use. The Data Analyst will do the same with the logical data model.

At the end of the project, the Data Analyst and DBA attend the final review meeting for the project, at which "lessons learned" are identified and documented, to benefit future projects.

What you've read in this book represents one step on a continuing journey. It is by no means the definitive explanation of how to do database development, Agile or otherwise. Technologies and methodologies continue to evolve, and our understanding of how best to do our work evolves along with them. In our organization, which has used the Scrum methodology (in conjunction with a well-defined project governance process) for many years, we are now experimenting with other approaches, such as Kanban. We are even going "back to the future", by incorporating some object-oriented methodologies (OOA, OOD) into our development approach, in an effort to reduce defects.

At any rate, it is — as they say — a journey, not a destination. Hopefully, you will take away some useful ideas and approaches from the reading of this book, adapting and tailoring them to fit your particular business and technology environment. None of what you've read in this book is carved in tablets of stone. Just try to keep the important, fundamental principles in mind, and let your understanding develop with experience. In the long run, it is a combination of practical experience and a commitment to excellence — rather than the adoption of any particular approach or technique — that offers the greatest guarantee of success.

I wish you success on your journey.

Agile Alliance. A wealth of information about Agile Development, its philosophy, and best practices can be found on the web site of the Agile Alliance at http://www.agilealliance.org/.

Agile Data. Information about traditional approaches to Agile database development (not all of which I agree with, obviously!) can be found at http://www.agiledata.org/.

Ambler, Scott. People interested in Agile database development should definitely read the writings of Scott Ambler, who is a pioneer in this field. His books include *Agile Database Techniques* (Wiley Publishing, 2003) and *Refactoring Databases: Evolutionary Database Design* (Addison-Wesley, 2006). He also has a web site at http://www.ambysoft.com.

DAMA International. DAMA International is the recognized source for education, certification, and information regarding best practices in the data management profession. Information about DAMA can be found on their web site at http://www.dama.org/.

DAMA-DMBOK. The DAMA DMBOK (Data Management Body of Knowledge) is a compendium of standards and best practices in data management. The DAMA-DMBOK is available in both print and CD-ROM form, and can be obtained from Technics Publications at http://www.technicspub.com/. Enterprise server editions are available.

Kanban. Kanban is an iterative technique for managing work-in-process (WIP). In other words, the Kanban approach manages work rather than Sprints or other project iterations. Information about Kanban can be found at http://www.limitedwipsociety.org/.

PMI-PMBOK. Information about project management best practices can be found at the web site of the Project Management Institute at http://www.pmi.org/. The PMI publishes the PMBOK (Project Management Body of Knowledge), a compendium of standards and best practices in the Project Management field.

Scrum. The Scrum approach to Agile Development organizes people into self-directing, cross-functional teams, and empowers them to set goals and manage tasks in the context of project iterations called Sprints. Information about Scrum can be found at http://www.Scrumalliance.org/. A good starter book on Scrum is *Agile Software Development With Scrum* by Ken Schwaber and Mike Beedle.

AD   Agile Development

Agile   An iterative approach to application (software) development, based on early and continuous delivery of working software.

Attribute   A characteristic or property of an Entity in a logical data model.

BI   Business Intelligence; the analysis and reporting of data in a way that allows the business to recognize and take advantage of new and changing market conditions.

BDUF   Big Design Up-Front; that is, creation of a large number of analysis and design artifacts at the beginning of a development project, before any actual coding begins.

CDM   Conceptual Data Model

CEO   Chief Executive Officer

CI   Continuous Integration; the ability to quickly integrate changes into a new build of the application, and deploy it.

CIO   Chief Information Officer

CLR   Common Language Runtime; as used in this book, the creation of database objects (such as stored procedures) written in application programming languages.

COTS	Commercial Off-the-Shelf Software
CRM	Customer Relationship Management
CRUD	Create, Read, Update, Delete; the four basic operations that are performed on database tables.
DA	Data Administration
DA	Data Analyst
DAMA	The Data Administration Management Association; the international organization for data management professionals.
DBA	Database Administrator (or, alternatively, Database Analyst).
DBMS	Database Management System; the software that enables users and applications to interact with databases.
DDL	Data Definition Language; code used to create databases and database objects.
DMBOK	The Data Management Body of Knowledge; a compendium of information and best practices in data and information management.
DQ	Data Quality

EA	Enterprise Architecture
EAI	Enterprise Application Integration
Entity	A business object (such as Customer or Product), as represented in a logical data model.
ERD	Entity Relationship Diagram
ERP	Enterprise Resource Planning
FSP	Fundamental Stored Procedure
IDE	Integrated Development Environment; a framework in which application development activities can be done (e.g., Microsoft's Visual Studio Team System).
IT	Information Technology
JIT	Just in Time, referring to the allocation of resources at the moment they are needed.
KPI	Key Performance Indicator
LDM	Logical Data Model
MDD	Model-Driven Development
MDM	Master Data Management
Metadata	Information about the characteristic properties of a data object or structure; usually contained within that object or

structure.

Object	Something that has characteristic properties (i.e., it contains data) and performs a function.
O-O	Object-Oriented
OOA	Object-Oriented Analysis
OOD	Object-Oriented Design
OLAP	Online Analytical Processing
OLTP	Online Transaction Processing
ORM	Object-Role Modeling; a technique for conceptual data modeling that focuses on business objects and roles.
ORM	Object-Relational Mapping; software that moves data between application data objects and the underlying relational database.
PDM	Physical Data Model
Persistence	The temporary or permanent storing of data outside of an application that creates or uses it.
PRISM	Performance, Reusability, Integrity, Security, Maintainability; the five fundamental principles of data management.
QA	Quality Assurance

RDBMS	Relational Database Management System; software that supports the creation and use of relational databases.
Refactor	To improve an application or database object without changing its behavior.
RFID	Radio Frequency Identifier; microchips containing both data and function (behavior) that can be embedded in objects and products to make them more intelligent.
ROI	Return On Investment
Scrum	An approach to Agile Development involving multiple development cycles (called Sprints).
SDLC	Systems Development Life Cycle
SLA	Service Level Agreement; an agreement between the business and one or more IT support groups as to the availability of applications and databases.
SOA	Service-Oriented Architecture
Sprint	In the Scrum approach to Agile, one iteration of a development project.
SQL	Structured Query Language; used to create objects and to query and manipulate data in relational databases.

SSAS	SQL Server Analysis Services; a Microsoft product used for analysis of data using OLAP cubes.
SSIS	SQL Server Integration Services; a Microsoft product used to integrate data from multiple disparate data sources.
SSRS	SQL Server Reporting Services; a Microsoft product used for reporting data via a web browser.
TCO	Total Cost of Ownership
TDD	Test-Driven Development, an approach to application development that encourages creation of test code in conjunction with application code, and continuous testing during development.
VDL	Virtual Data Layer
XML	Extensible Markup Language; a way of transmitting and/or storing data in text form.

Made in the USA
Middletown, DE
09 February 2017

子連れ狼

LONE
WOLF
AND

CUB

DISCARD

story
KAZUO KOIKE

art
GOSEKI KOJIMA

DARK HORSE COMICS

LON
v.20

translation
DANA LEWIS

lettering & retouch
DIGITAL CHAMELEON

cover illustration
MATT WAGNER

publisher
MIKE RICHARDSON

editor
TIM ERVIN-GORE

assistant editor
JEREMY BARLOW

consulting editor
TOREN SMITH for **STUDIO PROTEUS**

book design
DARIN FABRICK

art director
MARK COX

Published by Dark Horse Comics, Inc., in association
with MegaHouse and Koike Shoin Publishing Company.

Dark Horse Comics, Inc.
10956 SE Main Street, Milwaukie, OR 97222
www.darkhorse.com

First edition: March 2002
ISBN: 1-56971-592-0

1 3 5 7 9 10 8 6 4 2

Printed in Canada

Lone Wolf and Cub Vol. 20: A Taste of Poison

To find a comics shop in your area, call the
Comic Shop Locator Service toll-free at 1-888-266-4226.

$9.95
12/1/15
DC

i14123381

A TASTE
OF POISON

By KAZUO KOIKE
& GOSEKI KOJIMA

VOLUME
20

A NOTE TO READERS

Lone Wolf and Cub is famous for its carefully researched re-creation of Edo-Period Japan. To preserve the flavor of the work, we have chosen to retain many Edo-Period terms that have no direct equivalents in English. Japanese is written in a mix of Chinese ideograms and a syllabic writing system, resulting in numerous synonyms. In the glossary, you may encounter words with multiple meanings. These are words written with Chinese ideograms that are pronounced the same but carry different meanings. A Japanese reader seeing the different ideograms would know instantly which meaning it is, but these synonyms can cause confusion when Japanese is spelled out in our alphabet. *O-yurushi o* (please forgive us)!

TABLE OF CONTENTS

Good Fortune, Ill Fortune

ON THE SIXTEENTH OF JUNE, *KAJŌ-NO-SHUKUJITSU* WAS CELEBRATED AT EDO CASTLE.

WHEN TŌSHŌGŪ WAS STILL IN MIKAWA, THERE WAS A REVOLT, AND HIS ARMY HARD PRESSED.

IT WAS THE FIFTEENTH OF JUNE.

TŌSHŌGŪ'S ARMY WAS ROUTED. BUT HE TOOK SHELTER IN DAIJU TEMPLE, AND SO LIVED TO FIGHT AGAIN.

KREEE

BROOM

SPAK

THOK

THOK

TŌSHŌGŪ COULD ONLY UNIFY JAPAN YEARS LATER BECAUSE OF HIS NARROW ESCAPE THIS DAY...

...AND THUS TOKUGAWA CALLED THE SIXTEENTH OF JUNE *KAJŌ-NO-SHUKUJITSU,* THE "DAY OF GOOD FORTUNE."

ON THIS DAY, THE *SHŌGUN* PRESENTED *GO-KASHI* SWEETCAKES TO THE *GO-SANKE*, THE *FUDAI DAIMYŌ*, THE *TOZAMA DAIMYŌ*, THE *KŌTAI YORIAI*, AND THE *OMOTE-KŌKA SHOYAKU.*

FOR EACH GUEST...

THREE WHITE *DAI-MANJU.*

THREE POUNDED-RICE *AKOYA-MOCHI.*

THREE LARGE *UZURAYAKI.*

FIVE RED AND WHITE *YORIMIZU.*

FIVE SKEWERS OF BLUE *DAI-KINTON.*

AND FIVE TO SIX COATED *YŌKAN.*

PREPARATION AND DISTRIBUTION OF THE CAKES WAS OVERSEEN BY THE HEAD OF THE *KUCHIYAKU.*

THE *KUCHIYAKU* WERE THE TASTERS FOR THE *SHŌGUN* FAMILY. THEY WERE CALLED *KUCHIYAKU,* OR "OFFICIAL MOUTHS," BECAUSE THEY CHECKED FOR POISON WITH THEIR OWN TONGUES.

OUR LORD COMETH!

24

THE GO-SANKE-SAMA...!

26

27

OKUBLIO KAGA-NO-KAMI-*SAMA!*

SAKAI SANUKI-NO-KAMI-*SAMA!*

ANDŌ TSUSHIMA-NO-KAMI-*SAMA!*

ABE SURUGA-NO-KAMI-*SAMA!*

Ī SHŌSHŌ-
SAMA!

HOTTA
BUZEN-
NO-KAMI-
SAMA!

MATSUDAIRA
KAI-NO-KAMI-
SAMA!

INABA
SADO-
NO-KAMI-
SAMA!

MAKINO
TŌTŌMI-
NO-KAMI-
SAMA!

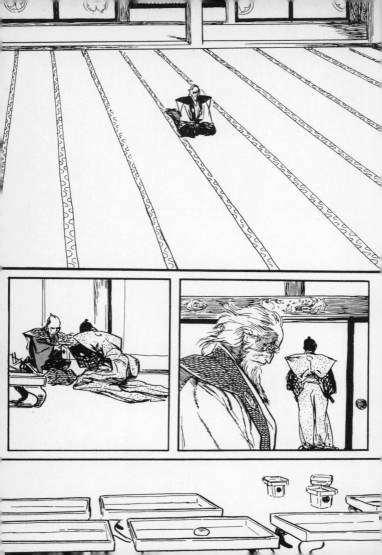

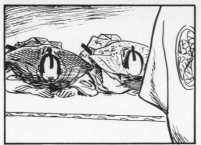

MY...
MY *LORD!*
PLEASE
WAIT!

SUSS
SUSS

YAGYŪ
RETSUDŌ
HAS NO
GO-KASHI.

FOOL! YOU BRING YOUR *BAD LUCK* TO MY *KAJŌ* FESTIVAL AND YOU THINK YOU DESERVE MY *CAKES?!*

MY LORD!!

JIJI! YOU'RE A *BROKEN-BACKED NAG!* I PITY YOU!

I LOAN YOU *ABE-NO-KAII.*

THE WOLF'S *HEAD!* IN TEN DAYS!

33

YAGYŪ-*SAMA*.

ABE TANOSHI SHALL HELP IN ANY WAY HE CAN.

MY THANKS.

IT'S SMALL WONDER OUR LORD IS ANGRY. FIRST ŌGAMI ITTŌ DESTROYS HIS *FIREWATCHERS*. THEN HE BUTCHERS MUKAI SHŌGEN AND HIS CREW...

...AND SAILS TO EDO ON OUR LORD'S OWN *SHIP!*

MM.

YAGYŪ-*SAMA*... YOU'VE LOST *FACE*. THE *DAIMYŌ* AND *JIKISAN HATAMOTO* PLOT AGAINST YOU.

ONLY FEAR OF YOUR REMAINING *POWER* RESTRAINS THEM.

MNN...
····

AND YOUR *POWER*, YAGYŪ-*SAMA*, DERIVES FROM OUR LORD'S DEEP *TRUST*. HE LETS YOU OFF EASILY...

...WHERE ANY *OTHER* MAN...
····

YOU ENJOY HIS TRUST AS WELL.

MY POISON TASTERS VET ALL OUR LORD EATS.

OF *COURSE* I DO!

I HEAR RUMORS YOU TAKE ADVANTAGE OF IT.

OH, WITH *WOMEN*, I SUPPOSE? LOOK AT ME! A FACE SO UGLY THEY ONCE CALLED ME *KAII THE FREAK!* IT'S NOT EASY TO FIND WILLING WOMEN.

BUT I ENJOY THE FLESH AS MUCH AS ANY MAN, AND MAYBE *MORE*. AND SO, PEOPLE *TALK*. THAT I *FORCE* WOMEN TO OBEY ...HAH! *RUMORS*.

BUT TO THE *POINT! YAGYŪ-SAMA*, WHEN THE *BAKKAKU* RE-CONVENES, YOU MAY BE *INVESTIGATED*.

THUS OUR LORD SAYS *TEN DAYS*.

HRM...

SO... WHAT WILL YOU DO?

WHAT DO YOU *THINK?!* I WILL *CRUSH* HIM!

HE'S LIKE A *RAT* IN A *TRAP* HERE IN EDO! WE'LL GET HIM AT *LAST!*

36

AND PLAY INTO HIS *HANDS*...?

WHAT?!

EDO'S RIGHT UNDER THE *SHŌGUN'S NOSE!* ITTŌ WOULD LIKE NOTHING *BETTER* THAN TO FIGHT YOU HERE.

ALREADY YOU'RE CRITICIZED FOR LETTING HIM ARRIVE ON OUR LORD'S *WARSHIP*— ANOTHER SUCH *DISASTER*, AND YOU'RE *FINISHED!*

MNN...!

THAT'S WHY ITTŌ CAME HERE! HE *WANTS* THE ATTENTION OF THE NATION, TO GET YOUR CLAN *DISBANDED!* IF YOU *FAIL* TO KILL HIM *NOW*...

YES... THE NAME OF MY *CLAN*...

AND *ŌGAMI* MUST HAVE PLANS, AS WELL.

WHAT'S BECOME OF ALL THE *GOLD* HE EARNED? NOBODY KNOWS.

HRRM...

SO YOU MUST BE *CAREFUL.*

I SEE WHY OUR LORD *TRUSTS* YOU, ABE-NO-KAII.

YOU'RE A CUNNING MAN...

NOW—DON'T YOU FIND IT *STRANGE?* A WANTED CRIMINAL DEFEATS *EVERYONE* THE *DAIKANSHO* AND THE YAGYŪ SEND AGAINST HIM, AND WALKS INTO EDO *UNSCATHED.* PEOPLE THINK ITTŌ HAS THE LUCK OF THE *DEVIL.* BUT OBJECTIVELY, CAN MERE *LUCK* EXPLAIN IT?

OR EVEN *STRENGTH...?*

BOTH, I DARE SAY...

WRONG! NO ONE IS THAT LUCKY!

NO SINGLE MAN DEFEATS AN ARMY!

THEN... WHAT?

HIS *BOY...* DAIGORO!

SHIDŌ CONDEMNS KILLING WOMEN AND CHILDREN.

AND *SAMURAI* CAN'T KILL A CHILD! SHAME BLUNTS THEIR SWORDS. IT'S OBVIOUS THEY'RE STUMBLING OVER THE BOY.

YOUR MEN, THE *DAIKANSHO'S* MEN... ALL TRUE *BUSHI*. IT'S *DAIGORO'S* POWER THAT KEEPS ŌGAMI ITTŌ ALIVE!

ME...
I'D TARGET
THE *BOY* FIRST,
THEN ITTŌ.

NO DOUBT
YOU'VE TRIED
TO TAKE THEM
ONLY BY FORCE
OF ARMS.

BUT WAR
ISN'T JUST
POWER. IT'S
CHANCE.

SO *EASY*
TO POISON
A CHILD...

ABE TANOSHI IS THE MASTER *POISONER* OF OUR AGE! HOW ELSE CAN I BE OUR LORD'S TASTER...?

HOH...!

NOW I SEE!

HEH HEH... LEAVE IT TO *ME*. ITTŌ'S CORPSE WILL LIE ROTTING UNDER THE STARS, WITH NONE THE *WISER*..

BWEH HEH HEH HEH!

41

HEH HEH HEH...
....

THEN... I ASK YOUR HELP. I'LL HAVE THE *MACHI-BUGYŌ* TRACK HIM DOWN...

HEH HEH... DON'T BOTHER.

I CAN FIND HIM *MYSELF.*

AND BESIDES...

IT'S THREE DAYS SINCE ITTŌ ENTERED EDO, JUDGING FROM WHEN THEY FOUND THE CREW.

AND ONLY *NOW* RETSUDŌ-*SAMA* ASKS THE *MACHI-BUGYŌ* TO FIND HIM...?

A LITTLE *SLOW*, ARE WE? OR DID YOU *MEAN* TO SAY THEY'VE BEEN SEARCHING *HIGH AND LOW*... WITHOUT RESULT?

HRM!

SO! NOT EVEN THE FULL MIGHT AND RESOURCES OF THE YAGYŪ CLAN CAN FIND HIM.

FRANKLY... THIS IS SO.

HIS FEINT COST US TWO DAYS. I'D SENT MY MEN TO FORTIFY KAWASAKI AND FUNABASHI...

...BUT THEY RETURNED LAST NIGHT, AND NOW THE HUNT IS ON.

WE'LL HAVE HIM SOON.

WILL YOU REALLY?

LAST TIME THIS MAN *ESCAPED* YOU AND HIJACKED A *WARSHIP!*

THEN YOU HAVE A *BETTER* IDEA?!

I *DO.* CURIOUS...?

OF *COURSE!*

THEN COME TO MY *COMPOUND...*

...IN *FRIENDSHIP.*

45

MNCH

MNCH

*ABE

MY MEN WILL BE HERE SHORTLY...

...FROM ACROSS ALL EDO.

ACROSS ALL EDO...?!

AND ALL TRUSTWORTHY...?

UNLIKE *YOUR* CLAN, YAGYŪ-*SAMA*, THEY'RE AS *HOPELESS* WITH A SWORD AS I AM. YET EDO'S VERY *LIFE* IS IN THEIR HANDS.

WHAT...?!

AH...
I SAID
IT WAS
URGENT.

AND SO—
HERE THEY
ARE.

THE RULERS OF EDO'S *KITCHENS!*

ECHIZENYA KAHEI, HEAD OF THE RICE DEALERS.

SIR!

YAOZEN OF THE GREEN-GROCERS.

UOKYU OF THE FISHMONGERS.

BARS! MISO SHOPS! BAKERIES, EATERIES...

...EVEN *CHEFS!* THEY CONTROL THEM *ALL!*

HOH...!

ŌGAMI ITTŌ'S STILL *HUMAN*. HE *EATS*... OR HE *DIES*.

THESE MEN HANDLE ALL THE FOOD IN EDO. THEY'LL FIND HIM... AND *SOON!*

TRULY A *KUCHI-YAKU*...

...ABE-NO-KAII-*SAMA!*

LISTEN *WELL, ALL* OF YOU!

THE CRIMINAL *LONE WOLF AND CUB*, ŌGAMI ITTŌ, FORMER EXECUTIONER FOR THE SHŌGUN, HAS ENTERED *EDO!*

53

ALERT YOUR PEOPLE AND *FIND* HIM!

IF HE COMES TO BUY RICE, OR FISH, OR VEGETABLES, *SELL* THEM. BUT *TAIL* HIM... AND TELL ME *INSTANTLY!*

HERE IS THE *WANTED POSTER!*

FWAP

FOCUS ON THE RIVERBANK AREAS!

UNDERSTAND?!

YES, ABE-NO-KAII-*SAMA!*

THEN *GO! NOW!!*

IN TWO *KOKU*, EVERY RICE DEALER, FISHMONGER, GREENGROCER...

...EVERY CANDY PEDDLER, FISHERMAN, AND PEASANT IN EDO WILL HAVE ORDERS.

THEY'LL TELL US WHERE ITTŌ IS.

HEH HEH... EVEN WOLVES HAVE TO *EAT!*

AND WHEN THEY *FIND* HIM...

THIS WAY, PLEASE.

56

THE *APOTHECARY* OF JAPAN'S GREATEST *POISONER,* ABE TANOSHI!

FEAST YOUR EYES, RETSUDŌ-SAMA!

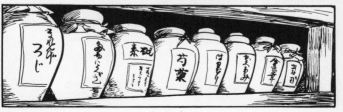

EVERY *KNOWN* POISON... AND ALL MY *OWN* SPECIAL MIXES.

FOR EXAMPLE... ADD *HABU* VIPER VENOM TO MONK'S HOOD— *TWICE* AS POTENT!

ANDROMEDA, GENISTA, YELLOW RHODODENDRON, IVY, *TAKENIGUSA*, KALOPANAX, *YUZURI*...

...I GREW THEM, EXTRACTED THEM, REFINED THEM TO BE *ODORLESS* AND *TASTELESS*.

HMM...
PERHAPS A
DEMONSTRA-
TION...?

HRG...!

SPSH

60

BWEH HEH HEH... *DAIGORO*? MAYBE EVEN *ITTŌ HIMSELF*...

BUT HOW WILL YOU *DELIVER* IT...?

CUT ITS SUPPLIES... AND BREAK THE ARMY.

JUST WATCH HOW I DO IT.

THERE IS MORE TO WAR THAN *POWER*.

LOGISTICS. WATER. AND *POISON*.

AND THE DAY I *DELIVER*, SOME GRACIOUS *SUPPORT...*?

BWEH HEH HEH!

I LEAVE IT TO YOU.

DON'T WORRY ABOUT A THING.

63

KRRKK

64

SO, RETSUDŌ! YOUR *EYE* JUST ABOUT POPPED OUT OF YOUR *HEAD...*

FIRST BURY ITTŌ, AND GET THE *YAGYŪ* LETTER.

AND *THEN...* YOU'RE *NEXT!*

...DIDN'T IT, OLD MAN?!

HEH, HEH... YOU DON'T HAVE A *CLUE.*

THE KUROKUWA AND THE ŌGAMI CLAN... ALREADY GONE.

JUST THE YAGYŪ LEFT.

IF I BRING *THEM* DOWN, THE ABE CLAN CONTROLS THE *NATION!*

OUR LORD ALREADY TRUSTS ME MORE THAN RETSUDŌ.

AND IF I KILL ITTŌ, THE YAGYŪ NAME WILL BE *WORTHLESS TRASH...* BWEH HEH HEH... *HA HA HA!*

66

AN EXCEEDINGLY *DEADLY* MAN. HE'S A THREAT TO US AS WELL.

JINNAI!

MY LORD!

WATCH ABE TANOSHI *CLOSELY.*

IF HE *DOES* KILL ITTŌ, THEN IN THAT VERY *INSTANT—*

—KILL THE
KUCHIYAKU!
EVERY ONE!

YES, MY
LORD!

KAJŌ-NO-
SHUKUJITSU...
AN AUSPICIOUS
DAY.

BUT FOR
WHOM...?

68

Lair of the Night- hawks

HEY, HANDSOME.

WANT SOME FUN?

≷PHEWW!≷ DON'T *SCARE* ME LIKE THAT.

HOW ABOUT IT? SLOW NIGHT, I'LL GIVE YOU A *DEAL*. CHEAP AS IT GETS.

LIKE WHAT YOU *SEE?*

OH *YEAH!* FRESHLY *PLUCKED,* LOOKS LIKE!

THAT'S *RIGHT.* IT'S MY FIRST NIGHT.

THINGS... *HAPPEN,* YOU KNOW?

IF THEY DIDN'T, WHO THE HELL WOULD DO *THIS?!*

SO, *OPENING NIGHT!* POX FREE!

BUT IF I DON'T HURRY HOME...

COME ON— HOW OFTEN DOES A GUY GET TO DO IT WITH A *FRESH* WOMAN?

LIKE THEY SAY— TRUE LOVE, ONCE IN A LIFE- TIME.

COME ON. *TRY* ME.

SORRY... IT'S BEEN WARM... AND IT'S MY ONLY KIMONO.

BUT MAYBE YOU *LIKE* IT THAT WAY...? HOT AND SWEATY...

JUST ONE REQUEST.

DON'T LOOK AT MY *BACK.* *EVER!* GOT IT?

OH, YEAH! S-SURE!

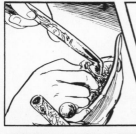

HEY,
LOVER BOY...
GOT A
LIGHT?

FFHH

WANT A
PUFF...?

SURE,
IF YOU
DON'T
MIND.

THIS
IS ABOUT
GONE...
I'LL
REFILL
IT.

PIHT

HSSS

80

WORKS
LIKE A
CHARM...!

83

IT'S ABOUT TIME FOR THOSE *YOTAKA* HAGS TO HIT THE STREETS...

BUT MAYBE I'LL TRY IT ON A COUPLE MORE GUYS...

≥HIC≤ FUGGIN' JERK... GONNA...

≥HIC≤ ≥URRP≤

HEY... *BIG BOY.*

84

HUH? WHADDYA WANT?!

YOU STINKIN' *NIGHTHAWKS* CREEP ME OUT.

NICE *TOY*. PERFECT LENGTH, GOOD HEFT. SPRINGY...

TALK *SWEET*, 'N' CARRY A *BIG STICK!* ⌇HIC⌇ *YOTAKA* DON'T GET MEAT LIKE *THIS*, HEH, HEH...

WANT IT?

SURE I WANT IT... AND I'M *CHEAP*.

HEY, FUCK YOU, SLUT!

IF *YOU* WANT SOMETHING, *YOU* PAY!

SELLER'S MARKET, HEH HEH...

DAMN... THEY'RE HERE.

HN...?

85

WHA—
WHAT
THE—?!

CLEAR *OUT*, JOHN-BOY!

YAIEE!!

YOU! WHO SAID YOU COULD WORK HERE?!

THIS RIVER'S *KAWA-MATAZA* TURF!

HMPH! MATAZA, MATAGURA, WHO *GIVES* A SHIT? SINCE WHEN DO NIGHTHAWKS RATE *TURF?!*

HEH HEH HEH. WHAT *NOW*, BITCH? THAT SPIDER'S GONNA BE CRYING TEARS OF *BLOOD!*

AUUHHN!

HEH HEH HEH... LOOKING A LITTLE *PALE*? I GUESS YOU'VE HEARD ABOUT OUR *INCENSE*!

FUCK YOU, YOU *WHORE*!

HEH... SHE'S GOT *GUTS*.

YOU READY...?

HEE, HEE! *YEAH*!

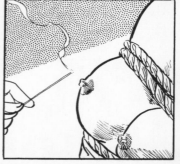

FIRST, WE BURN OFF YOUR *NIPPLES*, SEE? THEN WE WORK DOWN TO YOUR *PUSSY*, THEN *DEEP* INSIDE!

AND LAST, WE BURN OUT YOUR *EYEBALLS*... SO GET READY! OF COURSE, IF YOU *APOLOGIZE* NICELY ENOUGH, I *MIGHT* LET YOU JOIN MY GANG INSTEAD.

NO?! OKAY, THEN— *BURN HER!*

WA-WAIT! *STOP!*

SHUDDUP! IT'S TOO *LATE!*

I *KNOW!* BUT, A *SMOKE!* A LAST *SMOKE!*

HUH...?!

I GOT THE HABIT *BAD!*

I *LIVE* FOR *KIZAMI* TOBACCO! AND ONLY THE *BEST!*

I'VE FALLEN SO FAR, IT'S ALL I'VE *GOT. EXPENSIVE* SHIT, TOO. THAT'S WHY I SELL MYSELF— TO BUY IT!

SURE, WHY NOT?

WHERE IS IT?

IT'S IN MY SLEEVE.

HMPH! NICE *KISERU* PIPE! HMM... I WONDER WHAT GOOD *KIZAMI* IS LIKE...?

D-DAMN THOSE *SLUTS!!* IT'S ALL *GONE!*

HH! HH!

AUGGH!!

AAH... AHH!!

OOOH... *AAHH!!*

I... I WANT IT! IT *HURTS!!*

OH, GOD... I...I'M *DYING...*

KI... *KIZAMI!!* NNGGH...

BAM BAM

SKRRTCH

UHN...
. . . .

*ABE

101

P-PLEASE... OH GOD, *PLEASE!* I... CAN'T...

PLEASE, GOZEN-SAMA... YOUR *KIZAMI!!*

103

104

P...PLEASE...
GOD, *PLEASE*...
K-*KIZAM!!*

BTAM

I TOLD YOU *NEVER* TO COME HERE!

DID YOU *FORGET?!*

109

SKICH SKICH

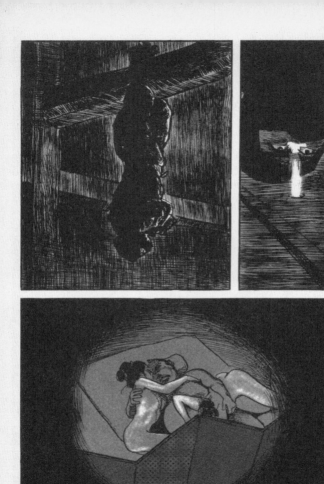

SHAKK

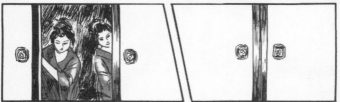

114

FORGIVE ME, GOZEN-SAMA...?

VERY WELL. BUT YOU ARE *NEVER* TO COME HERE AGAIN!

YES, MY LORD.

I'LL SEND YOU YOUR KIZAMI, AS USUAL.

BUT SINCE YOU'RE HERE, I WANT A REPORT.

FIRST... COME!

YES, MY LORD.

115

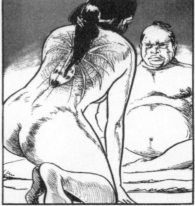

116

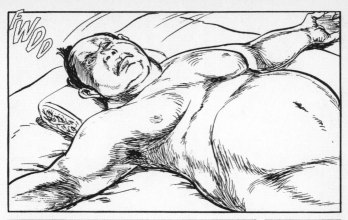

117

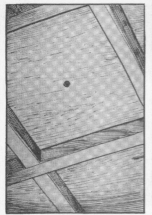

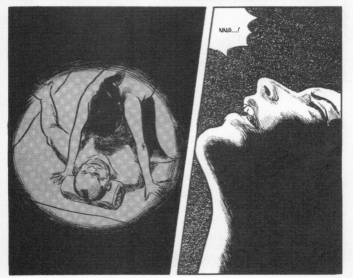

NNG...!

118

SO...
DID YOU TRY
THE *KIZAMI*
WITH MONK'S HOOD
AND *HABU*
VENOM...?

Y-YES, SIR...
I DID AS YOU...
COMMANDED...

AND THE
RESULTS
...?!

SOME GUY...
JUST...
ONE PUFF...

119

AAHN!!

HRM!

I...HOOKED THE NIGHTHAWKS ON YOUR *KIZAMI*... THE TYPE WITH *AFUYŌ*.

N-NOW THEY'LL DO WHATEVER I SAY... TO GET MORE. I'LL USE THEM.. AS PART OF MY *WEB*...

120

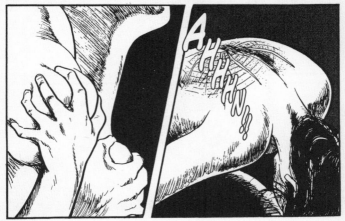

121

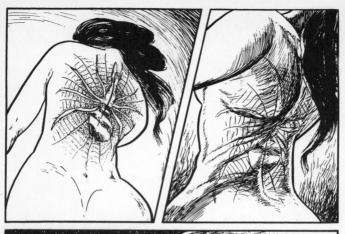

AS LONG
AS I HAVE...
YOUR SPECIAL
KIZAMI...
THEY'RE M-MINE...
TO COMMAND!

122

THEN I'LL SEND YOU ALL YOU NEED.

AHH! AH! AHHN!

BWEH HEH HEH HA HA HA!

LONE WOLF MOVES AT NIGHT.

WITH THE YAGYU AND THE *MACHI-BUGYŌ* AFTER HIM, HE HAS TO HIDE BY DAY.

MMM... AAH!!

SO I USE PEOPLE WHO *LIVE* BY NIGHT. *STRATEGY!*

NO *SWORDS,* NO *JITTE.* JUST *THERE* IN THE DARK, LIKE THE TREES AND GRASS...

NIGHTHAWKS!

123

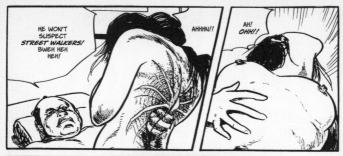

HE WON'T SUSPECT *STREET WALKERS!* BWEH HEH HEH!

AHHHN!!

AH! OHH!!

EVERY PERSON HANDLING FOOD IN EDO, WATCHING. THEY SPOT THEM. THE NIGHTHAWKS TRAP THEM. AND MY POISON KILLS FIRST *DAIGORO*...THEN ITTŌ *HIMSELF! UNDERSTAND,* O-TOSHI?! NO *MISTAKES!*

Y-YES, SIR... *OHH...!*

BWEH HEH HEH! STRUGGLE AWAY AS HE MIGHT, HE'S *TRAPPED,* LIKE A FLY IN A SILK SPIDER'S *WEB...*

124

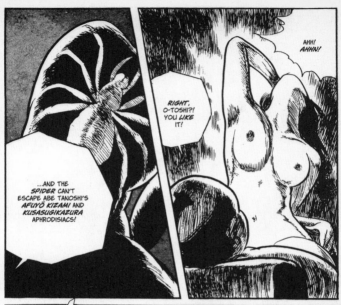

...AND THE *SPIDER* CAN'T ESCAPE ABE TANOSHI'S *AFUYŌ KIZAMI* AND *KUSASUGIKAZURA* APHRODISIACS!

RIGHT, O-TOSHI?! YOU *LIKE* IT!

AHH! AHHN!

BWEH HEH HEH HEH!

126

JINNAI...?

MY LORD.

HAS ABE-NO-KAII MADE HIS MOVE?

YES, MY LORD. HE USED A WOMAN THIEF CALLED "SILK SPIDER" TO HOOK THE NIGHTHAWKS ON *AFUYŌ*.

HE'LL HAVE THEM APPROACH LONE WOLF AND CUB, AND *POISON* THEM, STARTING WITH THE BOY.

HMM... *NIGHT-HAWKS.*

127

IS THERE *ANY COMMONER* IN EDO HE DOESN'T CONTROL? DANGEROUS *INDEED*.

BUT THUS PERHAPS PERFECT FOR KILLING *LONE WOLF*, MY LORD...

YES... *LONE WOLF,* VERSUS *ABE-NO-KAII.*

THIS I MUST *SEE!*

HEH HEH...

HEH HEH HEH!

128

Blighted

Leaves

*FOOD

*SAKE

THAT'S *CRAZY*. *LONE WOLF AND CUB*, HUH?

MAN... FIVE THOUSAND *RYŌ*!

SERIOUS TOUGH GUY!

MNCH MNCH

SEEMS LIKE *EDO* FOLK DON'T MUCH KNOW HIM.

THE *CAPITAL*, AND EVEN *NEWBORN BABES* DO!

FOLK PISS IN THEIR PANTS AT THAT NAME, LET ME TELL YOU!

NO WAY!

HE'S A *CONTRACT KILLER.* THE *BEST!*

DAMN... AND HIM WITH THAT CUTE *KID?* I DUNNO, DAD OR *NOT,* IT AIN'T *RIGHT* TO TAKE A KID ALONG ON *MURDERS.*

HEY, DOLL! ANOTHER BOWL OF *SOUP!*

COMING UP!

SECONDS ON THE *RICE,* HERE!

GOT YA!

SO, MASTER... WHAT IF WE *SPOT* HIM..?

WE TELL ABE TANOSHI, THE *KUCHI-YAKU.*

HUH? THE *POISON* TASTER?

NOT THE *BUGYŌ...?*

135

137

FOOD, PLEASE. BOILED VEGETABLES AND RICE WILL DO.

Y-YASSIR...

139

SO TELL THE *KUCHIYAKU*... HURRY!

G-G-G... GOTCHA!

140

141

IT'S ON THE TABLE.

AH... TH-*THANK* YOU, SIR!

142

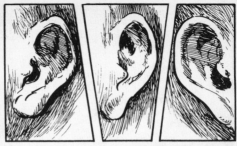

L-LONE WOLF AND CUB!

YEAH!! IT'S *GOTTA* BE!

THE *SPITTIN' IMAGE* OF THE POSTER!

MASTER! THE *KUCHIYAKU*...?

YAOSHICHI'S *HOOFIN'* IT THERE *NOW*!

AND *YOU* MEN! *TAIL* HIM... BUT *CAREFUL* LIKE!

TAKE *TURNS!* IF IT'S JUST *ONE GUY,* HE'LL *NOTICE...*

GOT YA, BOSS!

THE *KUCHIYAKU* LOOKS AFTER US! WE'LL TRACK THIS GUY INTO *HELL* IF HE SAYS SO!

DON'T GET *COCKY!* 'N' DON'T *LOSE* HIM!

WHA-?!

AIIEE!!

146

I EXPECTED YAGYŪ... BUT THE *DOKUMI KUCHIYAKU?!*

148

IN MY DAY IT WAS OLD *ABE GENMOTSU.*

ALWAYS UPRIGHT AND *MODEST...* A STERLING *GENTLEMAN.* WHY WOULD HE HUNT FOR THE *YAGYŪ...?*

GARA GARA GARA

IT'S BEEN FOUR DAYS SINCE WE SET FOOT IN EDO, AND THE YAGYŪ HAVEN'T YET STRUCK. THEY FEAR A *DISTURBANCE...?*

PERHAPS. AND YET, THAT IS UNLIKE *RETSUDŌ.* NO, THE *KUCHIYAKU* MUST BE OUR *NEW ENEMY...*

GARA GARA GARA

...AND *THEN* THE YAGYŪ.

149

YOU *LOST* LONE WOLF?!

YOU FOOLS!!

F-*FORGIVE* US, SIR! WE WERE S-SO *SCARED,* WE WERE *PETRIFIED!*

WE COULDN'T FOLLOW HIM...

M-M-MERCY, SIR...! MERCY!!

HAH! IT'S *NOTHING!* *SIGHTING* HIM IS PRIZE ENOUGH FOR NOW!

GET ME A MAP!!

151

YOUR SHOP'S *WHERE* ON SANYA-BORI..?

A... ABOUT A *CHO* FROM IMADO BRIDGE.

SO... *HERE.* ....

WHICH WAY DID HE *GO?!*

AWAY FROM THE BRIDGE, SIR...

HRM.

EVERY GREENGROCER, FISHMONGER, AND RICE DEALER FROM IMADO TO SHIN-YOSHIWARA'S SEARCHING THE SANYA-BORI, SIR.

YOU!! COME!!

CONTACT "SILK SPIDER" O-TOSHI!

HAVE HER NIGHTHAWKS SWEEP THE WEST BANK OF THE SUMIDA...

...AND ALONG NIHONZUTSUMI AND THE HORIKAWA FROM SHITAYA.

YES, MY LORD.

BWEH HEH HEH... THIS TIME YOU'VE FLOWN INTO MY *WEB*, LONE WOLF!

BWA HA HA HA!!

GARA GARA GARA

GARA GARA

GARA GARA

154

GARA GARA

KTNK THNK

160

WHAT THE
FUCK?!

HEY, THIS
IS *OUR* TURF!
WE *WORK* IN
THIS SHACK!

DAMN
SQUATTER!

I REGRET
THE OFFENSE.

163

REGRET?! YOU THINK THAT *SETTLES* IT?!

BURGLARS DON'T GET OFF SAYING *SORRY!*

YOU GOTTA *PAY UP* SOME RENT!

STOP *SQUAWLING!* YOU SOUND LIKE *CATS* IN *HEAT!*

WHAT'S THE PROBLEM?

HE'S *SQUATTING* IN *OUR* SHACK!

164

LET HIM BE.

HE'S GOT A *KID*. WE HELP *EACH OTHER* WHEN WE'RE DOWN AND OUT, RIGHT?

WE DON'T NEED IT NOW, ANYWAY.

IT'S OKAY, GO-*RŌNIN*-SAMA.

REST UP IF YOU LIKE.

AWW, DID WE WAKE YOU UP, CUTIE...?

I'M SORRY!

LET'S YOU AND AUNTIE BE *FRIENDS...* MM?

KLAPP *KLAPP* *KLAPP*

167

168

169

HERE, LITTLE BOY!

COME ON!

AUNTIE'S GOT A *PRESENT* FOR YOU! PUT OUT YOUR HAND...

IT'S A *MANJŪ*, SWEETIE.

IT'S FROM *IMADO-YA!* EDO'S YUMMIEST!

171

OH, SO *SOFT* AND SO *SWEET!* YOU'LL *LOVE* IT!

MM...? WANT IT?

COME ON... *TAKE IT.*

WHAT? DON'T *LIKE* IT?

OR... YOU NEVER *HAD* ONE BEFORE?

SEE? FULL OF *ANKO!* IT'S SO DELICIOUS!

I...
I DON'T...
YOUR SON DOESN'T
LIKE *MANJŪ*...?

THEN... HAVE A CUP, GO-RŌNIN-SAN.

SOMETIMES EVEN WE NIGHTHAWKS HAVE TO DROWN OUR SORROWS.

THINK OF *HOME*, OLD *LOVERS*... A FALLEN WOMAN HAS ONLY HER TEARS, MM?

PLEASE. DOWN ONE WITH ME.

I DON'T DRINK. BUT I HONOR THE SPIRIT.

I'VE HAD *ENOUGH* OF YOUR *SHIT!!*

WHAT'S *WRONG* WITH YOU *TWO?!* YOUR *BRAT* WON'T EAT MY *MANJŪ,* AND *DADDY'S* SO HIGH AND *MIGHTY* HE WON'T EVEN *DRINK?* OR...JUST NOT WITH *ME?!*

IS *THAT* IT? EVEN *BEGGAR SAMURAI* DON'T DRINK WITH *NIGHTHAWKS?!*

175

I *TOLD* YOU NOT TO WASTE ANY *SYMPATHY* ON HIM!

WE SHOULD'A JUST *SHAKEN* HIM *DOWN!*

WELL, YOU'RE *DAMN WELL* GONNA *DRINK!*

AND YOUR *KID'S* GONNA EAT MY *MANJŪ!* WE'RE BEING *NICE* TO YOU, DAMN IT!

I'M NOT ALLOWED ALCOHOL.

BUT IF YOU THINK ME A *SAMURAI*, I'LL DRINK LIKE A *SAMURAI*.

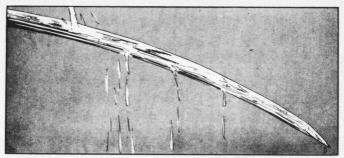

MY CHILD AND I DON'T LIVE TO EAT— WE EAT TO LIVE.

WE MERELY EAT ENOUGH TO SUSTAIN LIFE. *NO LUXURIES!*

HE'S NEVER TASTED A *MANJŪ*, AND THUS HAS NO DESIRE FOR ONE.

WE APPRECIATE YOUR ACT OF KINDNESS. NOW... FORGET US.

180

GO-RŌNIN-SAN!

GARA GARA

YOU'RE *LONE WOLF AND CUB*... AREN'T YOU?

I, I *KNEW* IT!

I SHOULDN'T GET INVOLVED, BUT...THE *LAW'S* AFTER YOU!

POSTERS *EVERYWHERE!*

WAIT! *PLEASE!*

GARA GARA

IT'S *DANGEROUS* OUT THERE!

EDO'S *CRAWLING* WITH COPS!

HOW ABOUT THIS... STAY WITH US *NIGHTHAWKS!*

WE'LL SHELTER YOU... *FEED* YOU, EVEN!

YOU NEED **SOME** PLACE TO STAY, NO?

SO, WE **TRADE!** YOU CAN BE OUR **BODYGUARD.**

IT'S **TOUGH** OUT HERE. CREEPY JOHNS, ALL THOSE CHEAP **HOODS.**

WELL ...?

183

THE BRANCHES INTERTWINE, FLOWERING WITH ALL THEIR STRENGTH IN THE TOO SHORT SUMMER.

BUT SOMETIMES THERE'S ONE *BLIGHTED LEAF*. A *SINGLE* LEAF THAT WITHERS AN ENTIRE THICKET.

IF WE STAYED, *WE* WOULD BE THAT BLIGHTED LEAF, DESTROYING YOU ALL.

BUT WE
THANK YOU.

GARA
GARA

WELL,
SHIT!

SO...THE "SILK SPIDER" CAN'T DELIVER HER *BITE,* EH?

THEN I'LL HAVE TO GO MYSELF.

IT *ITCHES*.
SCRATCH!

NOW *SUCK*.

187

YES... I'LL HAVE TO GO *MYSELF*...

the hundred
and first

Abe-
No-
Kaii

193

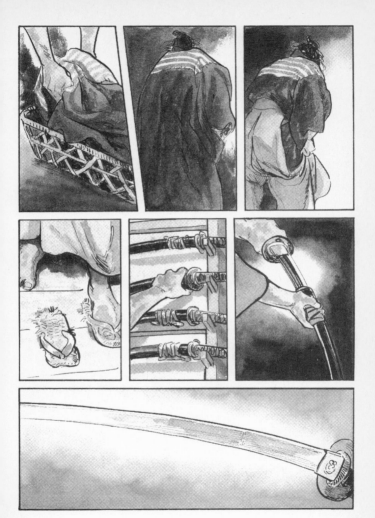

195

197

NNG...!

HNNG...

C-CAN'T... MOVE...

GOING... NUMB...

BWEH HEH HEH HEH!

NNK... KRKK!

204

CAN'T MOVE, CAN'T *JUMP*.

EH, MY *YAGYŪ LAPDOG?*

IF YOU THOUGHT *MAKIBISHI* WERE JUST FOR *SHINOBI*, *BIG* MISTAKE. ABE-NO-KAII LIKES THEM, TOO.

MAYBE I'M NOT AS *AGILE* AS YOU NINJA...

...BUT MY TOYS ARE *MUCH* MORE EFFECTIVE. IT'S THE *VIPER VENOM*, YOU SEE?

JUST A *SMIDGEN* IN THE BLOOD, AND YOU'RE ALL *NUMB*. RIGHT? CAN'T EVEN WAGGLE YOUR *TONGUE!* HEH HEH...

HAH! I SAW THROUGH RETSUDŌ *AGES* AGO! HE FIGURED LONE WOLF AND I WOULD FIGHT IT OUT, AND *HE'D* KILL THE *VICTOR.* THAT'S WHY YOU'RE TAILING ME, EH?

I'VE BEEN LETTING YOU RUN LOOSE SO RETSUDŌ WOULD THINK I FELL FOR IT. "CATCH THE SHARKS WHILE THEY FIGHT," HE THINKS. BUT THINK *AGAIN,* OLD MAN!

BWA HA HA! THE INVINCIBLE *YAGYŪ RETSUDŌ,* AFRAID OF *ME!* BUT HE'S *RIGHT!* HE *SHOULD* BE!

AFTER I BURY THE *WOLF,* HEH HEH...

...I BURY *HIM,* LAST OF THE YAGYŪ!

THEN... THE POWER OF THE SHŌGUNATE, IN *MY* HANDS!

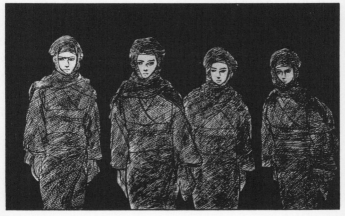

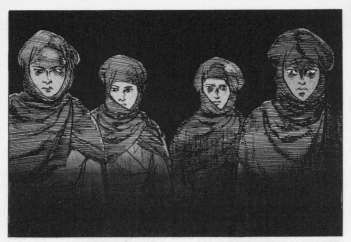

ENSLAVE HIM TO AFUYŌ!

HE'S A TRAINED *SHINOBI*, SO KEEP HIM *PARALYZED*.

THEY SAY YOU GUYS RIP UP YOUR FACES AND DIE WHEN YOU'RE CAUGHT, KEEPING YOUR IDENTITY SECRET TO THE LAST.

TOO BAD YOU'RE *PARALYZED!*

AND AFTER SMOKING MY SPECIAL *KIZAMI* YOU'LL TAKE ORDERS LIKE A *DOG!*

BWEH HEH HEH.. A *SHINOBI'S* TRAINING VERSUS *AFUYŌ...* NO CONTEST!

THEN I'LL USE HIM TO MANIPULATE THAT CURSED *RETSUDŌ!*

209

DAMMIT. IF *HE* WON'T DRINK, AND HIS KID WON'T EVEN EAT *MANJŪ*, HOW CAN I *POISON* THEM?

FACE IT— YOU HAVE *FAILED*, O-TOSHI!

IT'S
ME.

G-
GOZEN-
SAMA!

≥PHEWW≤
HAVEN'T
WALKED
LIKE THAT
IN AGES.

SIR...
THOSE
CLOTHES
...?

FROM NOW ON
I RUN THE SHOW.
HE'S TOO TOUGH
FOR YOU.

212

I...
I HAVE
NO EXCUSE,
MY LORD...

SO...
LONE
WOLF AND
CUB?

I HAVE
THE NIGHTHAWKS
TAILING HIM. THERE
SHOULD BE A
REPORT SOON...

HE...
HE'S STILL
HEADED
DOWNRIVER!

I THINK
HE'S GONNA
WALK ALL
NIGHT!

SHALL WE TRY A TRAP...?

WHAT HAPPENS IF WE SCATTER *THESE* ON A DARK PATH...? HEH HEH...

GOZEN-SAMA! PLEASE LET *ME* DO IT!

NO. BOTCH IT AGAIN AND HE MIGHT NOTICE.

POISON ONLY WORKS WHEN THE POISONER'S UNKNOWN. KNOW THE *POISONER,* KNOW HIS *POISON.*

FIND A *BOAT!* WE'LL CUT HIM OFF!

214

216

HEH HEH... HE WON'T DIE *THIS* EASILY. IT'S JUST A *TEST*.

WORTH A TRY, THOUGH. SOMETIMES EVEN *PROS* SLIP UP.

BUT... NOT EVEN A *WOLF*... NOT IN THE *DARK!*

THE YAGYŪ AND THE KUROKUWA TRIED *EVERY* TRICK.

HE'S NOT *HUMAN*, HE'S A *REAL* WOLF. IF A WOLF SNIFFED THE GROUND, IT'D FIND THEM.

EITHER WAY, WE LEARN SOMETHING.

BWEH HEH HEH. NOW IT'S GETTING *ENTERTAINING!*

217

OKAY, LET'S PULL OUT.

AREN'T WE STAYING TO WATCH ...?!

IDIOT! HE'D SENSE US!

HE EVEN SPOTTED THE KUROKUWA *NINJA*, DIDN'T HE?

WE'RE *AMATEURS*. HE'D FEEL US IN AN *INSTANT*.

WE'LL PULL IN DOWNSTREAM. CHECK BACK LATER.

THINK, WOMAN! DO *HUNTERS* SIT BY THEIR *TRAPS*?

I'M TAKING A NAP.

YAWWWNN...

GARA GARA   GARA GARA

GARA GARA GARA

GARA GARA GARA

THKK

DAIGORO!
DON'T
MOVE!

STAY
IN THE
CART!

225

228

YAWWWWN!

. . . .

WELL...

LET'S GO SEE WHAT WE *CAUGHT.*

KRIK

KRIK

230

232

HRM!!

HMM...
....

....
....

HE FELT
A WHEEL HIT
A *MAKIBISHI*...
THEN, THE INSTANT
HE FELT *PRESSURE*
ON HIS SANDALS...

234

...HE LEAPED.

UHRMM... A *WOLF'S* REFLEXES. *INHUMAN!*

BUT THEN... WHY *LEAVE* THEM?

IT'S A *CHALLENGE!*

235

A MESSAGE FROM LONE WOLF— "THIS WON'T WORK TWICE!"

HE'LL GO *BAREFOOT* NOW.

HE SEES THROUGH *WALLS*, THEY SAY.

AND THROUGH HIS SANDALS! *NOW* HE'LL TRAIN HIS *FEET.*

I...I'VE NEVER BEEN AFRAID IN MY *LIFE.* AND AT LAST, AN OPPONENT THAT SCARES ME TO *DEATH!*

HEH HEH HEH... *HA HA HA!!*

NO WONDER RETSUDŌ CAN'T TOUCH HIM. *DEADLY!*

236

I *LOVE* IT! LET ME *AT HIM!* HEH HEH HEH!

BUAHAHA HA HA!

DAMN... I'M *THIRSTY.* THE BIG BAD WOLF SCARED ME *DRY.*

WATER, O-TOSHI!

I-I'M SORRY... I DIDN'T BRING ANY.

NO WELLS OR SPRINGS NEARBY...

NOT EVEN A *HOUSE...*

YOURS WILL DO FINE!

237

WELL, *HURRY UP!* IT'S NOT THE *FIRST* TIME!

Y... YES, MY LORD.

238

NOT...
YET...

NOT
YET...?

YOU *IDIOT!*
A GROWN WOMAN
WHO CAN'T *PEE* ON
COMMAND?!

ALMOST...
THERE...

GULP

GULP

GULP
GULP

SALTY. THAT MEANS YOU'RE *TIRED.*

GIVES ME AN IDEA... MAN OR WOLF, HE HAS TO *SHIT* AND *PISS.*

SAME WITH HIS *CUB.* DUMPS A LOAD, WIPES HIS BUTT! WE'LL SEND A NIGHTHAWK AHEAD BY BOAT, AND WAIT...

WHEN THE CUB LEAVES PAPA WOLF TO DO IT, SHE SIDLES UP ALL FRIENDLY, AND HELPS *WIPE* HIM...

...USING PAPER TREATED WITH *THIS!*

THIS POISON IS A FINE POWDER, BUT IT WILL DISSOLVE AND INVADE THE INTESTINES. KILLS HIM *DEAD!*

EVEN IF PAPA WOLF'S WATCHING, IT'S JUST A WORTHLESS *NIGHTHAWK.* HE WON'T SUSPECT A THING... HEH, HEH...

I'LL DO IT, MY LORD!

NO, HE'D RECOGNIZE YOU.

LONE WOLF'S *CUB...* KILLED GOING *POTTY!*

BWE HEH HEH *HEH HEH!*

GARA GARA GARA

OH! ALREADY OCCUPIED? MIND IF WE SHARE...? HEE HEE!

UUHNG!

UHNNNGG!

HERE... I'VE GOT SOME PAPER—

DAMN!

I SEE,
I SEE.
NEVER RELY
ON OTHERS!
HEH, HEH...

BUT
THAT'S FINE.
WHY *RUSH IT*
WHEN YOU'RE
HAVING *FUN,*
EH?

AND
MORE TO
COME.

A Taste of Poison

255

258

AAH, *ASEBI!*
A *LOVELY* POISON...
DISSOLVE IT IN WATER,
AND IT SPREADS
A HUNDRED
TIMES OVER.

ONE TOUCH
AND IT'S *OVER!*
DON'T GO NEAR
THE WATER...
BWE HEH HEH!

260

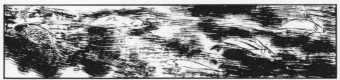

DAMN!
SEEMS IT'S
TRUE—

—THE GODS
SMILE ON
FOOLS AND
CHILDREN.

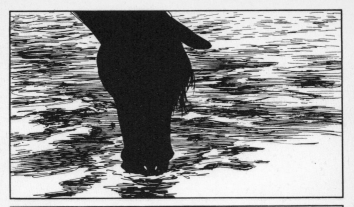

HRRK!

NOT EVEN RETSUDŌ IS *THIS* EVIL.

ONLY A *MONSTER* WOULD POISON A RIVER AND KILL PERHAPS *THOUSANDS* OF INNOCENTS TO GET ONE MAN!

HOW MANY PEOPLE WILL DIE DOWNSTREAM...? AND THOSE *MAKIBISHI* IN THE NIGHT... *ANYONE* COULD HAVE WALKED THERE.

271

DAIGORO!
STAY *BACK!*

SHAK
KCHAK

G-GOZEN-SAMA! WE...WE FAILED AGAIN...

NOT SO! WE FOUND THE WOLF'S WEAKNESS—

—HE REFUSES TO SACRIFICE *OTHERS* ON HIS QUEST!

LOOK AT HIM FLAIL.

SKREEK

BTAM

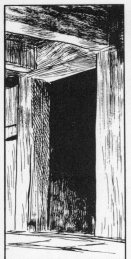

285

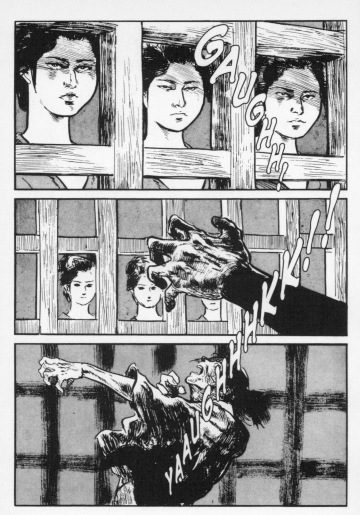

286

HRGH...
· · · ·

KIZAMI!!
GIVE ME
KIZAMI!!!!

NNGH...!

AUGHH!!

GRRRCH

287

P-PLEASE! GIVE IT TO ME!!

KIZAMI!!

OR... OR I'LL DIE!! I'LL DIIIE!!

AGGH! AUGH!!

288

WELL...?

THE SIXTH WITHDRAWAL PHASE.

AAAHHNNN!

BWEH HEH HEH!

A *SHINOBI*, TRAINED TO TEAR OFF HIS OWN *FACE* WHEN CAPTURED... BROKEN BY A PINCH OF *AFUYO*.

HEH HEH... *HURTS*, DOES IT?

AGGH!

KIZAMI! P-PLEASE! *PLEASE!!* AUHHG!!

YOU HAVE *TWO WAYS* TO ESCAPE THIS AGONY.

BITE YOUR TONGUE OFF AND *DIE*... OR *BETRAY* THE YAGYU.

WHAT WILL IT BE...?

NNG... KIZAMI! *KIZAMIIII!!*

HEH... A *SHINOBI* WHO CAN'T BITE HIS TONGUE.

BWAH HA HA!!

OKAY—
GIVE HIM
SOME.

HAHH!
HAHH!

NNG!

FHHF!

HHHF!

YOUR *NAME!*

S-SUDARE JINNAI. I SERVE RETSUDŌ-SAMA...

WHAT WERE RETSUDŌ'S *ORDERS?!*

292

OBSERVE ABE-NO-KAII BATTLE THE LONE WOLF...

...AND THEN...

...IF KAII *KILLS* THE WOLF...

WHAT *THEN?!*

TO KILL *HIM!!*

BWEH HEH HEH...!

BWAH HA HA HA!

I *KNEW* IT! AM I NOT *BRILLIANT?!*

BWA HA HA HA!

NOW *LISTEN,* JINNAI!

NO LONGER A *SHINOBI!!* AN *ADDICT!*

UNDER-STAND?!

NOW GO, JINNAI. DON'T LET RETSUDŌ SUSPECT.

REPORT TO HIM AS BEFORE. ONLY NOW, YOU SPY ON *HIM...* FOR *ME!*

JINNAI...?

MY LORD.
I MAKE MY
REPORT.

YES...?

ABE-NO-KAII
SEEKS TO
POISON
LONE WOLF
AND CUB.

HE'S
LOCATED THEM,
AND TAILS THEM
WITH THE WOMAN
THIEF "SILK SPIDER,"
AND THE *YOTAKA*.

297

I SUSPECT THAT IN TIME, HE'LL SUCCEED.

KEEP WATCHING. WAIT UNTIL HE KILLS LONE WOLF...

...THEN *STRIKE!*

RETSUDŌ-SAMA...

...I'VE DONE EVERYTHING I CAN FOR YOU.

J-JINNAI?!

WHAT ARE YOU—

I HAVE... NO *EXCUSE*...

I FELL INTO ABE-NO-KAII'S POISONED TRAP. I'M AN *ADDICT*, NEVER TO BE A *SHINOBI* AGAIN.

AN...
ADDICT?

TO *AFUYŌ*,
MY LORD!

I MADE
HIM THINK I
WAS HIS AND
GOT THIS FAR...
BUT NO
FARTHER.

ABE-NO-KAII KNOWS YOUR *HEART*, RETSUDŌ-*SAMA!*

HE KNOWS HE'S *NEXT* TO DIE AFTER HE KILLS LONE WOLF AND *CUB!*

HRNG!

R-RETSUDŌ-*SAMA!* THIRTY *YEARS* I'VE SERVED THE YAGYU. I'M A *SHINOBI...* NEVER ONCE DID I SPEAK MY MIND.

BUT AS I LEAVE THIS WORLD, THERE'S *ONE* THING I *MUST SAY!*

THEN SPEAK!

DON'T LET ABE-NO-KAII KILL *LONE WOLF!*

THE YAGYŪ AND ŌGAMI ITTŌ ARE *BLOOD ENEMIES*. TO PURGE THIS HATRED AND SAVE THE CLAN, YOU MUST FIGHT HIM *YOURSELF!*

PEOPLE WILL WHISPER THROUGHOUT JAPAN... "THE WARRIOR YAGYŪ USED A *POISONER* TO DEFEAT LONE WOLF!" YOU'LL BE A *LAUGHING STOCK!*

WILL YOUR CHILDREN— KURANDO, HYŌGO, GUNBEI, AND SAYAKA-*SAMA*— REJOICE IN THEIR GRAVES? THEIR LIVES LOST IN PURSUIT OF THIS SHAMEFUL END?

RETSUDŌ-*SAMA!* KILL ITTŌ *YOURSELF!*

304

ABE-NO-KAII IS NO *SAMURAI!* HE'LL STOP AT NOTHING FOR POWER. HE'S A *BEAST*, DEVOID OF *SHIDŌ!*

SEE HOW HE THOUGHT HE COULD TURN ME WITH *AFUYŌ*.

NO *BUSHI*, NO *SHINOBI*, WOULD SURRENDER TO *AFUYŌ*... BUT HE DOESN'T *UNDERSTAND!* DON'T LET SUCH A BEAST KILL ŌGAMI ITTŌ!

ITTŌ'S A *BUSHI* AMONG *BUSHI!* LIKE THE *YAGYŪ!*

HE HAS THE *YAGYŪ LETTER*, YET HE DOESN'T USE IT. BECAUSE HE'S A MAN OF *HONOR!*

RETSUDŌ-SAMA...! RECONSIDER!

305

FORGIVE ME, JINNAI. YOU SPOKE THE TRUTH. I WAS ABOUT TO HEAP *SHAME* UPON SHAME.

YES... I SHALL KILL ŌGAMI ITTŌ!

BUT NOW... BEFORE THAT... ABE-NO-KAII!

*ABE

HEH HEH...
SO MUCH FOR
THE *YAGYŪ*.
AND NOW,
THE *CLIMAX!*

IT'S TIME
TO *BURY*
LONE WOLF
AND CUB,
ONCE AND
FOR ALL!

BWEH
HEH HEH!
*BWAHH
HAH HAH
HAH!*

LONE WOLF AND CUB BOOK TWENTY: THE END
TO BE CONTINUED

GLOSSARY

afuyō
A type of opiate drug.

anko
Sweet red bean paste.

asebi
Pieris japonica. Japanese andromeda, a broad-leaved evergreen shrub. Andromedotoxins (grayanotoxins) are water-soluble diterpenoid compounds. Leaves and flower nectar are sources of the toxin.

bakkaku
The government. The shogun, his councilors, and his senior officials.

buke
A samurai household.

bushi
A samurai. A member of the warrior class.

bushidō
The way of the warrior. Also known as *shidō*.

cho
Approximately 300 meters.

daikan
An official who collected taxes owed to Edo and oversaw public works, agriculture, and other projects administered by the central government.

daikansho
The office of the *daikan*.

daimyō
A feudal lord.

dokumi
Poison taster.

Edo
The capital of medieval Japan and the seat of the shōgunate. The site of modern-day Tokyo.

Fudai daimyō
The inner circle of clans pledging allegiance to the Tokugawa. The Fudai clans were Tokugawa allies even before Tokugawa Ieyasu's decisive victory of Sekigahara that launched the Tokugawa shogunate.

go-kashi
Cakes and candy. The *"go-"* is an honorific because the cakes come from the shōgun. There are several categories of *wagashi* (Japanese sweetcakes): *Manju* have sweet paste from *azuki* red beans, wrapped in a soft flour shell. *Mochi* are made from pounded rice, often with sweet paste inside. *Yōkan* is a semi-hardened, sweet jelly. There are hundreds of kinds of *wagashi*, often unique to the towns where they are made.

han
A feudal domain.

honorifics

Japan is a class and status society, and proper forms of address are critical. Common markers of respect are the prefixes *o* and *go*, and a wide range of suffixes. Some of the suffixes you will encounter in *Lone Wolf and Cub*:

chan – for children, young women, and close friends

dono – archaic; used for higher-ranked or highly respected figures

san – the most common, used among equals or near-equals

sama – used for superiors

sensei – used for teachers, masters, respected entertainers, and politicians.

jiji

Old man. Grandfather. Both intimate…and condescending.

jikisan hatamoto

Daimyō directly serving the shōgun, with the right to meet him face to face. Their title, "standard bearers," came from history, when the warriors who would be promoted in peacetime to *hatamoto* had been the most trusted allies of Tokugawa Ieyasu, the first Tokugawa shōgun.

jitte

A specialized weapon carried by street cops. About 18 inches long, with no cutting edge — just two prongs designed to catch and snap off an opponent's sword blade.

kajō

Good fortune. June 16 was a popular folk festival long before Ieyasu's narrow escape. In its original incarnation, sixteen sweetcakes were offered to the gods to ward off disease, and eaten afterwards.

kizami

Tobacco was extremely expensive in early Japan, and the preferred form was finely shredded, hair-like *kizami*, rolled into tiny balls and smoked by inhaling deeply in a few quick puffs.

koku

A bale of rice. The traditional measure of a *han*'s wealth, a measure of its agricultural land and productivity.

kōtai yoriai

Retainers of *hatamoto daimyō* based in Edo for their lords' visits to the capital.

kusasugikazura

Asparagus cochinchinensis.

machi-bugyō

The Edo city commissioner, combining the post of mayor and chief of police. A post held in monthly rotation by two senior Tokugawa vassals, in charge of administration, maintaining the peace, and enforcing the law in Edo. Their rule extended only to commoners; samurai in Edo were controlled by their own *daimyō* and his officers. The *machi-bugyō* had an administrative staff and a small force of armed policemen at his disposal.

makibishi

Caltrops. A traditional ninja weapon, designed to always leave a point up. Intended to slow down pursuers.

omote-kōke

Untitled shogunal liaison officers in charge of protocol and relations with the imperial court in Kyōto.

rōnin

A masterless samurai. Literally, "one adrift on the waves." Members of the samurai caste who have lost their masters through the dissolution of *han*, expulsion for misbehavior, or other reasons. Prohibited from working as farmers or merchants under the strict Confucian caste system imposed by the Tokugawa shōgunate, many impoverished *rōnin* became "hired guns" for whom the code of the samurai was nothing but empty words.

sankyo sanke

The three sub-branches of the Tokugawa clan. When there was no heir to the main Tokugawa line, one would be picked from two of these clans, while the *fuku*-shōgun (Vice-shōgun) always came from the third.

shinobi

A generic term for ninja, meaning "one who moves in secrecy." Ninja had their heyday in the time of warring states before the rise of the Tokugawa clan. Originally mercenaries serving different warlords, by the Edo period they were in the service of the central government. The most famous *shinobi* were the ninja of Iga and Kaga, north of Kyoto. The Kurokuwa that appear in *Lone Wolf and Cub* were officially the laborers and manual workers in Edo Castle. Whether they truly served as a secret spy corps is lost in history.

shoyaku

The other titled posts in the shogunate.

takenigusa

Macleaya cordata.

Tōshōgū

Tokugawa Ieyasu.

Tozama daimyō

Daimyō who rallied to the Tokugawa side only after the Tokugawa victory at Sekigahara.

vet

To examine or appraise expertly.

yakuza

Japan's criminal syndicates. In the Edo period, *yakuza* were a common part of the landscape, running houses of gambling and prostitution. As long as they did not overstep their bounds, they were tolerated by the authorities, a tradition little changed in modern Japan.

yotaka

Literally, "nighthawk." Streetwalkers, among the lowest ranks of Edo period prostitutes.

yuzuri

Daphniphyllum macropodum.

KAZUO KOIKE

Though widely respected as a powerful writer of graphic fiction, Kazuo Koike has spent a lifetime reaching beyond the bounds of the comics medium. Aside from co-creating and writing the successful *Lone Wolf and Cub* and *Crying Freeman* manga, Koike has hosted television programs; founded a golf magazine; produced movies; written popular fiction, poetry, and screenplays; and mentored some of Japan's best manga talent.

Lone Wolf and Cub was first serialized in Japan in 1970 (under the title *Kozure Okami*) in *Manga Action* magazine and continued its hugely popular run for many years, being collected as the stories were published, and reprinted worldwide. Koike collected numerous awards for his work on the series throughout the next decade. Starting in 1972, Koike adapted the popular manga into a series of six films, the *Baby Cart Assassin* saga, garnering widespread commercial success and critical acclaim for his screenwriting.

This wasn't Koike's only foray into film and video. In 1996, *Crying Freeman*, the manga Koike created with artist Ryoichi Ikegami, was produced in Hollywood and released to commercial success in Europe and is currently awaiting release in America.

And to give something back to the medium that gave him so much, Koike started the *Gekiga Sonjuku*, a college course aimed at helping talented writers and artists — such as *Ranma 1/2* creator Rumiko Takahashi — break into the comics field.

The driving focus of Koike's narrative is character development, and his commitment to character is clear: "Comics are carried by characters. If a character is well created, the comic becomes a hit." Kazuo Koike's continued success in comics and literature has proven this philosophy true.

GOSEKI KOJIMA

Goseki Kojima was born on November 3, 1928, the very same day as the godfather of Japanese comics, Osamu Tezuka. While just out of junior high school, the self-taught Kojima began painting advertising posters for movie theaters to pay his bills.

In 1950, Kojima moved to Tokyo, where the postwar devastation had given rise to special manga forms for audiences too poor to buy the new manga magazines. Kojima created art for *kami-shibai*, or "paper-play" narrators, who would use manga story sheets to present narrated street plays. Kojima moved on to creating works for the *kashi-bon* market, bookstores that rented out books, magazines, and manga to mostly low-income readers. He soon became highly popular among *kashi-bon* readers.

In 1967, Kojima broke into the magazine market with his series *Dojinki*. As the manga magazine market grew and diversified, he turned out a steady stream of popular series.

In 1970, in collaboration with Kazuo Koike, Kojima began the work that would seal his reputation, *Kozure Okami* (*Lone Wolf and Cub*). Before long the story had become a gigantic hit, eventually spinning off a television series, six motion pictures, and even theme song records. Koike and Kojima were soon dubbed the "golden duo" and produced success after success on their way to the pinnacle of the manga world.

When *Manga Japan* magazine was launched in 1994, Kojima was asked to serve as consultant, and he helped train the next generation of manga artists.

In his final years, Kojima turned to creating original graphic novels based on the movies of his favorite director, Akira Kurosawa. Kojima passed away on January 5, 2000 at the age of 71.

THE RONIN REPORT

By David S. Hofhine

An Authentic Example of a Dotanuki School Sword: part one

For the last several years, I have been working full time as a professional *togishi* (Japanese sword polisher) and have recently had the rare pleasure and honor of working on an authentic Dotanuki school *katana*. This is the same Dotanuki school of sword-smithery that is often mentioned in the *Lone Wolf and Cub* series, and which allegedly produced the *katana* sword that was used by Itto Ogami. Hence, this article is something of a sequel to the essay originally presented in *Lone Wolf and Cub* volume twelve entitled "The Dotanuki Sword of Lone Wolf and Cub."

To give a complete description of this particular sword and its unique Higo school mountings, it will be necessary to give a short overview on the subject of Japanese sword-smithery and what goes into a Japanese *koshirae* (sword mounting). Japanese swords present a very deep field of study. There are many top universities in Japan that offer advanced post-graduate degrees in sword study, and within this field has grown an enormous vocabulary of terms to describe how certain features of a blade look. Terms such as "wind-blown sand" and "moonlight reflecting on still water" are two examples of the descriptive terms used. There are, in fact, entire books devoted to defining the hundreds of terms used by sword aficionados. I will be using primarily English equivalents to facilitate understanding by the occidental reader, but will also include basic Japanese terms as needed to describe this sword and its features as accurately as possible.

Forging a good sword is difficult. To maintain a good cutting ability and to stand up to heavy use, the cutting edge must be very hard. In addition to having a hard edge, the blade must also be so tough it will not easily break. Finally, a blade must be rigid, yet resistant to bending, and if bent should spring back into shape to a reasonable degree.

These characteristics are not necessarily compatible, and therein lies the problem. For example, as steel is made to be harder, it also becomes more brittle. Many different steps must be taken while forging a blade to arrive at a balance that holds all of the best characteristics of a finished sword and fewest of the worst. Each step in the forging process has an effect on the overall appearance and functionality of the finished blade. Ancient Japanese swordsmiths made numerous ingenious innovations to solve these problems, resulting in the Japanese sword's famous attributes as a weapon and its unique physical characteristics.

The Dotanuki described in this article would be defined as a *katana*, that is, the classical "samurai sword" with a single edged, curved blade, usually about 25" to 29" long (fig. 1). Traditionally, a *katana*

Fig. 1   is also defined by a ridge, called a *shinogi*, which runs the full length of the blade, separating the bevel of the lower surface from the flat part of the upper surface. This particular *katana* has a blade length of 26 3/8", measured from the tip of the point to the notch where the blade ends and the tang begins, and is very similar to the *katana* depicted throughout *Lone Wolf and Cub*.

Fig. 2

sword, is the tempering pattern, or *hamon*, that runs along the cutting edge of the blade (fig. 2). The edge of a Japanese sword is hardened in a process called *yaki-ire*. First, the body and back edge of the blade are covered in a clay mixture to partially insulate it from heat. Then the exposed edge is hardened by heating it to a great temperature followed by a quick cooling in water. This process leaves a pattern along the cutting edge of the blade that is the hallmark of a traditionally forged Japanese blade.

The hardened edge is actually a type of crystalline steel known to modern science as *martensite*, and is the same sort of steel that modern razor blades are made of. It is about as hard as steel can get, but unfortunately it is brittle and will crack and chip rather then bend or dent. The body of the blade, having been protected by the clay insulator, remains a softer and more flexible type of steel known as *pearlite*. The shape of the *hamon* is formed by the boundary where the *martensite* meets the *pearlite*. This combination of a tough flexible body and an extremely hardened edge is one of the keys to the Japanese sword's extraordinary cutting ability.

Bringing out the details of the *hamon* is a primary goal of the sword polisher. There are two styles of finish for the temper line, *sashikomi* and *keisho*. *Sashikomi* is a natural finish that lets the shape of the temper line stand out on its own with little enhancement. *Keisho* finish, on the other hand, uses little slips of fine polishing stone